# CURRENT ISSUES IN PLANNING

# Current Issues in Planning

**Edited by
Sylvia Trench and Taner Oc**

Gower

Published by
Gower Publishing Company Limited
Gower House
Croft Road
Aldershot
Hants GU11 3HR
England

Gower Publishing Company
Old Post Road
Brookfield
Vermont 05036
USA

British Library Cataloguing in Publication Data
Current issues in planning.
    1. Environment planning
    I. Trench, Sylvia, *1935*– II. Oc, Taner, *1944*–
*711*

ISBN 0566 05794 8

Printed in Great Britain by
Billing & Sons Ltd, Worcester

# Contents

## Part 1   Strategies for Pedestrians

## Part II   Jobs for the Inner Cities

# Contents

# Foreword

I hope that the Institute of Planning Studies will continue to promote seminars such as those reported here. In this series subjects have been raised and practical solutions explored with results which will be helpful to all those in planning practice.

In looking at the increasing use of the private car and the absence of any meaningful policies to mitigate its consequences, the seminar on 'Strategies for Pedestrians' was concerned with a topical subject. It is also a subject which can now be examined in the light of the advancing ideas about equal opportunities and the weight we give to those who must compete on such unequal terms against the car. We should continue to examine policies in this way in the hope of promoting better practices and with a view to questioning so much of the spurious objectivity employed in transport planning.

Few subjects have figured so prominently for so long in relation to the inner cities as job creation, and rightly so. Unemployment is the cause of much in urban degeneration, yet despite volumes of works and good intentions, progress in seeking and implementing practical solutions is slow. In the meantime much damage is being done; many are beginning to talk in terms of a permanent 'underclass'. The seminar on 'Jobs for the Inner Cities' revealed much about the variety of enterprises being directed by public agencies towards specific remedies. Some, it is clear, are not content to place their faith only in a general increase in economic activity. While there are successes to report, the seminar revealed some very serious problems indeed. Local government enterprise has often much to learn. One hopes that the spirit of direct help to those most in need will not be prejudiced and that we shall see a refinement and development of good practices, and a speedy abandonment of those which demand so much in resources with little effect.

Few subjects could be so conspicuously and sadly lacking sufficient attention and practical solution as that of homelessness. We must hope that the Institute of Planning Studies will continue to find opportunities to promote enquiry and discussion. It is becoming increasingly difficult for public agencies to establish and operate policies which will produce direct results. With the acceptance of the growth of an underclass, we seem to be retreating from the problem of homelessness rather than facing it. Yet in many places throughout the country, good practices have been built up, and new ideas are being explored with the housing associations and the charitable organizations. Again we should be identifying these allowing the best to be developed.

Addressing pressing social, economic and environmental problems is to be applauded but it is particularly commendable when a seminar series also takes up the relationship between the planners and the development industry itself; it is only within a better understanding between these that practical solutions will be found and put into operation in reasonable time. Thankfully it is a theme consistently explored these days and, as we see from the chapters herein, there is much to be learnt, and a great deal of progress to be made. The conditions were probably never better to develop a better understanding and I hope that we shall see seminars in the future when the two sides are brought together in a joint concern for the kinds of issue and problems addressed in these earlier papers.

John Dean
Past President, The Royal Town Planning Institute
Special Professor, Institute of Planning Studies,
University of Nottingham
City Planning Officer, Leicester

# Preface

This book has developed out of a series of seminars run at the Institute of Planning Studies in Nottingham University as part of its Continuing Professional Development Programme for planners. Each of the sections was the subject of a separate seminar and most of the contributors first gave their paper there. Some of the chapters have been rewritten from the transcripts of the seminar proceedings; others have been revised by the authors in the light of the discussion at the time or of subsequent developments, and a few have been commissioned after the event to extend the discussion on particular aspects. The editors would like to thank all those who attended the seminars whose ideas and interest have provided the stimulus for what is to follow.

The aim of the seminars was to offer the Institute of Planning's postgraduate students and the professional planners who attended, a flavour of some of the current arguments in planning policy circles and to introduce relevant recent research. Each of the seminars brought together a variety of speakers who were involved with the problem under discussion from a different aspect, some with academic research and others with practical policy implementation at various levels. The aim was not so much to provide balance where this would involve rehashing well known long standing arguments or information, but to present some of the most important ideas under discussion at the present time. Now that the results are to be made available to a wider audience the purpose is still the same.

We are aware that it is customary especially in the introductory sections to play safe and write carefully measured prose. We make no apology for departing from this practice. Many of the chapters are self-consciously committed in their style, and so are our introductions. This is deliberate. There is no shortage in the planning literature of bland prose and lengthy generalizations. Indeed in our experience of teaching postgraduate students over many years we have become increasingly concerned with the need for direct statements and straightforward arguments.

For this reason, although this is a responsible academic publication backed by research and written by people who have considerable relevant expertise it is intentionally written as far as possible in a way that will keep the reader alert to the realities behind the issues.

Sylvia Trench
Taner Oc

# Acknowledgements

This book was conceived as a result of the enthusiastic support of the planners participating in our continuous Professional Development seminars and we have had Professor J. C. Moughtin's strong support and encouragement. We are most grateful to him and to all the contributors to the seminars and to the book.

The demanding task of transforming the transcriptions of seminar contributions to well argued chapters of a book was made much easier by Jenny Chambers's continued assistance. We are also grateful to Sarah Tittle for her secretarial help, including weekends, Peter Whitehouse for illustrations, and Helen Appleton for carefully checking the manuscript and for much helpful advice.

We are grateful to Praeger Publications for permission to reproduce in Chapter 4 part of 'A Strategic Approach to Child Pedestrian Safety', by Howarth and Lightburn from *Road Safety: Research and Practice* (eds. Foot, Chapman and Wade 1981).

We are also grateful to LEDIS, the Local Economic Development Information Service, for contributing the information sheets reproduced in Appendices I and II for Chapter 8.

# Contributors

*Peter Ambrose* is Lecturer in Urban Studies, University of Sussex. He is the author of *The Quiet Revolution* (Chatto and Windus, 1974), *The Property Machine* (Penguin, 1975), and *Whatever Happened to Planning?* (Methuen & Co. Ltd, 1986).

*Peter Austin* came to the Institute of Planning Studies, University of Nottingham, with an Honours degree in Science Resources from Birmingham University. He was awarded an MA in Environmental Planning in 1986. He worked for Middlesbrough Borough Council from 1986 to 1988.

*Philip Bean* is Senior Lecturer in the Department of Social Policy and Administration, School of Social Studies, University of Nottingham. Before that he was a research officer for the Medical Research Council and a probation officer in the Inner London Probation and After-Care Service. He has had numerous Visiting Professorships. His main interests are in the fields of criminology, mental health, and social philosophy where he has published widely. Publications include: *Compulsory Admissions to Mental Hospitals* (John Wiley), 1980); and *Mental Disorder and Legal Control* (Cambridge University Press, 1986).

*Martin Binks* is Lecturer in Economics in the Department of Economics, University of Nottingham. He has been actively involved with research on small firms since his work for the Wilson Committee in 1978. Since 1981 he has been the Director of Nottingham University's Small Firms Unit.

*Brian Dabson* is Managing Director of the Centre for Employment Initiatives. Before that he worked as a town planner and spent 13 years in local government in Glasgow, Warwick and Merseyside before moving to CEI in 1983.

*Frederick Davies* came to the Institute of Planning Studies, University of Nottingham, with an Honours degree in Economics from Stirling University and obtained an MA in Environmental Planning in 1988.

*John Dean* has been City Planning Officer, Leicester, since 1973. He was President of the Royal Town Planning Institute in 1987. He has been a member of the Council of the Royal Town Planning Institute since 1978. He has worked as a town planner in Manchester and Cheshire and as an engineer at Bolton and Cheltenham. He has also been the Chairman of both the RTPI's Education and Public Relations Boards. He has been Special Professor at the Institute of Planning Studies, University of Nottingham since 1986.

*Frank Doherty* has been Chief Executive of the Greater Nottingham Cooperative Society since March 1977. He is a Director of the Cooperative Wholesale Society and the Cooperative Bank. He is a chartered accountant.

*John Ferris* is Lecturer in the Department of Social Policy and Administration, School of Social Studies, University of Nottingham. He has published in the fields of housing, urban planning and social policy. His current research interests include housing policy and homelessness.

*Mayer Hillman* is Senior Research Fellow at the Policy Studies Institute (formerly Political and Economic Planning). He is principally engaged in research on transport, energy and health policies. Before joining PEP in 1970 he was an architect planner in private practice. He is the author or co-author of many publications on these subjects, including *Personal Mobility and Transport Policy*, 1973; *Walking is Transport*, 1979; *Energy and Personal Travel: obstacles to conservation*, 1983; and *Danger on the Road: the needless scourge*, 1984.

*David Hoath* is Reader in Law at the University of Sheffield, and is a solicitor. He has a particular interest in housing law, and has written three books on the subject including *Homelessness* (Sweet and Maxwell, 1983). He is currently involved in writing a book on public sector housing law, which includes detailed treatment of the law relating to homelessness.

*John Holmes* is Group Planning Director of Wilson Bowden plc. Until

1987 he was Director of Planning for Broxtowe Borough Council and before that Deputy Director of Planning at Charnwood Borough Council, Leicestershire.

*Ian Howarth* has been Professor and Head of Department of Psychology, University of Nottingham since 1964. He has also been Director of the Accident Research Unit since 1972 and Director of the Blind Mobility Unit since 1970. He has published widely in the area of accident research. His qualifications include MA, D.Phil, FBPsS and C.Psychol.

*Kai Lemberg* is Special Advisor to the City of Copenhagen, and Professor at Roskilde University Centre in Denmark and at the Nord Plan Institute in Stockholm. He was Chief City Planner for Copenhagen from 1968 to 1988. He is a co-author of *Nordic Democracy* (Danish Institute, Copenhagen 1981). He is an economist and planner.

*Nathaniel Lichfield* is Professor Emeritus of the Economics of Environmental Planning, University of London, and founding partner, Nathaniel Lichfield and Partners, planning, development, urban design and economic consultants. Before establishing the practice, he worked in a private development company, local government and central government. His main publications are: *The Economics of Planned Development* (Estates Gazette, 1956), with Peter Kettle and Michael Whitbread, *Evaluation of the Planning Process* (Pergamon, 1975), with Haim Darin-Drabkin, *Land Policy and Planning* (George Allen & Unwin, 1980), *Economics and Urban Conservation* (Cambridge University Press, forthcoming).

*David Miller* is Deputy Director of the Centre for Local Economic Strategies. He has held a number of academic and local government posts in the field of regional and local economic development; he has been involved in several major research projects on local authority economic development policy and has published a number of articles on the subject.

*Patricia Mounser* is Research Associate with the Department of Psychiatry, University of Nottingham. Before that she was Research Assistant in the Department of Medicine, University of Nottingham. She is currently examining the referral process with the Medical System for a PhD thesis. Her main interests are in health and health services, mental health and community care policy. She has published in these and related areas.

*Taner Oc* is Senior Lecturer in Planning at the Institute of Planning Studies, University of Nottingham. His current research and recent publications examine 'ethnic minorities and planning'. He has taught at Middle East Technical University, Queen's University of Belfast and George Washington University. He has qualifications in architecture, planning and social sciences. He is a member of the International Society of City and Regional Planners.

*Susie Ohlenschlager* is the Recycling Officer for Oxfordshire County Council and secretary of Transport 2000 International. Before that she worked for Transport 2000 compiling Transport Retort and was specially concerned with road safety for cyclists and pedestrians. She also worked for ROSPA, and for a cycling pressure group, and she developed the cycleways curriculum for primary schools.

*Anthony Ramsay* is Lecturer in Planning at Strathclyde University. He practised for 19 years, in local government and in new towns, first as a civil engineer and then as a town planner. He is a leading member of the International Federation of Pedestrians and is also a member of the Pedestrians Association's National Executive. In the last few years he has acted as consultant to the National Consumer Council and to a special committee of the European Parliament on pedestrian-related matters.

*Sylvia Trench* is Lecturer in Economics and Transport Policy at the Institute of Planning Studies, University of Nottingham. She worked previously at Political and Economic Planning, the National Economic Development Office and the Department of Economic Affairs. In recent years her research has been mainly concerned with public transport and she has contributed articles to various journals.

*David Whynes* is Senior Lecturer in Economics at the University of Nottingham. He has published extensively in the fields of economic development, political economy and social policy. His current research interests include homelessness, drug control and policy and cost-effectiveness appraisal in health treatments.

*Douglas Wright* is Housing Development Manager for the Nationwide Building Society. He has been employed by the Nationwide Building Society for 14 years in various capacities, including that of Branch Manager, and for the last two-and-a-half years as Housing Development Manager. The

Housing Development Manager role has now developed to meet the specific requirements of Nationwide Housing Trust which is a subsidiary company of Nationwide Anglia Building Society undertaking the construction of housing developments.

# PART I
# STRATEGIES FOR PEDESTRIANS

# Introduction

*Sylvia Trench*

Pedestrians have a hard time in most urban areas. This is partly because so little is done *for* them. It is also because so much is done *against* them. Land use and traffic planning which is concerned with provision for vehicles and access for car owners is not just ignoring pedestrians in a neutral way; it is very often creating barriers of distance and physical layout which make it much more difficult to walk about.[1] This section deals with the consequences of planning policies which fail to take account of their impact on pedestrians as well as with policies which are designed to make specific provision for them.

Walking accounts for around 75 per cent of all journeys of less than one mile despite the obstacles and deterrents (Hillman and Whalley, 1979). The range of facilities and important destinations that are within this radius is clearly an important determinant of the proportion of journeys that will be made on foot as opposed to car or public transport for those who have a choice. It is also a major determinant of the quality of life for those who do not have a choice of transport. Planning land use in such a way that more facilities are in walking distance of where people live therefore has a double pay-off, and trends which reduce the number of places people can conveniently walk to carry a double penalty.

It is sad therefore that so little attention is paid in current land use planning to Perry and Stein's concepts of neighbourhood developments with shops, library, doctor, and so on, in easy walking distance. As long ago as 1929 Perry was advocating that developments should be based on a neighbourhood unit where facilities would be located within a quarter of a mile of the furthest dwelling (Perry, 1929). By 1942 Stein had taken this idea further in his plan for Radburn where amenities were placed in easy walking distance of homes and there was also a degree of pedestrian vehicular segregation, (Stein, 1942). After the war many of the early new towns' designs used a version of the Radburn principle.

1

Market pressures in the private sector and the pursuit of economies of scale at the point of supply in the public sector are taking more and more facilities further away from the would-be pedestrian. As local post offices and corner shops close, as education departments opt for larger schools farther away, as doctors group in bigger and better but more distant health centres and health authorities close down smaller hospitals, the range of opportunities within walking distance continues to shrink. Some of these trends are occurring generally, but they are also exacerbated by reducing residential densities. Research shows a clear relationship between the range of facilities within walking distance and density (Hillman and Whalley, 1979). Unfortunately these matters are rarely discussed in planning circles at present.

Provision for pedestrians has always been a low priority for engineers and planners. It is less glamorous, and less prestigious than building roads or bridges. Although it is relatively cheap that does not count for much in a world where men are often judged by the size of their budgets.[2] Even the very limited provision of the pedestrian precinct has only recently become widely accepted and the exclusion of traffic from busy narrow shopping streets is still a matter of controversy. The notion that people count for more when they are encased in a ton and a half of metal than when they are on their own two legs, dies hard in modern thinking.

There is a widely held presumption that keeping traffic moving is the highest priority in transport planning. This is evident in policy decisions about big matters like aggregate spending on road building compared with the trivial amounts spent on provision for pedestrians. But it is more immediately noticeable in little matters like siting bus stops and crossings a distance away from where people want to be, and sending pedestrians over bridges and under subways in order not to slow down traffic by providing for pedestrian movements at busy junctions or on the level.

Few of those who are responsible realize that these policies imply a discriminatory valuation of people's time. If this had to be explicitly stated it would amount to saying that a man in a comfortable car, protected from the weather, with his heater and car stereo must always have his time counted as more valuable than that of a woman (and it is a woman more often than not) on her feet, in the cold and wet perhaps carrying heavy bags or pushing a pram.

The implied value judgement that a person's time is worth more if he is in a car than if she is on her feet is by no means self-evident, though conventional techniques used for economic evaluation of transport

2

investments give this a spurious credibility. Time savings for pedestrians were not included in evaluations for road investments until 1987, and even now the convention is followed that non-working time is valued at only 43 per cent of the time of people travelling during paid working hours.[3]

Even so it is doubtful if many of the schemes which cause pedestrians to climb up stairs and down ramps and detour around iron railings in the interests of keeping the traffic moving, would in fact show an overall gain in a cost-benefit calculation. These decisions are conventionally taken on the basis of spurious 'technical' criteria or design standards whose basis of determination is rarely made clear. Whatever its basis it certainly owes nothing to the notion that all people are equal let alone any notions of social justice like taking into account the relative hardships involved to different groups of people as a result of traffic management schemes.

It is an everyday consequence of traffic management schemes that the elderly, lame and heavy laden should climb and limp and heave in order that fit, middle-aged, seated and heated men listening to their radios and speaking on their car phones should be spared small amounts of delay.

Another common perverse priority is that given to goods vehicles. Schemes often exempt delivery vehicles from the general exclusion of vehicles where there is no back access to shops. The idea that they should be unable to deliver during peak shopping hours is considered unacceptable to the shopkeepers who are usually vociferous in opposing schemes in the early stages; so also is the idea that they would have to trolley goods from the end of the street instead of from the side of the road. Many people involved with planning policy have a gut feeling that the movement of goods must in itself be more important than the movement of people because it seems more directly related to a saleable end product.

These blanket exemptions open up the pedestrian area to a large number of goods vehicles only a very few of which are engaged in delivering heavy goods if indeed they are delivering goods at all. One study found that exemption for goods vehicles meant that a vehicle was entering a very short pedestrian zone on average once every five minutes so that most pedestrians would meet at least one during their visit. It would be fallacious to assume that most of these vehicles were engaged in some vital economic activity. Of the 46 vehicles carefully watched over a four-hour period, 18 drove straight through without stopping. Of the remaining 28, only 17 were observed to be making an actual delivery and many of these were seen to be of items small and light enough to be easily carried in from outside the area (Institute of Planning Studies, 1987).

In the same scheme it was decided to exclude disabled holders of orange badges as they were now so numerous, and to require seriously incapacitated persons to make a special application to the County Council for a supplementary disabled permit for vehicular access. Taxis which previously had a rank in the street were excluded and to date (two years later) have no proper taxi rank and are not supposed to drive in to pick up or set down even disabled passengers. It does not seem to have occurred to anyone that delivery vehicles could equally well have been restricted to those who made out a special case of hardship, and that, for example, carrying a few flower bouquets for 50 yards is probably less of a hardship than asking a disabled or elderly person to walk from the car park or find a non-existent taxi rank.

If these priorities make little sense as a social policy, so also does the basic neglect of pedestrians make little sense in terms of overall transport strategy. Mayer Hillman's contribution leads off the discussion with a refreshing first principles approach to transport policy. If walking were a new idea to be compared with existing transport modes, policy makers would be leaping over one another to introduce and promote it because it fits so well all the stated objects of transport policy and scores so highly on grounds of economy, environmental impact and health.

No one in this country has researched more or written better on issues related to the movement of people than Mayer Hillman. His *Personal Mobility and Transport Policy* in 1973 was the first major transport study to concern itself with the movement of people as opposed to vehicles which had been (and largely still are) the main preoccupation of transport planners. His *Walking Is Transport* in 1979 is also essential reading for anyone seriously interested in human scale transport policy.

His conclusion on policy strategy for walking must therefore command respect and set the tone for the discussion which follows in later chapters and which pick up some more specific issues.

Susie Ohlenschlager was asked to write specifically about women. There is no need to get into an arid argument about whether pedestrians are relatively neglected because so many of them are women or whether women are getting a raw deal in transport terms because they have less access to cars than men and because the nature of their work involves more walking. It is clear that as a group many more of them are adversely affected by the way in which pedestrians are treated.

As Susie Ohlenschlager points out, pedestrians have very little political clout and are not organized into powerful pressure groups. Motorists on

4

the other hand have not one but several well financed, generously staffed organizations to speak publicly and lobby privately for them, and the goods vehicle industry is similarly represented by well-heeled bodies. Mayer Hillman reminds us that no industry exists to make a profit from walking.

Women seem to find it as hard to organize and finance campaigns for their transport and environmental needs as they do to get trade unions to organize and represent their employment problems and for much the same reasons. Most women have less free time to attend meetings, less access to a car to get there and less disposable income to cover subscriptions and donations. So the fact that a very large proportion of pedestrians are women is both a part of the explanation of the under-provision for this sector and an indictment of the way the nation treats those who do the most part of its shopping, pram pushing and child escort duties. It is also a measure of its response to the knowledge that a group known to be vulnerable to attack is making many of its trips, rightly or wrongly, in a certain degree of fear.

If women are a vulnerable group, children are even more in need of special protection. Most of today's adults have grown up with road safety drills and in turn passed on the Green Cross Code to their children. It seems natural to assume that further progress in reducing accidents means working harder at teaching children to be even more careful, and to place the onus of accident prevention on the children themselves.

Ian Howarth, a psychology professor whose department at Nottingham University has been involved in research on human factors' aspects of road safety for over 15 years, has contributed a chapter which turns all these preconceptions upside down. He draws on his own and other academic research projects to show that children have in fact very well developed accident-avoiding strategies in the presence of vehicles but that motorists are observed to take very little avoiding action — slowing down, hooting or swerving away from the kerb — in the presence of children. It is not the behaviour of the victims that needs to be improved.

He goes on to develop a radical and imaginative policy for making motorists watch out for children. This combines a change in the law with altering the physical layout of residential streets in a way which both makes a legal presumption of drivers' responsibility workable and which also makes the streets themselves safer for children.

John Dean, as ex-President of the Royal Town Planning Institute and Leicester City Council's Chief Planning Officer, contributes a professional planner's perspective. Our cities are organized for the young and fit, and they are only a minority of the population. The groups with special problems as pedestrians — the elderly, disabled and pram pushing members of the community — outnumber them and anyway planning for those who have problems will not impede the progress of the others. He describes how Leicester has developed an approach to provision for pedestrians which starts by identifying the needs of the most vulnerable groups and then tries to alter the physical environment to give them an easier passage.

Schemes for pedestrians play a key role in Leicester's City Centre Action Plan. It is also about to introduce a British version of the Dutch 'woonerf' — a way of civilizing residential streets without totally excluding access traffic, through using the street layout and furniture to enforce the precedence of pedestrians.

Chapter 5 is written by Kai Lemberg who was the Chief Planner for Copenhagen when it led Europe with one of the earliest and eventually most successful pedestrian schemes in a large European capital city. He tells how it came about despite the opposition of the traders at the beginning and with their enthusiastic support towards the end. After a fiercely contested experiment he tells how in 1964 'the shopkeepers had thanked the Town Hall for not listening to them in 1962' and carried on with the scheme despite their earlier protests.

This turnabout will be familiar to anyone who has been closely involved with a shopping street pedestrianization scheme. It remains one of the peculiarities of planning politics that shopkeepers seem to be instinctively hostile to such proposals and invite their customers to join their campaign of opposition to provisions which would allow these same customers to shop in greater comfort and safety. Time after time, however, their fears of reduced turnover are proved wrong and there is a happy coincidence of greater profit and improved amenity. The case study charts the different stages the scheme passed through and measures some of the effects on traffic flows and pollution in the area.

The discussion of the pedestrianization strategies is completed by a review of successful and unsuccessful features of different schemes. This section is contributed by Anthony Ramsay, a transport planner with a worldwide experience of pedestrian schemes who looks both at the detail and the scope of a variety of schemes and draws out some general rules for good practice.

Both precincts and segregation for pedestrians sound like good ways of meeting the demand for provision for walking. They can often be no more than a token recognition of pedestrians' needs if they are not based on proper studies of behaviour of pedestrian traffic comparable with the studies of vehicular traffic used for road planning. Many mistakes have been made. Anthony Ramsay describes cases where provision is too small or too cluttered for the numbers of pedestrians or for their natural social groupings; precincts which are stuck on the edge of main roads or bypasses; segregation may mean extra walking or climbing and may just be a device for getting people out of the way of fast-moving traffic.

A worrying trend which on the face of it looks as though it would be beneficial to pedestrians is the growing provision of enclosed shopping malls. These often become more than an extra collection of shops; they may become the main centre for the town's shopping and therefore a focal point of activity (McDougall, Slack and Trench, 1974). When these are privately owned and closed, as they usually are, at night, the town loses a most important pedestrian thoroughfare. Anthony Ramsay fears many pedestrians have extended journeys and long detours as a result of this policy.

A problem often arises about what to do with the buses which had previously stopped along pedestrianized shopping streets. He describes problems in Oxford and also in Leeds, where a minibus penetrating the area aroused so much hostility it was eventually withdrawn. Kai Lemberg referred to the same problem in Copenhagen where the bus company had opposed the exclusion of buses, and John Dean found the same problem in Leicester where many people specifically mentioned their dislike of 'incomplete' traffic exclusion in a participation exercise.

This kind of problem is an interesting example of how issues cannot be simply polarized as a choice between car owners and the rest. There are conflicts of interest between the different parts of 'the rest'. Cyclists in pedestrian areas cause a lot of problems; the tactile paving which helps blind people hurts sufferers from arthritis and so on. These issues are not simply solved by a single principle or preference. Much depends on the numbers and distances involved and these can be measured.

It is not necessary to be a full-blooded utilitarian to accept that the numbers of people and the distances involved should be measured and compared. Excluding buses, as Anthony Ramsay points out, involves little hardship where routes penetrate close by on crossing streets; on the other hand admitting cyclists may mean that they are allowed to disconcert and even intimidate elderly pedestrians for a gain of as little as 20 seconds per head (Institute of Planning Studies, 1987) and it is hard to see how exclusion in this case could be reasonably opposed. Studies which put some orders of magnitude on the demands of each of the affected groups may help to produce decisions which are less rule of thumb than is often the case.

There has been some progress in relation to leisure and recreational walks. Anthony Ramsay describes some pleasant schemes but he argues that they are no substitute for strategic through routes which allow people to walk to and from their main daily round of work, shopping and school journeys.

This is really the theme of the whole section on strategies. Pedestrians are not pet animals to be thrown occasional crumbs of preferential treatment or to be confined within a protected game reserve and open to attack outside. Everyone is a pedestrian for part of the time and those who spend more time than others in this role are on the whole people who are more deserving of consideration because they have a more difficult time than the average person. Planners and engineers must begin to give the problems of their movement over the whole of their journey from origin to destination the same kind of consideration they have been accustomed to give to motor traffic.

## NOTES

1   This is sometimes even taken to the extent of erecting iron railings or cementing rounded stones at the sides of roads as a deterrent or barbaric punishment for the pedestrian who goes where she was not supposed to go.
2   Nottinghamshire County Council dealt with this problem by the setting up of a separate environmental improvements group in 1982 with its own annual budget of £1.5m. Most of its projects are concerned with pedestrian schemes. The result has been a programme which carries some of the prestige and political identification that are more usually associated with roads and bridges.
3   The convention is to value walking time at double that for in-vehicle time, meaning that on average, a pedestrian moving outside paid working hours would have her time valued at 86 per cent of that of a lorry driver waiting

## REFERENCES

Hillman, M. and Whalley, A. 1973, *Personal Mobility and Transport Policy*, Political and Economic Planning.
Hillman, M. and Whalley, A. 1979, *Walking is Transport*, Policy Studies Institute.
Institute of Planning Studies 1987, *Pedestrianization in Beeston High Road* Report of Environmental Analysis Elective (unpublished).
MacDougall, M. Slack, A. and Trench, S. 1974, 'The Victoria Centre',

*Journal of the Town and Country Planning Association,* February.

Perry, C. 1929, *The Neighbourhood Unit*, vol. 7 Neighbourhood and Community Planning, Regional Survey of New York and Its Environs, New York.

Stein, C.S. 1942, 'City Patterns, Past and Future', *New Pencil Points*, June.

# 1

# The pedestrian in public policy

*Mayer Hillman*

Suppose the Secretary of State for Transport were to instruct his civil servants to analyse the outcome of current transport policy in terms of the extent to which it had furthered the social, economic and environmental objectives explicit or implicit in the 1977 White Paper, *Transport Policy:*

> improving the environment; avoiding the waste of finite fuel; lowering the private and public costs of travel; minimising the extent of suffering and anxiety from road accidents; and providing for the transport needs of people without a car (Department of Transport, 1977).

A response to this request could be established by looking at the available evidence in the Department of Transport's own statistical volumes which, while by no means comprehensive, do provide a good indication of the rate of progress (Department of Transport, published annually). They would have to tell him that in the last ten years there has been a drift away from most of the objectives, continuing the trends from the previous decade, though generally at a less alarming rate.

## ENVIRONMENT

Far from improving, the evidence suggests that the environment has deteriorated. Two indices, the extent of air pollution and the volume of traffic noise, can be used to establish what changes have occurred with regard to that part of environmental quality which is influenced by modifications of transport patterns over the last ten years.

In spite of improving standards, Table 1.1 shows that, other than those of sulphur dioxide and lead, the annual tonnages of pollutants expelled into the air by motor vehicles, has risen by about a fifth during the decade. Owing to the decrease in air pollutants from most of the other main sources, the proportion attributable to road traffic has increased to such an extent that, by 1985, of all man made processes, road traffic contributed 84 per cent of the carbon monoxide, 26 per cent of the hydrocarbons, and 40 per cent of the nitrogen oxides.

**Table 1.1   Changes in air pollution and road traffic mileage, 1976 – 86**

| Air pollution (th tonnes) | 1976 | 1985 | % change 1976 – 85 |
|---|---|---|---|
| Carbon monoxide | 3,729 | 4,521 | + 21 |
| Hydrocarbons | 449 | 545 | + 21 |
| Nitrogen dioxides | 604 | 740 | + 22 |
| Sulphur | 50 | 40 | – 20 |
| Lead | 7.6 | 6.5 | – 14 |
| | | | |
| Traffic mileage (bn vehicle km) | 1976 | 1986 | 1976 – 86 |
| Articulated lorries | 5.5 | 6.9 | + 25 |
| Motor cycles | 4.7 | 5.4 | + 15 |
| Cars and taxis | 173.4 | 242.4 | + 40 |
| All mileage | 220.4 | 297.7 | + 35 |

The second index that can be used to measure environmental quality is the volume of road traffic. Some indication of the change in noise from motor vehicles can be obtained from the annual figures of traffic levels derived from the Department of Transport's roadside traffic counts. While these figures can serve only as approximate indicators of this as some improvement in reducing engine noise has been made in recent years, they are fairly reliable for this purpose. It can be seen in the table that total vehicle mileage has risen by over a third between 1976 and 1986. Even if it were judged that 1976 levels were acceptable, it is extremely unlikely that average noise emissions from vehicles has been reduced to this extent. It can be seen, too, that the mileages of heavy lorries and motor cycles — the two sources of traffic noise judged in a national survey to cause particular annoyance in the home[1] — have also continued to rise at an alarming rate.

## ENERGY CONSERVATION

Transport has made increasing demands on supplies of finite fuel. Higher oil prices, together with the recession from the mid-1970s, have lead to petroleum consumption for all purposes other than for transport being nearly halved as domestic and industrial users have introduced conservation measures, switched to alternative fuels, and reduced their overall demand for energy. However, as can be seen in Table 1.2, consumption for transport during the decade has increased by over a quarter with the result that, whereas the proportion used for cars in 1976 was only 28 per cent of the total, by 1986 the proportion had increased to 40 per cent.

### Table 1.2   Changes in petroleum consumption, 1976 – 86

| Petroleum use (m tonnes) | 1976 | 1986 | % change 1976 – 86 |
|---|---|---|---|
| Motor Spirit | 16.9 | 21.5 | + 27 |
| DERV | 5.6 | 7.9 | + 41 |
| Aviation fuel | 4.1 | 5.5 | + 34 |
| All transport uses | 28.6 | 36.7 | + 28 |
| All non-transport uses | 32.1 | 17.3 | − 46 |

The increase in consumption for cars was the most significant of all transport uses in terms of tonnage. This is explained by the continued growth in car ownership and in the average mileage per car which, in combination, have outweighed the effects of improved fuel efficiency through better car and engine design (Hillman and Whalley, 1982).

# ECONOMY IN EXPENDITURE

Expenditure on transport continues to rise. During the decade, total expenditure on personal travel — that is public expenditure together with users' expenditure less motor taxes, to eliminate overlap of these expeditures — has risen by nearly a third in real terms. Close examination of the figures set out in Table 1.3 shows that the predominant element — users' expenditure on cars — has risen by two-fifths, and their expenditure on rail has risen to a similar extent to the decline in their expenditure on buses and coaches. Public expenditure on roads too has increased, though not to such an extent as that on private transport.

**Table 1.3   Changes in users' and government expenditure on personal motorized travel, 1976 – 86**

| Users' expenditure (£ bn) | 1976 | 1986 | % change 1976 – 86 |
|---|---|---|---|
| Cars (including taxis and hire cars) | 23.1 | 32.7 | + 41 |
| Buses and coaches | 2.6 | 2.3 | − 12 |
| Rail | 1.6 | 1.8 | + 14 |
| All | 27.2 | 36.8 | + 35 |
| **Public expenditure (£ bn)** | **1976/7** | **1986/7** | |
| Revenue support to public transport | 0.45 | 0.43 | − 5 |
| All expenditure on roads | 2.96 | 3.18 | + 8 |
| capital costs | 1.75 | 1.75 | 0 |
| current costs | 1.21 | 1.43 | + 18 |

Comparison of users' expenditure with public expenditure in 1976 and 1986 shows that the additional expenditure by users was many times higher than any savings effected in public expenditure. Thus, while governments have continued to pour money into roads and into maintaining much of the revenue support for public transport, users' expenditure on private transport has risen markedly, with the small fall in their expenditure on public transport making hardly any difference to their overall expenditure on personal travel.

13

The extent of progress in reducing the adverse physical and mental consequences of travel can be monitored from records of transport accidents. As Table 1.4 shows, road casualties have declined overall by 14 per cent during the decade in question. However, there has been an increase in the number of cyclists killed or seriously injured.

**Table 1.4  Deaths and serious injuries in road accidents, 1976 – 86**

| Type of road users | 1976 '000s | 1986 '000s | % change 1976 – 86 |
|---|---|---|---|
| Car users | 34.9 | 29.7 | – 15 |
| Pedestrians | 20.6 | 19.1 | – 7 |
| Two-wheel motor vehicle users | 19.9 | 16.5 | – 17 |
| Cyclists | 4.9 | 5.3 | + 8 |
| Bus passengers | 1.2 | 0.8 | – 35 |
| All road users | 86.1 | 74.1 | – 14 |

## SUFFERING AND ANXIETY

No evidence is available on whether the overall fall in casualties has resulted in people feeling safer when travelling, or being less anxious for instance about allowing children to get about on their own. Fear of traffic is known to encourage parents to restrict their children from making their own way to and from school, and elsewhere, for several years beyond the age at which they are physically competent to do so (Hillman, Henderson and Whalley, 1976).

Although there is no comprehensive record of changes in vehicle speeds during the decade, the evidence that is available indicates that these too have risen: it has been estimated that, nationally, they are increasing on average by 1.5 per cent per annum (Tanner, 1981). It seems likely that the combination of this rise with the increase in traffic levels has heightened public perception of danger and of the risks entailed in personal travel. In turn, this has led to the distortion of many people's preferred patterns of travel, for example, discouraging cycle use, and to the restrictions on children's independent travel.

## EQUITY

There is no sign either of progress towards the final objective of providing for the transport needs of people without a car. As can be seen in Table 1.5, levels of car ownership, both per household and per person, have risen by about a fifth so that nearly two in three of all households own a car and there is an average of one car for every three people. Over half the adult population hold a driving licence whereas, ten years ago, only two in five did. In these ways, more people have been able to maximize their personal freedom in travel.

**Table 1.5   Changes in access to transport and in consumer travel cost indices, 1976 – 86**

| Access to motor transport | 1976 | 1986 | % change 1976 – 86 |
|---|---|---|---|
| Cars (per 100 population) | 25.8 | 31.5 | + 22 |
| Car-owning households (per cent) | 56 | 63 | + 7 |
| Bus km run (bns) | 3.5 | 3.3 | − 7 |
| Buses in use (ths) | 75.5 | 67.8 | − 10 |
| Passenger train (m.km) | 305 | 312 | + 2 |
| Passenger rail routes (th.km) | 14.4 | 14.3 | − 1 |
| Consumer travel cost indices compared with all consumer cost indices | | | |
| Car travel | 100 | 102 | + 2 |
| Rail travel | 100 | 98 | − 2 |
| Bus and coach travel | 100 | 124 | + 24 |

However, this still obviously leaves nearly two in five households without a car, half of all adults without a licence, and most people without a car of their own. The gap between their mobility, ease of access and costs of travel − most of them are heavily dependent on getting about on foot or by public transport − and the equivalent of those with a car has continued to widen generally (Hillman, Henderson and Whalley, 1976). As the table shows, public transport services have continued to decline in terms of the number of vehicles in use and their mileage, the only obvious areas of improvement being in British Rail's 'Inter-City' services and in the extension of the network of coach services. But stage service bus mileage and routes, on which by far the highest proportion of public transport journeys are made, have continued to decline.

Unfortunately, there are few records of changes in the accessibility of public and commercial facilities to the population that they are intended to serve. These would be invaluable as indicators of the ease with which they can be reached on foot. But it is known that their numbers have declined during the decade, so it can be reasonably assumed that they have also declined in geographical accessibility, especially as there has also been an expansion of the housing areas served. Thus, there are now fewer facilities conveniently accessible on foot.

The costs of travel have risen both for private and especially for public transport. The average running cost of travel per user kilometre by car, predominantly for petrol, was far lower than the cost of travel by public transport in 1976, and this gap has widened further during the decade.

## NEW POLICIES

Having surveyed this evidence, the Secretary of State might well deduce that new policies were urgently needed: he could conclude that there was a need for his Department to invest in research and development to find a form of transport which would be more likely to further the objectives noted earlier. He would be looking for a travel method which was environmentally benign, consumed little energy, was cheap to use and to cater for, did not generate danger in use, and was universally available.

It would not be fanciful to assume that someone would draw his attention to *walking*. After all, it not only fulfils all these prerequisites but also has the virtue of serving a social function. What would the Secretary of State do in the circumstances? Would he refuse to be drawn into discussion on the merits of walking on the grounds that that would be a frivolous subject, or would he ask his civil servants to carefully scrutinize this mode? In what respects would they consider walking unsatisfactory?

## HOW GOOD IS WALKING?

First, it would be found wanting because travellers using their own two feet are more exposed to the weather than those travelling in motor vehicles.

Second, walking would be judged to be relatively unsafe, with road accident statistics cited in support of this. And third, it would be argued that most of those who were using this form of transport are restricted to a catchment area of one or two miles.

Were these civil servants to be objective in their assessment, they would also note that comparatively little research has been carried out on walking. In one of the few available studies (Hillman and Whalley, 1979) they would find that, on average, about a third of all journeys are made on foot and that, for those without access to a car, this proportion rises to about a half, and for many children and old people higher still. However, they would have to admit that the significance of walking continues to be largely unrecognized in public policy – other than, on safety grounds, by the provision of road crossings and, on grounds of amenity, by the creation of some pedestrian precincts. Even here it would be recognized that the motivation stems more from a concern about the sufficiency of road space in central areas to cater for traffic than about the need to cater for walking as a transport mode.

Closer attention to the role of walking would soon reveal that a substantial proportion of the population are concerned about the quality, convenience and safety of the pedestrian environment; that pedestrians have to contend with increasing volumes of traffic moving at ever higher speeds, and that, as pedestrians, half a million receive medical treatment each year because of accidents of one form or another (Plowden and Hillman, 1984).

## PUBLIC POLICY

The Secretary of State could well wish to establish how this lamentable situation had arisen, given the attractions of walking, particularly from the public viewpoint, and would wish to be informed as to the savings that could be achieved by enabling and encouraging transfer from motorized to non-motorized forms of travel.

He would be likely to find out – though not necessarily from his own civil servants – that among the reasons for the oversight of the significance of walking was his own Department's predilection for motorized travel, especially by car; the judgement of its advisors that, at the heart of transport policy, there is perceived to be an overriding need to cater for the growth in this form of travel by investing vast sums of public – or even private – money in road building; and underlying this, questionable assumptions about the extent of availability of the car and the impact of its use on general freedom of movement. His attention would also be drawn to the oversight of the significance of land use and location planning in terms of their impact on patterns of travel and people's ability to reach their destinations on foot.

He would perhaps realize that walking as a mode of travel has the disadvantage that it is cheap to cater for and so has no commercial lobby promoting provision for it, and that this has inevitably led to its lowly status in transport policy and the lack of appreciation of its relevance to the objectives of transport policy noted in the introduction.

## POLICIES TO PROMOTE WALKING

In reaching the conclusion that walking is deserving of proper recognition as an outstanding transport mode, the Secretary of State could be expected to wish to see what changes were necessary to create an environment conductive to walking. It would appear that there are three components: convenience, access and safety.

He would be very likely to be advised that an overriding consideration would be the need to incorporate walking into the planning and transport processes of local and central government with, for instance, a requirement that, at the planning stage, pedestrian impact statements, assessing the implications of proposals for the convenience of people getting about on foot, have to be made.

He would wish to see pedestrian priority areas established, and would want local authorities to create environments in which the convenience and safety of pedestrians were not reduced at every road junction, by providing for them a well maintained and uninterrupted network, free of danger, noise and pollution, by such measures as raising road intersections to pavement level, with priority thereby given to people on foot. Where pedestrians had to run the gauntlet of motor traffic, he would require significantly lower speed limits, taking advantage of the many technical means of enforcing these without recourse to more traffic police (Plowden and Hillman, 1984).

Finally, it would be put to him that the most crucial element in encouraging walking lay in the maintenance and promotion of local opportunities to meet people's travel needs. He would be informed of the wide benefits in this context of easily accessible shops, schools, leisure facilities and so on.

It is not inconceivable that an open minded Secretary of State would recognize how virtuous walking is and how beneficial it would be to reverse current priorities, and accord it a central place in both transport and planning policies and practice.

## NOTE

1   This survey found a strong correlation between traffic volume and the proportion of respondents who were sufficiently bothered to shut doors and windows (Morton-Williams et al, 1978).

## REFERENCES

Department of Transport 1977, *Transport Policy*, HMSO, London Cmnd 6836.
Department of Transport, *Transport Statistics, Great Britain*, annually, HMSO, London
Hillman, M. and Whalley, A. 1979, *Walking is Transport,* Policy Studies Institute.
Hillman, M. and Whalley, A. 1982, *Energy and Personal Travel: obstacles to conservation*, Policy Studies Institute.
Hillman, M., Henderson, I. and Whalley, A. 1976, *Transport Realities and Planning Policy*, Political and Economic Planning.
Morton-Williams, J. et al 1978, *Road Traffic and the Environment*, Social Community and Planning Research.
Plowden, S. and Hillman, M. 1984, *Danger on the Road: The Needless Scourge*, Policy Studies Institute.
Tanner, J. 1981, *Methods of forecasting kilometres per car*, Transport and Road Research Laboratory Report LR968.

# 2
# Walking in the city
*John Dean*

The great majority of pedestrian preference schemes are brought about simply to create convenience for pedestrians. They are there to provide a valuable space for shoppers to enjoy a reasonable environment and so that trade can flourish and avoid the deterioration which chronic congestion brings.

In some places, of course, the sheer weight of numbers means that pedestrian flows assert themselves; thus there is self-regulation. Some town centre markets are good examples of this: without any traffic orders, the flow of pedestrians in and around such places regulates the speed of vehicles and imposes an accepted responsibility on drivers to proceed with due care.

Rarely, however, are areas improved simply for the sake of amenity. Of course, pedestrian preference schemes introduce opportunities to create better amenities; to plant trees, to erect seats and in some places even introduce such features as fountains. Schemes are also used to enhance the conservation of buildings if there is such potential in the area. Rarely, however, is a real piazza created with space and buildings in harmony.

Compared with the combination of town planning and architecture in the Renaissance and the Baroque periods there is something missing in towns today and the idea of creating delight and enjoyment in towns has been lost. The point is illustrated by the way Patrick Leigh-Fermor described one of the German towns in 1934:

> Except for the fierce keep on the rock, the entire town was built for pleasure and splendour. Beauty, space and amenity lay all about (Leigh-Fermor, 1979). [This is a long way from current ideas in town building.]

Pedestrian preference[1] schemes have usually been concerned with convenience, safety and trade. Most developments have been ad hoc, utilizing opportunities where they arise. They have not been part of a strategy. There are signs that this is changing and postwar suburbs and estates often reflected some pattern and logic in the provision of an overall plan for pedestrian movements. This kind of thinking now needs to be applied to town centres. Pedestrians need links between car parks, bus stations, important points in the traffic system and land uses generally. Even if full pedestrian preference cannot always be applied to such links, the routes could be made more attractive to pedestrians.

However pedestrian convenience is usually secondary to commercial ends when political and economic priorities are balanced. Pedestrian preference is always more acceptable when it is clear that car use threatens trading itself. But a more radical approach is needed.

Much urban design is based on the convenience and priorities of the young fit male. This is the predominant design model for controlled pedestrian crossings, for the detailed layout of spaces and roads and for the way public transport is organized. But this is design for a small minority of the population.

In a big city like Leicester, for instance, where there are about 290 000 residents, there are only 57 000 men between the ages of 15 and 44 years and yet these are the ones who form the model for design. The groups with less ability to get around are the people over 65, the disabled and the women who can be expected to be dealing with buggies or prams or carrying loads of shopping, often both. The total of people in these categories in Leicester comes to about 66 000. Obviously designing to allow these people to get about more easily is not going to seriously inconvenience the others. Leicester is beginning to design for a broader client group. Three examples from recent schemes and policies will illustrate this newer and more progressive approach.

## THE CITY CENTRE ACTION PROGRAMME AND PEDESTRIAN PREFERENCE

The City Centre Action Programme is a ten-year plan for Leicester's central area. It indicates the main areas where the City and County Councils intend to invest as a guide to other organizations and individuals whose own investment decisions will affect the prospects of the city centre in the twenty-first century.

A key part of the programme is the phased creation of a pedestrian preference zone affecting nearly the whole of the central shopping area. This will involve the removal of all but essential traffic at certain times. Between 11.00 am and 4.00 pm only certain classes of vehicle would be permitted to enter the zone including emergency services, buses, cycles, vehicles displaying orange badges and permit holders. Permits will be given to taxis, specialized cash delivery vehicles and vehicles delivering perishables, some refuse collection vehicles, occupiers of off-street parking in the zone, builders and statutory undertakers. Following its gradual implementation starting in 1989 a range of street improvements will be possible, from pavement widening and extensions to loading-only streets and streets completely free of vehicles between 11.00 am and 4.00 pm.

It is intended to follow this scheme with the creation of a new network of footpaths linking car parks, shopping areas and open spaces. The aim would be to provide a system of attractive, and direct walkways, which will also be easier for disabled people to use, between all major pedestrian starting points and destinations within the central area. It is also intended to improve pedestrian links across the central ring road. Better and safer means of crossing the ring road will be provided to accommodate the large number of journeys made daily on foot from the surrounding residential areas, for instance, from the Polytechnic and the railway station, into the city centre. Existing bridges and subways will be made more attractive by better lighting and surfaces and new crossings installed in more convenient locations.

The needs of the disabled will be considered whenever pedestrian links are being developed or improved: paths will be ramped and include handrails whenever necessary, and dropped kerbs will be incorporated at entry or crossing points. This would also benefit women who often have to move around the city centre encumbered with prams, children and heavy shopping.

## A 'WOONERF' SCHEME: WORTHINGTON STREET, LEICESTER

The scheme involves the application of the Dutch 'woonerf'[2] principle to a typical Victorian terraced street in Leicester's inner area; it is being transformed into an area principally for the relaxation and enjoyment of its residents through the creation of an open space environment but without closing it to traffic. The two overriding objectives have been:

- to deter through traffic and encourage vehicles using the street to travel slowly and carefully; and
- to improve the environment for the benefit of residents and pedestrians.

The scheme has complemented the achievements of the Council's 'housing renewal strategy' in the area and has had the full support of local residents. It has transformed Worthington Street from a vehicular 'rat run' into one of Leicester's quieter and more attractive backwaters.

Attempts were made to introduce legislation, akin to that which exists in Holland, by a new type of Order which would limit speeds to a very low level and make it obligatory to give way to pedestrians. This was proposed in the Leicestershire Bill but was unsuccessful. Instead design measures using existing legislation will be used to try to emphasize pedestrian priority over vehicles.

The traditional carriageway and kerb-defined footpaths have been replaced with a new brick surface without any kerbs and a range of different colours has been used to define areas to which vehicles are restricted. Vehicular speed restraint is enforced by the narrowness of the carriageway — just wide enough for two-way traffic — its snaking zig-zag passage along the street and by the installation of ramps at two strategic points.

The ramps are marked by brick planters decorated with embosed brick courses. These complement the decorative brickwork of adjacent buildings and emphasize the conscious attempt to ensure that all the details reflect the materials and features of the local architecture.

Clay pavers bordered with soldier courses of red brick form the roadway. Parking bays (39 in number) are picked out in dark brown paving and cast iron bollards and railings help to define these and also add a traditional touch to the street scene. Distinct buff-coloured pavers create contiguous forecourts to the houses themselves.

Victorian style street lighting has been installed and trees and shrubs have been planted to soften the overall design. Hanging baskets and window boxes are to be mounted on house fronts where owners have agreed to maintain them, thereby adding to the attraction of the street.

The street contains about 82 terraced houses. The cost was £180 000.

# PLANNING FOR WOMEN

Work is well advanced in the City Planning Department on ways in which the Planning Service can be improved for women and girls. Draft design guidelines have been prepared to highlight those features of the built environment which are particularly important to women, and which should be recognized and incorporated into private and public developments. The guidelines were sent to women's groups and other interested organizations in the city and a series of public meetings held for feedback.

At the same time a joint officer/police working party has been meeting to discuss crime prevention and planning. The vulnerability of the female pedestrian is recognized as a serious issue, and one which could be improved by the adoption of certain planning practices. Safety problems and possible solutions were discussed at the consultation meetings which produced a number of generally accepted views on pedestrian schemes.

Totally traffic-free areas in parts of the centre were welcomed and extensions asked for both in and out of the city centre. Another matter raised, which is not only of concern to women, was that they had reservations about partial pedestrianization. The centre of the road was seen as the vehicular route and pedestrians felt unsafe when forced off the former pavements by parked vehicles. In any confrontation the vehicle would win! 'Why not a 10.00 am to 4.00 pm vehicle exclusion zone?' asked someone.

A 'Buses only' area was seen as particularly hazardous. Minibuses were driven fast and often erratically. It was particularly difficult for the disabled to cross. The message from the meetings is that women pedestrians wish to use areas which are known to be safe from traffic and want controlled crossings of trafficked areas rather than having to rely on their own agility, drivers' goodwill or force of numbers.

The multi-storey car parks were condemned unanimously on grounds of personal safety of pedestrians. A sense of isolation, lack of accessible, sympathetic officials, and the dingy construction and finish of the car parks increased the sense of fear. This problem would not appear in any statistics as frightening experiences were rarely reported. Car parks appear to be designed for cars going in and out, whereas they should be designed for the pedestrian, the product of the parking process.

The consultations also highlighted the need for car parks and bus stops to be located close to shopping areas and for the routes between to be safe from traffic and attack with no dark alleys.

Safety was also an issue in pedestrian areas away from the city centre. The Worthington Street Woonerf, for example, provided a comfortable daytime environment but the lack of surveillance from passing traffic made it less acceptable for some pedestrians at night. The solution could be perhaps to ensure that alternative more frequented routes were available for pedestrians at night.

Planning applications are now monitored to assess their impact on the female pedestrian in terms of convenience of movement and safety. The results of the consultations will enable the fine tuning of existing and future pedestrian schemes. The design guidelines and a future crime and planning document (Leicester City Council, 1989) will continue to improve facilities for the pedestrian woman.

## NOTES

1   This term covers any schemes which significantly increase the degree of freedom of movement for pedestrians ranging from vehicle loading restrictions for the main part of the day to making streets completely free of traffic.
2   See Appendix to Chapter 6.

## REFERENCES

Leicester City Council 1989, 'Safety, Access and Facilities for All' *Design Guidelines*
Leicester City Council 1989, *Crime Prevention by Planning and Design*, April
Leigh-Fermor, Patrick 1979, *A Time of Gifts*, Penguin.

# 3
# Women also travel

*Susie Ohlenschlager*

This chapter is about women as pedestrians. Men are by no means exempt from the problems being discussed here since walking is ultimately the most important mode of travel for both sexes in a society where 37 per cent of all households do not possess a car. However since 70 per cent of women do not possess a driving licence they are worse affected by the problems of pedestrians.

## GENDER AND TRAVEL PATTERNS

Women are far more dependent than men on walking as a mode of transport and they also face different and very specific problems. Despite the marked differences between the travel patterns and travel needs of women and men, women have played virtually no part in planning their walking environment. The professions which plan and design residential areas and shopping centres are male-dominated.

In certain age groups gender is a stronger influence on travel patterns than economic status (see Tables 3.1 and 3.2). For example, the difference between the wealthiest and the average household in the proportion of their journeys made by car, 58 per cent and 42 per cent respectively, is less than the difference between men and women. Men between the ages of 30 and 59 undertake 66 per cent of all their journeys by car while women in the same age group use a car for only 43 per cent of all their journeys.

Even more striking figures have been revealed by the GLC survey specifically about women and transport (Greater London Council,

1985). This survey showed that 87 per cent of women undertook the whole of their journey on foot at least once a week, compared with only 7 per cent on British Rail, and 27 per cent by car (Greater London Council, 1985).

Table 3.1   Percentage of total journeys made by different modes

|  | Men aged 21 – 64 | Women aged 21 – 59 |
|---|---|---|
| Type of journey | % | % |
| Walk/cycle | 25 | 42 |
| Public transport | 9 | 14 |
| Car | 64 | 44 |
| Other | 2 | 1 |
|  | 100 | 100 |
| Journeys to/from work |  |  |
| Walk/cycle | 20 | 31 |
| Public transport | 14 | 26 |
| Car | 63 | 41 |
| Other | 3 | 1 |
|  | 100 | 100 |
| Shopping journeys |  |  |
| Walk/cycle | 35 | 53 |
| Public transport | 8 | 15 |
| Car | 56 | 31 |
| Other | 2 | 1 |
|  | 100 | 100 |

Source: Potter and Lester, 1983.

Table 3.2   Percentage of journeys by different modes according to household income and gender

|  | Walk | Public transport | Car |
|---|---|---|---|
| Income | % | % | % |
| All households | 39 | 14 | 42 |
| Household income over £10 000 pa | 27 | 11 | 58 |
| Gender |  |  |  |
| Men aged 30 – 59 | 21 | 9 | 66 |
| Women aged 30 – 59 | 39 | 15 | 43 |

Source: Potter and Lester, 1983.

The GLC survey showed that shopping for essential goods is the main travel purpose for women, and that 42 per cent of women walk all the way. Escorting children forms a significant proportion of all journeys.

The pedestrian accident rate for women and girls is lower than for men despite the fact that women do more walking then men. Some studies have attempted to link this difference to inherited or acquired behaviour differences between the sexes, such as men walking diagonally across roads.

## IMPLICATIONS FOR WOMEN

It is clear from figures alone that walking is immensely important for women, and that for the greatest part of their walking trips women are shopping or escorting children. The importance of these two types of trip, shopping trips and trips with children, has enormous implications for the way in which towns and cities and transport networks linking facilities should be designed.

But what about the implications of all these figures for women themselves? It is very tempting for planners and politicians of all persuasions to fall into the trap of assuming that walking is merely the mode of last resort, done most by the most disadvantaged sectors of society. This view is reinforced by the fact that often people do walk because public transport is so bad that they have no choice.

### Enjoyment

However the GLC survey revealed that the women questioned enjoyed walking. It is always easy to forget this when we talk in lofty terms about transport policy. After all, the reasons for enjoying walking in smelly, dangerous, congested urban areas, on streets which are often fouled by dogs, are not immediately obvious. But the fact is that walking offers many opportunities for social interaction. Cars cannot fulfil that function, although of course public transport and also cycling can. The opportunities for social interaction are also very important for children, as are the opportunities — although sadly limited by the dangers — of play and discovery along the way. Walking is also a healthy form of exercise, even though pollution must to some extent negate the benefits.

And finally, walking offers independence; it costs nothing, and enables women and children to get around without having to rely on someone else.

Women and their families can derive many benefits from walking: social interaction, exercise, independence. But there are a number of difficulties and dangers which hinder them from enjoying it to the full.

## Safety

Take for example the fear of harassment. The GLC survey revealed that only 15 per cent of women felt safe walking at night. By contrast, 37 per cent felt safe in a bus. The younger age groups were even more worried, with only 11 per cent of 16−19 year olds feeling safe when walking at night. The added stress of allowing children out on the streets is also a factor that needs to be taken into account.

Public perceptions of poor pedestrian conditions have recently been revealed in a large-scale consultation exercise on public attitudes to traffic problems. Four independent road assessment studies into different areas of London were commissioned by the Department of Transport. All four studies revealed pedestrians' perceptions of danger, difficulties in crossing the road, the disturbance they suffered from noise, pollution, and severance. In one study, for example, the problems for pedestrians of danger and severance were listed as a problem second in importance only to the lack of a good public transport system (Department of Transport, December 1986).

## OBSTACLES FOR WALKERS

While these London road assessment studies give a picture of the general problems for pedestrians, there are some more specific ones, all of which will be encountered by men too, but to a lesser extent since they do overall less walking:

- high kerbs, narrow footways;
- pavement parking;
- stairs and confusing walkways;
- subways and footbridges (these are difficult to use, for different reasons);
- severance, when barriers or heavy traffic separate two sides of the road;

- speed of traffic (increases danger, risk of accident and threat, also difficulty crossing road when accompanying small children or carrying heavy loads);
- distance of bus stops from shopping facilities;
- traffic lights and confusing intersections;
- intrusion from heavy lorries;
- pollution;
- fear of harassment.

Why is this list of problems so long? Why have so many mistakes been made? It is not simply that the growth of the transport network has been influenced largely by men, who are only now getting an idea of women's specific travel needs. While car driving — a more prestigious masculine pursuit than walking — has increased, walking has inexorably slipped to the bottom of the list. It has become a third-rate mode of travel in the road user hierarchy.

## ROAD USER HIERARCHY

Basically this is a question of who has power. The road lobby — the lobby for motorized transport — is rich and powerful. Its members include industrial and road haulage interests as well as the wealthy consumer organizations for car owners. And the individual car driver has power. Motor vehicles are the biggest, the fastest, the strongest on the roads. Therefore, inevitably, it seems, pedestrians must defer to them to save their own skin, although they do not always succeed in doing that.

So at two levels motor transport comes out top of the hierarchy. On the roads the driver whether male or female is supreme. And in the corridors of power too, the road lobby is bigger and stronger than any other road user lobby.

## THE ROAD LOBBY

There is another reason why motor vehicles are accorded high priority. It is said that the economy depends on lorries; lorries and cars need bigger and faster roads to feed the economy and to reduce congestion and accidents. Because it is possible to estimate the costs of accident savings and time savings to drivers, road building or improvements can be justified on economic grounds. But pedestrian and cyclist time in current cost-benefit analysis techniques were not given any value at all until 1987.[1] This is why one can read of road schemes being justified, while the accompanying cycle lane or pedestrian facility is not.

## PRACTICAL IMPROVEMENTS

However more recently, a gradual, almost imperceptible shift in attitudes has begun to take place. The present road safety minister acknowledges that pedestrians have had a raw deal. It seems, therefore, a good time to draw up a list of the kind of changes needed to give women in their role as pedestrians a better deal:

1. dropped kerbs for easy negotiation by people with prams and shopping trolleys and disabled people;
2. increases in green man crossing times;
3. traffic restraint in residential streets and on main roads;
4. better pavement maintenance;
5. better street lighting;
6. stricter controls on air and noise pollution;
7. parking control and pavement parking control;
8. speed humps.

## CONCLUSIONS

Transport policy makers, locally and nationally, have a duty to give pedestrians in general, and the specific needs of women and children in particular, a much higher priority.

The value of pedestrian time needs to be given parity with that of other road users in cost-benefit analysis. But even before that stage is reached, more consultation with women would improve decision making. The GLC women's survey, and even the London Road Assessment Studies, which were the Government's first attempt at this scale of consultation, have set a precedent for far more extensive consultations of those who too often get left out.

Ultimately, of course, there is a need to encourage more women to enter the planning and engineering professions.

## NOTES

1 Now the Department of Transport has published new values of time which do put a value on pedestrian and cyclist time: Values for journey time savings and accident prevention (Department of Transport, 1987).

## REFERENCES

Department of Transport 1986, *London Road Assessment Studies*, Stage One.
Department of Transport 1987, *Values for Journey Time Savings and Accident Prevention*, March.
Greater London Council, 1985, *Women on the Move: Results of Survey by the GLC Women's Committee*, vols 1–9 and London Strategic Policy Unit vol.10
Potter, S. and Lester, N. 1983, *Vital Travel Statistics, Transport 2000 Ltd.*

# 4

# Making residential areas safer for children

*Ian Howarth*

This chapter[1] is concerned with the problem of road accidents to children. It will be argued that the conventional approach to the problem through education and exhortation directed at children and parents has a limited value which has probably by now been exhausted. By contrast very little effort has been devoted up to now to altering the behaviour of drivers and research suggests that policies directed at motorists would be more likely to reduce child accident rates.

## ACCIDENTS IN RESIDENTIAL AREAS

The majority of accidents to children occur on residential roads. Figure 4.1 shows the age distribution of children who are killed or injured on major and minor roads. Most accidents to children under 11 occur on minor roads. Grayson (1975) has shown that 60 per cent of pedestrian accidents to children under the age of 15 occur within a quarter of a mile of their own home. In addition, it has been found (Routledge, Repetto-Wright and Howarth, 1974; Routledge, Repetto-Wright, Lightburn and Howarth, 1977 unpublished) that the behaviour of children at the ages of five to seven years, the most vulnerable ages, is quite different on major and on minor roads.

The children have an effective strategy for crossing roads where there is light traffic, but are incapable of crossing a busy road in safety. By the age of 11 children can usually cope with busy roads, using an adult

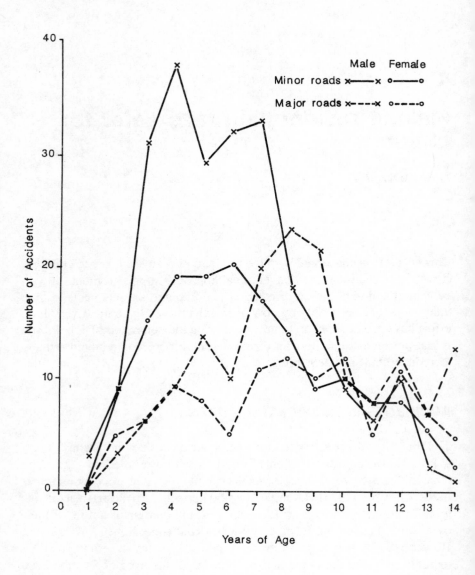

Source: C I Howarth & A Lightburn (1981).

**Figure 4.1   Number of accidents to pedestrians aged
0 to 14 years on major and minor roads 1971–76**

road-crossing strategy. The strategy which the younger children use is that which they are formally taught in the Green Cross Code or other safety-training schemes. However, the instruction to 'wait until the road is clear' is inappropriate on busy roads as it results in an almost indefinite delay which children are no more prepared to tolerate than adults.

The adult road-crossing strategy, which children learn informally despite deliberate instruction not to do so, is to step into the road in anticipation of a gap in the traffic and to pass swiftly through the gap as close as possible to the rear bumper of one car, and as far as possible from the front bumper of the following car.

Howarth and Lightburn (1981) have tried to take account of this evidence and suggest that the most effective measures for children will be those which can be applied to residential roads, and that any measures appropriate to such roads will be quite different from those which are appropriate on busy roads.

## WHO CAUSES ACCIDENTS?

It is commonly assumed that accidents to child pedestrians are due in large part to the heedlessness of the children. This assumption must be questioned in the light of recent research. Three separate studies, (Howarth and Lightburn, 1980; Howarth, 1985) using different observational techniques, have studied a large number of road crossings which children made, or attempted to make, at a time when a car was either within 20 yards or between 20 and 100 yards away when the child came to the kerb. The results were quite clear. No driver could be seen to take any avoiding action, either swerving or braking, unless the child was within 20 yards of the vehicle at the moment he signified his intention to cross the road. Since 20 yards is approximately the stopping distance of cars travelling at 25 miles per hour, this study shows that drivers never take marked and clearly visible avoiding action until it is too late to stop.

In contrast, the children frequently take avoiding action when the vehicle is between 20 and 100 yards away at the moment when the child reaches the kerb. The most common action for the child is to wait for the car to pass, but occasionally the child will do something more complicated, such as stepping ir o the road and then stepping back. If the car is within 20 yards of the child when the child steps off the kerb, the children nearly always wait for the car to pass, and the drivers quite frequently swerve or brake. However even on the most favourable interpretation, the action

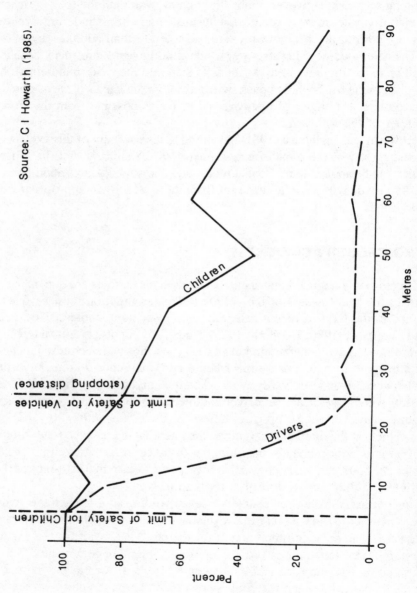

Source: C I Howarth (1985).

**Figure 4.2 The percentages of drivers and child pedestrians taking avoiding action**

taken by the children is more frequent, more vigorous and more effective (see figure 4.2). Further radar measurements of car speeds outside schools confirm this (Thompson, Fraser and Howarth, 1985).

It has been shown that the ratio of potential accidents to actual accidents is at least 10 000:1 (this figure was termed the probability of an accident per potential encounter with a car, *Pa/c* in the paper by Howarth, Routledge and Repetto-Wright, 1974). That is, all but one in 10 000 potential accidents are avoided by action on someone's part. Evidence suggests (Howarth and Lightburn, 1980; Howarth and Repetto-Wright, 1978; Howarth, 1985) that most of the avoiding is done by the children rather than the drivers, who should have a more realistic recognition of their responsiblity for pedestrian accidents, particularly on minor roads.

## MAKING DRIVERS MORE CAREFUL

Drivers might be induced to exercise such a responsibility for the care of children by changing the law with respect to child pedestrian accidents, by introducing the concept of *res ipsa loquitur* (Howarth and Gunn, 1982), the presumption of negligence unless proved otherwise.

It is clear that this doctrine, mild though it is, would be quite unworkable and possibly dangerous if it were applied to the busy roads we have called 'traffic routes'. But it should not be too difficult to have this measure accepted in relation to quiet 'residential' roads, provided drivers are given clear indications of the status of the road in question.

The distinction between 'residential' roads and 'traffic routes' implies a different attitude to the design, care and maintenance of the roads in the different areas. Some progress is already being made by developing design standards that emphasize the residential nature of access roads (Department of the Environment, 1977). In the long run these changes may reduce the amount spent on the upkeep of residential roads but, in the context of an integrated package, improve their safety and convenience.

It has been calculated that only 14.5 per cent of all vehicle journeys are on minor roads. An even smaller proportion will be on the designated 'residential' roads which are being suggested. Although the measures which are being proposed must reduce speeds on these roads, the effect on total vehicle journey times will be very small, while the reduction in child pedestrian accidents is potentially very great. The reduced speeds may also reduce the severity of any vehicle accidents which occur on these roads.

## PARKED CARS

Parked cars cause considerable problems for child pedestrians, particularly those at the most vulnerable ages. The conventional explanation for this is that the parked cars prevent motorists from seeing children who are about to cross the road. However, if it is true that motorists make little attempt to avoid children even when they can see them, then the reduced visibility of the child is unlikely to be important.

An alternative explanation is that the road-crossing strategies used by children are confused by the presence of a parked car. They are also told, 'try not to cross near parked cars', but in many residential areas this is impossible. They are told to stop at the kerb and look to see if the road is clear, but if they are near a parked car they will be unable to see. The sensible strategy, which most adults use, is to stop at the outside margin of the parked vehicle and look round it to see if the road is clear. If the equivalent of a second kerb were used to define the area of the road in which cars could park, then unambiguous and easily understood instructions could be given to children which would enable them to cross safely in the vicinity of parked cars.

## AN INTEGRATED LEGAL AND DESIGN STRATEGY

In the light of the evidence that road design needs to give drivers physical cues for behaviour, and that residential road designation is needed to make a change in law acceptable, a proposal for an integrated legal and design strategy is outlined below:

1  The measures will be limited to residential roads which do not form part of any major traffic route.
2  These roads will be clearly labelled as belonging to residential areas. The important point is to leave no-one, pedestrian or motorist, in any doubt about the status of the road, which will be either 'residential' or 'traffic route'. Signs on entering or leaving such areas, road markings, and characteristics such as width and sharpness of corners could all be used for this purpose.
3  Children must be made aware of the distinction between the two classes of road and dissuaded from crossing those which are designated 'traffic routes'. When they are old enough they can be allowed to cross

'Residential' roads using the safety drills in the Green Cross Code, or any developments of it.

4   Drivers must be told that on residential roads child pedestrians have priority to the extent that, if they injure a child, the driver will be presumed negligent unless he can prove otherwise. (This particular proposal, which applies the doctrine of *res ipsa loquitur* to these situations is described in greater detail in Howarth and Gunn, 1982.) This change must be given the force of law and will therefore require new legislation. It will impose on drivers a greater responsibility for avoiding accidents in these areas, and will make it much less likely that the defence, 'The child ran heedlessly into the road and there was nothing I could do to avoid the accident', will succeed in any criminal action which follows from an accident. There will be no need to enforce the legislation in any other way.

5   The Highway Code must be amended so as to make quite clear to motorists what are their additional responsibilities in these residential areas.

6   Different policies must be adopted towards roadworks on 'residential' roads and on 'traffic routes'. On the latter the safety and ease of passage of traffic must continue to have priority. On residential roads greater attention must be paid to the needs of pedestrians. No dramatic new expenditure may be required since in many cases a policy of benign neglect will serve almost as well. Pavement corners should not be rounded; roads should not be widened in these areas. More positively, as in some general improvement areas, changes should be designed to slow down rather than speed up the traffic by narrowing roads, sharpening pavement corners, using speed humps, and so on.

7   Regulations about car parking should be made consistent with the status of roads as 'residential' or 'traffic routes'. As a general rule parking should be minimized on 'traffic routes'. Conversely, parking should be allowed on 'residential' roads but measures should be taken to ensure that parking does not increase the danger to pedestrians. One way to do this would be to designate 'parking' zones on one or both sides of the 'residential' road. These zones could be marked, as in some continental countries, by a 'double kerb' system which separates the highway from a parking zone by a low kerb, and the parking zone from the footpath by a higher kerb. The same effect could be produced more cheaply by the use of paint or small bollards. This measure

would have the effect of narrowing the road and hence slowing traffic in residential areas. It would also have the effect of making it easier to teach children to pause and assess the situation before they cross from a parking zone to the highway.

## PUBLIC ACCEPTANCE

People are very pessimistic about the effect of legal measures, but this is because of the difficulty of enforcement and the problem of public acceptance. The legal measures being suggested here will not need to be enforced, although they will affect any proceedings which take place after an accident. Public acceptance should be relatively easy to obtain if the designated residential roads are reasonably chosen. It ought not to be too difficult to persuade drivers that their behaviour should be markedly different on different classes of road, and their acceptance will be made easier if the status of the different areas is clearly marked.

## NOTE

1   Some of this material was originally published in C.I. Howarth and A. Lightburn, 'A Strategic Approach to Child Pedestrian Safety,' in *ROAD SAFETY Research and Practice,* Hugh C. Foot, Antony J. Chapman, & Frances M. Wade, eds. (Praeger Publishers, New York, 1981), pp. 127–34. Copyright 1981 by Praeger Publishers. Used with permission.

## REFERENCES

Department of the Environment, 1977, *Design Bulletin 32* on Residential Roads and Footpaths, London, HMSO.

Grayson, G. 1975, *The Hampshire Child Pedestrian Accident Study,* Laboratory Report 668, Transport and Road Research Laboratory.

Howarth, C.I. 1985, 'Interactions between Drivers and Pedestrians: Some new approaches to Pedestrian Safety' in Evans, L. and Schwing, R. (ed.) in *Human Behaviour and Traffic Safety*, Plenum.

Howarth, C.I. and Gunn, M. 1982, 'Pedestrian Safety and the Law' in Chapman, A., Wade, F. and Foot, H. (eds.) *Pedestrian Accidents,* Wiley.

Howarth, C.I. and Repetto-Wright, R. 1978, 'The Measurement of Risk and the Attribution of Responsibility for Child Pedestrian Accidents', *Safety Education,* vol.144, no.1.

Howarth, C.I., Routledge, D. and Repetto-Wright, R. 1974, 'An Analysis of Road Accidents involving Child Pedestrians', *Ergonomics*, vol. 17.

Howarth, C.I. and Lightburn, A. 1980, 'How Drivers Respond to Pedestrians and Vice Versa' in, Osborne D. and Levis J. (ed.), *Human Factors in Transport Research vol. 2 User Factors: Comfort, The Environment and Behaviour,* Academic Press.

Howarth, C.I. and Lightburn, A. 1981, 'A Strategic Approach to Child Pedestrian Safety' in Foot, H., Chapman, A. and Wade, F. (eds.), *Road Safety; Research and Practice*, Eastbourne, Praeger.

Routledge, D., Repetto-Wright, R. and Howarth, C.I. 1974, 'The exposure of young children to accident risk as pedestrians', *Ergonomics*, vol. 17.

Routledge, D., Repetto-Wright, R., Lightburn, A. and Howarth, C.I. 1977, 'The development of road crossing skill by child pedestrians', *Proc. of the Int. Conf. on Pedestrian Safety*, Haifa, Israel.

Thompson, S. Fraser, E. and Howarth, C.I. 1986 'Driver Behaviour in the Presence of Child and Adult Pedestrians', *Ergonomics*, vol.28, no. 9.

# 5
# Lessons from Copenhagen
*Kai Lemberg*

Copenhagen got its first pedestrian street in the central city area during the period of rapid private motorization in the 1960s. It was the main shopping street in the mediaeval town called *Strøget*, which means Mall or Main Street. For a long time it had been a tradition every year during the month of December to close Strøget for vehicular traffic to increase the attractiveness of the Christmas trade, as speciality shops and department stores were located all along the street. This had worked without problems.

About 1960, proposals were made by town planners and in the City Council to make this pedestrian status of Strøget permanent instead of just a Christmas phenomenon. The proponents pointed to small, but successful, examples of pedestrian shopping streets like Lijnbaan in Rotterdam and from 1961 Kalvestraat in Amsterdam, and to the attractiveness of old, car-free cities like Venice and Dubrovnik.

## OPPOSITION TO PEDESTRIANIZATION

However, the proposals raised a storm of protests. First to protest were the shopkeepers along Strøget, who firmly believed that taking away the car shoppers and leaving only poor pedestrians in their street would reduce their turnover and ruin business. Besides, the police rejected the idea as impossible to carry out in practice, because the parallel streets were too narrow to take over the motor traffic banned from Strøget, and they feared the streets would be permanently congested. The chief city engineer was of the same opinion, and maintained that a number of crossings in the area would experience intolerable delays and cause traffic jams. Even the company which ran the municipal buses and trams, while welcoming the ban on cars and vans, argued that their existing bus routes through Strøget should remain in the street among the pedestrians, and that they would lose passengers by running through secondary streets. In fact, all the experts, except some town planners, objected heavily and warned against pedestrianization.

## A ONE-YEAR EXPERIMENT

However, the Mayor for Planning and Traffic,[1] a Conservative called Alfred Wassard, was convinced by those advocating pedestrianization and was supported by Social Democrats in the City Council. So it was decided to close Strøget by 17 November 1962 to all vehicle traffic (except ambulances, police and fire brigade emergency vehicles) from 11.00 am to 4.00 am. Even bicycles were to be excluded. During the morning hours of 4.00 am to 11.00 am, delivery vans and trucks were allowed, but not ordinary cars or taxis. Because of the many protests and warnings, pedestrianization was to be an experiment for one year. No counts or background analyses had been carried out before the rather sudden political decision, so no before-and-after studies are available.

The experiment soon turned out to be a great success in commercial terms as well as in town and transportation planning. The general public and the press were enthusiastic and shopkeepers experienced increased turnover and profits. The expected traffic jams and difficulties failed to materialize. Copenhageners as well as tourists enjoyed the pedestrianized Strøget as a new central city attraction. By 1964 − after the shopkeepers had thanked the Town Hall for not listening to them in 1962 − it was decided, without any opposition, to make Strøget a permanent pedestrian street.

Encouraged by this success, but after years of hesitation, two small pedestrian areas in the core of the central city were added in 1968: *Fiolstraede*, a narrow street with antique shops and university bookstalls, and *Gråbrødretorv*, a quiet square with no shops, but a huge tree and a couple of outdoor restaurants (see Figure 5.1). Fiolstraede, however, was not completely closed for vehicle traffic. Delivery vans were allowed access, mainly because a department store had its goods entrance in the street.

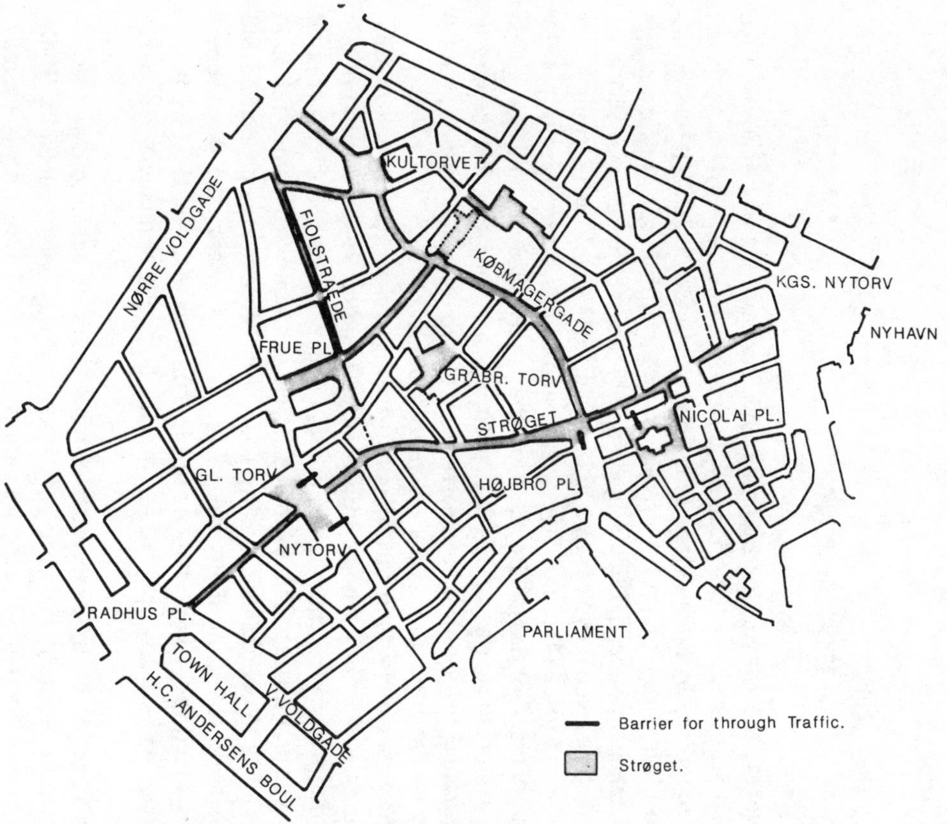

**Figure 5.1  Copenhagen pedestrian streets CBD 1980**

NYHAVN

KGS. NYTORV

NICOLAI PL.

Barrier for through Traffic.

Strøget.

KØBMAGERGADE

PARLIAMENT

GRÅBR. TORV

STRØGET

HØJBRO PL.

KULTORVET

FIOLSTRÆDE

FRUE PL.

NYTORV

GL. TORV

V. VOLDGADE

NØRRE VOLDGADE

RADHUS PL.

TOWN HALL

H.C. ANDERSENS BOUL.

44

# LONG-TERM PLANNING

In the meantime, the Copenhagen Planning Department had been established in 1968, and began the comprehensive analysis and planning of pedestrian streets and motor vehicle restraints in the central city of Copenhagen. The main results of its studies were the following.

In 1970 some 132 000 persons arrived in the central city area by car each day at an average of 1.3 persons per car. Of the total, 35 000 were commuters needing all-day parking, 13 000 were residents primarily needing night parking, and 84 000 were private and commercial visitors and customers needing short-term parking. To meet these demands 27 000 legal parking spaces (public, private and kerbside) were available in the central city area between the harbour and the ribbon of lakes of which only 4 300 were in the mediaeval town, in the central city core (see Figure 5.1).

Even allowing for several parking spaces to be used by successive car visitors during the day and others by commuters during day hours and by residents during the night, there must have been extensive illegal parking. This relationship between traffic flows and parking spaces explains why the number of cars arriving in the central city area had already reached its maximum by 1964: there were no more parking spaces available, and through traffic was increasingly choosing other routes.

New traffic counts in 1980 showed a total of 240 000 persons per day arriving in the mediaeval town, of whom 50 000 were by car, 20 000 were by bus and 130 000 were pedestrians, the majority of whom came from the four S-train stations surrounding the mediaeval town. The mediaeval town parking capacity in 1980 was 2 400 public spaces, mostly in streets and squares, but 460 in multi-storey car parks and underground garages, and 2300 private spaces, of which 300 were in multi-storey car parks and underground garages, and the rest were in yards. There were 1700 on the public kerbside. In the central city outside the core were 7050 public and 3340 private spaces (see Figure 5.2).

After pedestrianization of Strøget, the number of daytime pedestrians increased. Between 1962 and 1967, the number rose by between 35 per cent and 45 per cent to 23 000. The vehicular traffic of 8600 motor vehicles, 1000 mopeds and 4000 bikes in 1962 disappeared from Strøget. The interesting point is that traffic counts showed that only about 75 per cent of this former motor vehicle traffic appeared on other streets. The rest must have chosen more distant routes, changed to public transport or stayed at home.

## Strategies for Pedestrians

Numbers of Pedestrians Entering and Leaving the Mediaeval Town 1980.

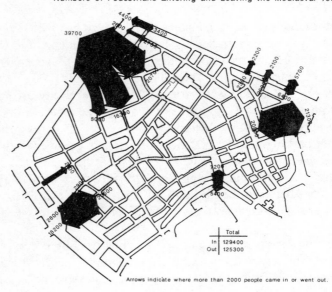

| | Total |
|---|---|
| In | 129400 |
| Out | 125300 |

Arrows indicate where more than 2000 people came in or went out.

Numbers of Cars Entering and Leaving the Mediaeval Town 1980.

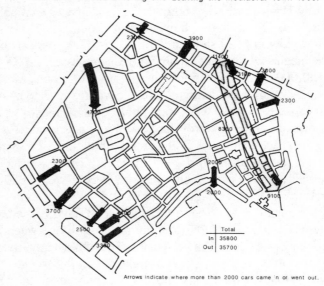

| | Total |
|---|---|
| In | 35800 |
| Out | 35700 |

Arrows indicate where more than 2000 cars came in or went out.

46

Numbers of Cyclist & Mopeds Entering and Leaving the Mediaeval Town 1980.

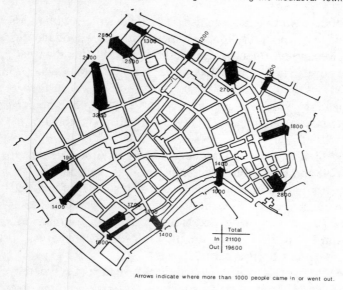

|  | Total |
|---|---|
| In | 21100 |
| Out | 19600 |

Arrows indicate where more than 1000 people came in or went out.

Numbers of Other Vehicles Entering and Leaving the Mediaeval Town 1980.
( Vans, Trucks, Taxis ).

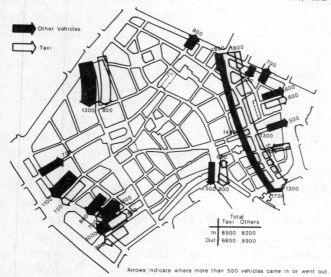

Other Vehicles

Taxi

| | Total | |
|---|---|---|
| | Taxi | Others |
| In | 6500 | 8200 |
| Out | 6800 | 8900 |

Arrows indicate where more than 500 vehicles came in or went out.

**Figure 5.2   Numbers of people entering and leaving the mediaeval town daily, 1980**

## ENVIRONMENTAL EFFECTS

Measures of air pollution have demonstrated that streets with motor vehicle traffic have considerably higher concentrations of soot and dust, carbon monoxide and nitrogen oxides, and other pollutants than pedestrian streets. The noise in inner city streets with traffic seems to be about 75dB(A) during most day hours, compared with about 65dB(A) in Strøget after pedestrianization, which roughly means that subjectively perceived noise levels in the pedestrian street are between a half and a third of the level in traffic streets.

No traffic break-downs or long delays were reported, neither for cars nor for buses, and no serious complaints came from operators of goods vehicles nor from morning hour pedestrians. The number of reported traffic accidents in the mediaeval town dropped from 158 in 1960 to 105 in 1963, while in the surrounding ring streets and squares the number increased slightly, from 112 to 122. Even without a full statistical analysis it seems likely that there has been a net decrease.

The concept of pedestrianization and the whole idea of restricting motor vehicle traffic instead of increasing street capacity and of giving preference to walking, cycling and the use of public transport, contrasted with traditional traffic engineering ideology but matched well with the growing awareness during the late 1960s and the 1970s of the value of the urban environment. These tendencies coincided with declining commercial attractiveness of inner city shopping streets compared with the new car-accessible and traffic-free suburban shopping centres.

So the interests of commerce and of ordinary people were both met by the creation of inner city pedestrian streets. In 1972 three barriers to stop the passage of vehicular traffic were introduced in the mediaeval town area, following examples from Bremen and Gothenburg. The point was to prevent or complicate the through traffic of vans and cars but to exempt buses and cycles to give them an advantage. In the early 1970s, parking meters were introduced in central areas. In 1973 the inefficient police control of parking was replaced by a new and very efficient system.

At international level the issues of pedestrianization and inner city traffic regulations against traffic congestion were taken up during the 1970s by several organizations. In the OECD an extensive exchange of experiences and views took place at expert level and later at ministerial level, resulting in the publication of *Better Towns with Less Traffic* (OECD, 1975). The Council of Europe included these themes in its 'Urban Renaissance' campaign. A wave of central city pedestrianization was pouring over European countries: West Germany, Sweden, the Netherlands, the UK and eventually almost all countries, even the USA and Canada.

## SHOPKEEPERS CHANGE SIDES

In Copenhagen the next steps in pedestrianization were taken in 1973 — this time, however, at the initiative of the shopkeepers! The Association of Businessmen in *Købmagergade* — Copenhagen's number two shopping street, running perpendicular to Strøget — asked the Council to pedestrianize their street, arguing that otherwise they would be unable to compete with Strøget. Once more the police, traffic experts and the municipal bus company warned the Mayor against this addition to the pedestrian network; but Mayor Wassard agreed to the request of the shopkeepers and was supported by the new Copenhagen City Centre Business Organization, the press and the General Planning Department. Consequently, Købmagergade and three smaller streets were pedestrianized. However, the warnings from police and traffic engineers and the lack of rear access for goods deliveries to shops in Købmagergade resulted in their becoming second-class pedestrian streets: contrary to Strøget, where all motor vehicle traffic is prohibited between 11.00 am and 4.00 am, delivery vehicles were admitted all day, like in Fiolstraede. To prevent this from creating illegal through traffic in Købmagergade, the street was split up in stretches with one-way traffic in opposite directions. A bus route on the street was removed to a parallel street.

During the 1970s Strøget and other pedestrian streets were repaved. The former carriageways and sidewalks, separated by gutters, were replaced by flagstones from facade to facade, and street furniture was added. The city provided benches, low walls, flower decorations and so on and cleared some smaller squares for parked cars. Private shopkeepers, restaurants and banks got permission to place showcases, advertisement boards and signs, outdoor summer restaurants and plants in the street area. At the initiative of private business some arcades, passages and small pedestrian precincts in yards and suchlike were also established. Copenhagen City Centre cooperated with the municipal traffic and planning authorities and published its own proposals for future city plans and design. These included more space for pedestrians, especially by opening some courts for pedestrian passage and new activities like small shops, exhibitions, handicraft workshops, etc.

Since the mid-1970s only one more public street in central Copenhagen has been pedestrianized. The sunny northern side of *Nyhavn*, a street with old, small houses and many tourist pubs along an old inner harbour basin, was pedestrianized in 1980. While Fiolstraede, Købmagergade and part of Strøget have heavy flows of commuting pedestrians in morning and late afternoon hours, plus shoppers and tourists all day long, Nyhavn is crowded with tourists, and the remaining pedestrian streets and precincts have much smaller flows.

## EFFECTS ON TRADE

Pedestrianization has changed the image of the streets and made them more popular. Although highly specialized outlets like a violin builder and an expensive high fashion department store have moved out, new activities have moved in, like small fast food restaurants, tourist shops, and youth fashion shops. During the early 1970s following the legalization of pornography, there was also an influx of porn shops and cinemas, but most of these have since disappeared. An interesting feature is that the neighbouring narrow streets north of Strøget, with old fashioned cheap flats, shops for things like daily food and small offices, which were not pedestrianized, have experienced a virtual revival with shops and restaurants orientated towards young people — Indian and other exotic clothes, psychedelic art objects, leather goods and so on. This area, however, is becoming threatened by office and service trades pushing forward — assisted by the city with local plans permitting change from dwellings to service trades.

## RESIDENTIAL STREETS

In 1976 an amendment to the Traffic Code made it possible for streets in residential areas to suspend the usual rules for traffic management to create integrated vehicle, bicycle and pedestrian traffic, but on the terms of the pedestrians and the cyclists — not on the car drivers' terms as in ordinary mixed traffic streets. The inspiration for this reform came from the Netherlands, where the concept of *Woonerf*, that is of treating some residential streets as accessories to the dwellings rather than as space for traffic, was carried out in traffic practice, first in Delft and Gouda and eventually in other Dutch cities (see Appendix to Chapter 6).

In Denmark, two new types of residential streets were introduced with integrated traffic: *quiet streets* with vehicle speed limits of 30 kilometres per hour, kerbside parking spaces and physical hindrances, including humps (sleeping policemen); and *play-and-stay streets*, primarily to be used by children and adults for outdoor recreation, with a speed limit of 15 kilometres per hour and a road design with trees, benches, flower containers and other street furniture. While in the suburbs many streets have been given back to people in this way, restricted finances have limited the number of such streets in Copenhagen. In the central city area only very few such streets exist.

## THE CHANGING CHARACTER OF THE AREA

During recent years certain problems have occurred in Strøget and other pedestrian streets. They are overcrowded and less clean, because of the overloading of Strøget and Købmagergade by showcases and signs from the shops, and sometimes with street musicians and artists and hawking. New mass unemployment among young people, hardship for social security receivers and a general sharpening of social and political conflicts may be part of the background. Besides, commercialization tends to 'internationalize' Strøget, and it is beginning to lose its Danish and local identity.

On the other hand, improved techniques have considerably diminished pollution stemming from traffic, and plans have been prepared to improve conditions for pedestrians, bicycles and public transport in the big squares like the Town Hall Square and Kongens Nytorv, which are still dominated by motor vehicle traffic.

During the last few years, rapidly increasing prices for a few premises in the mediaeval town, followed by a general increase of site values for taxation, have been squeezing out many small and specialized shops to the advantage of banks, travel agencies and offices. Planners and politicians are now reacting against these trends and are asking for more control over the commercial uses of pedestrian streets so that more can be done to improve their environmental quality rather than allowing shop owners to reap the benefits.

## NOTE

1  Copenhagen has seven mayors each with a different area of responsibility.

## REFERENCES

Lemberg, K. rev. 1973, *Pedestrian streets and other motor vehicle traffic constraints in central Copenhagen*, Københavns Kommune, Generalplan-laegnings Afdeling.
OECD 1975, *Better Towns With Less Traffic,* Proceedings of Conference, Paris.

# 6
# Evaluating pedestrianization schemes

*Anthony Ramsay*

The way in which society deals with facilities for walking is an index of its very civilization. But until very recently, most town planners regarded pedestrian affairs as irrelevant, marginal or the responsibility of others. This was the result of several factors.

First, municipal engineers were traditionally responsible for a broad range of functions, while town planning as a profession developed much later. Second, the motor car and the motor industry have been accorded a high degree of political favour from the early part of this century (Plowden, 1971). Third, 'traffic science' was conceived by electrical engineers in the USA as auto-centred and this led to their perception of pedestrians simply as obstacles to the progress of motor traffic through the street network (Matson et al, 1955). Last, town planning schools and schools of civil engineering have failed to address this subject seriously enough in research, writing or teaching.

Thanks mainly to original thinkers like Sir Colin Buchanan, Kai Lemberg, Paul Ritter and Alfie Wood (1958, 1973, 1964 and 1970 respectively), more positive policies for pedestrians are being developed. Over the last 30 years a large number of schemes to provide for pedestrians has been introduced in towns and cities in Europe, America and other parts of the world with varying degrees of success. The author has made a detailed study of twelve cities in Western Europe as well as extensive studies in the UK, North America and Africa. This chapter will draw on experience of over 25 years' research and teaching on pedestrianization schemes worldwide to see what lessons can be learned about how such schemes should be designed and implemented.

There is more to a successful pedestrian scheme than the simple exclusion of vehicles. Now that there is experience of a wide variety of approaches in different cities it becomes possible to analyse some of the pitfalls and identify some of the features which have contributed to the success of the better schemes.

## STREETSCAPING

There are several different approaches to the amount of paraphernalia that should be provided in a pedestrian street. This is to some extent a matter of cultural tradition and personal opinion. The traditional approach to street design in Japan aims for an integration in the visual sense of the street surface and the street elevations; and consequently for an absence of interrupting objects in the space between frontages (Fujiki, 1984). On the other hand, the prevalent philosophy in Western Europe sees planting as a generally valuable, even vital, component in the streetscape with the softness of the plants acting as a natural foil to the hardness of the paved and built surfaces (Boyer, 1973; OECD, 1974).

The piazza at La Défense in Paris exemplifies one extreme − a vast expanse of barren concrete paving, surrounded by tower blocks up to 45 storeys high. Though intended to do the opposite, the few isolated sculptures serve only to emphasize the dwarfing effect of the buildings. The small precinct in Marple (east of Stockport) illustrates the opposite approach, with so many trees, shrubs and benches crammed in that there is hardly enough space for pedestrians to make their way through.

In a Western European context, perhaps the most important point to make is about the provision of seating and off-line areas for standing. There is an almost insatiable demand for seating in pedestrian streets at busy periods and this is illustrated by the heavy use made of the copious supply of seating at Merseyway precinct in Stockport. The layout of the squares related to the famous mall in München Altstadt shows the ease with which lower seating heights for younger children can be incorporated in an overall schema (Perkin, 1973).

In North West Europe, the question of protection from rainstorms and strong winds is almost as important. The spectacular double-winged roof over the town centre piazza at Glenrothes New Town was eventually replaced because of its unfortunate capacity for attracting rain and wind rather than for excluding them. The Danes use canopies along and across the street to achieve a sense of enclosure while affording basic shelter, as at Viborg town centre (Ramsay and Stevenson, 1976). Likewise in Australasia, colonnades, known there as verandahs, are commonly provided in central areas to provide shade (Perrott, Lyon, Timlock and Kesa, 1972).

Studies show that people tend to prefer positions for sitting or standing from which a range of interesting actions and views can be witnessed (Gehl et al, 1968). This implies that public seating should be placed towards the edge of public areas facing inwards and, certainly in northern climes, preferably facing the sun.

From an ergonomic standpoint, a high proportion of seats should have back support. In a surprising number of instances, benching without any back is chosen by the designer for aesthetic reasons or for robustness against vandals. A widely applicable solution is the type of seat made from a sheet of curved steel, perforated to maximize drainage and looking at its most elegant when painted black.

## PEDESTRIANS AS TRAFFIC

The social aspect of pedestrian traffic is usually overlooked, since traffic engineers are used to assessing capacity in crude, mechanistic terms. With vehicular traffic, the social unit is commonly the driver and accompanying passengers so that the traffic unit coincides with the social unit. However pedestrians often travel in groups and prefer to walk side by side in these groups. The formulae which define the capacity of sections of walking routes assume that there will be no adherence of one pedestrian to another and grossly underestimate the socially acceptable width of footway.

A similar oversight also shows up in the contrasting treatment of 'parked' vehicles compared with 'parked' pedestrians. Vehicles parked on-street cause congestion so traffic engineers do their best to induce drivers to park them off-street. The corresponding phenomenon for pedestrian traffic is not acknowledged; consequently off-track space for standing to chat or for other reasons is not specifically allowed for.

On the contrary, the effective width for walking is commonly reduced by street furniture and the extra clearance which people instinctively allow in walking past or round such objects. A faint sign of hope has emerged in Italy — a municipal code has recently been formulated for Rome with the aim of minimizing such permanent obstructions and also temporary obstruction from road or building works.

Moreover experience shows that when people discover how well they can relax in central streets once the traffic is removed, street entertainments and other events are attracted which consume yet more of the space available.

The variation in pedestrian flows complicates the picture even further and is also often overlooked. The number of pedestrians fluctuates from month to month, from day to day, from hour to hour and from minute to minute. The pattern of these fluctuations varies greatly depending on life-styles and land uses. While traffic engineers go to considerable lengths to establish what these patterns are for motorized traffic, they usually determine street layouts without any prior survey or accurate assessment of pedestrian flow patterns.

Conscious attemps have been made in places as far apart as Barnsley and Copenhagen, Manchester and Utrecht, to establish what are the patterns of pedestrian flow. In the early days at least, these were the exceptions. Even now many central pedestrianized streets are created as an incidental (or even accidental) result of new bypass schemes. The designer fails to recognize the increased importance of pedestrians relative to vehicular traffic on the original route. The high street of Kilmarnock is a typical result of this phenomenon. Sadly, in some cases the opportunity to pedestrianize subsequent to bypassing is overlooked altogether, as at Auchterarder in Scotland.

The retention or introduction of regular access for vehicles creates many problems. It limits freedom of paving and planting layout. It also requires not only the frequent interruption of pedestrian flows but also an annoyingly frequent disruption of walking routes for the purpose of repairing breaks and depressions in the surface.


## PUBLIC OR PRIVATE CONTROL?

Since the property boom of the early 1960s, purpose-designed pedestrian-only shoping precincts have been created in nearly every town centre in the UK (Ramsay 1986, Roberts 1981, Smith 1985). The largest of these, like Brent Cross in London and the Arndale Centre in central Manchester, are of such huge dimensions as to be primary and strategic influences on the urban structure. Accordingly the issue of who owns and controls the sub-network of pedestrian routes within the precinct becomes critical.

Public authorities have frequently agreed to commercial schemes in which the access routes for pedestrians inside an enclosed centre are controlled by the private sector, for example the Brunel Centre at Thamesdown and Plaza Centre at East Kilbride. Unless the centre contains premises designed for evening and weekend use as at the Merrion Centre in Leeds, the management policy is then almost certain to be one of locking the entrances outside daytime business hours to prevent vandalism and minimize costs of patrol and maintenance. The public then loses the right to walk there after hours. The earlier phases of Cumbernauld town centre incorporated penthouse flats, access to which caused problems because of the conflict with a lock-up policy. The flats were eventually abandoned and given over to a more compatible use.

On balance such decisions on the part of the public authorities are likely to be against the interest of local citizens, because these malls, by their very nature and central location, are amongst the most strategic sections in the entire pedestrian network. This is especially important for the many people who are disabled or have difficulty walking and who would find the required detour particularly arduous and distressing.

## THE SEGREGATION ISSUE

The principle of segregation in transport planning is long-established since the middle of last century when bridges and fencing protected the public from standard gauge railway. This principle was adopted in official postwar Ministry manuals on road layout, but the enthusiasm of the local authorities to put it into practice varied widely. For an encyclopaedic account of schemes throughout the world for the physical separation of pedestrian and vehicular traffic see Ritter, 1964.

There was a successful experiment in Delft in the early 1970s of a compromise solution to the problem of traffic access within older residential areas. The technique used there has become internationally known by its Dutch name of *woonerf*, meaning residential yard. (For a fuller explanation see Appendix, also ANWB, 1977; Kwiatkowski, 1985 and Luikens et al, 1981.) This has led to a more generalized debate in European professional circles about the relative merits of integration and separation.

In essence, the proponents of integration argued that full physical segregation amounted to overkill; that some means of persuading or forcing motorists to drive very slowly on streets off the main vehicular network would solve the problem at least as well as the previous 'all-or-nothing' orthodoxy: safety and amenity for pedestrians would thus be enhanced without the need for expensive underpasses or other construction work.

To some extent this reaction confused principle with method; not all segregated schemes are well planned, but it is a mistake to condemn all segregation because of a few bad designs. Admittedly some segregation schemes have gone too far. This was especially true of multi-tiered schemes in large shopping centres like those at Cergy-Pontoise and Evry, two new towns about 30 km from Paris.

In these centres there are two different levels for mechanized traffic arriving — one for trains and one for road vehicles. Pedestrians circulate horizontally on the third and fourth levels. Although this resolves potential conflicts between different traffic modes, it generates vertical flows of pedestrian traffic or increases their extent. This adds to the costs of constructing, maintaining and operating the centres, and causes inconvenience to pedestrians due to the implied waiting or detouring. These problems are particularly serious in the early phase of Cumbernauld's town centre when uses were stacked one on top of the other. The unsystematic layout of steps, ramps and lifts makes going from the approach footpath, bus stop or car parking bay to the nearest shopping floors unduly complicated.

In the late 1960s, the central areas of Leeds, Liverpool and London used upper-level walkways as the principal means of achieving segregation. However town planners soon came to realize the futility of pedestrians being jerked up into the air only to have to descend again as they approached their next target destination. Until all shopkeepers could be persuaded to move their main entrances up one floor, such schemes would be bound to fail. These strategies have been quietly abandoned.

In contrast Eaton Center in downtown Toronto has a well thought out layout which helps to streamline pedestrian flows despite the number of floors. Moreover there is a special justification for underground walking facilities or other types of climate protection in a country which has such a harsh winter period as Canada's. Substantial networks have been developed in Montreal and Toronto with this factor in mind. Underground links are automatically protected by tunnel; high-level viaducts known as 'skywalks' are fully enclosed and other links at intermediate levels tend to be sited within enclosed malls such as the Eaton Center.

Not all segregated layouts are good *ipso facto*. By the mid-1960s, transport planners had become preoccupied with the rate of growth of motor traffic and too readily believed that all layouts on the pedestrian precinct principle were good, irrespective of location. Cconsequently there was a rash of miniature precincts abutting busy main roads and major junctions which, due to their poor location and the pedestrian traffic they generated, actually increased the degree of pedestrian vehicle conflicts.

The worst examples were supermarket projects where the developer had included a parade of several small shops to contrive a precinct to increase the site's attractiveness and improve his chances of getting planning permission. Examples of this sort can be found on the east side of Bury New Road north from Manchester.

## NETWORKS FOR WALKING

Those municipalities which have embarked on central area pedestrianization programmes with enthusiasm have generally followed through with further extensions until a sizeable pedestrian-only zone is established. The most obvious examples in Great Britain are Cardiff and Leeds; there are also many examples elsewhere, such as Ålborg and Randers in Denmark and Hanover in West Germany (see OECD, 1974).

Another example on a smaller scale is Milngavie, a small town on the north-western outskirts of Greater Glasgow. A web of footpaths radiates from the pedestrianized main street to link with nearby car parks and residential areas.

In Denmark, Holstebro in northern Jutland represents one of the finest instances of consistent and persistent municipal endeavour in this field. The central area is strongly pedestrianized, with complementary ring roads; and the most recently developed sector in the north-west boasts a comprehensive path system for walking and cycling. Then there are the British new towns — Corby, Cumbernauld, Erskine (a new community 10 km west of Glasgow), Stevenage and Washington. These have all featured comprehensive path systems from the start. Several others like Glenrothes adopted similar strategies at an intermediate review stage.

In other places, the attitude to pedestrianizing strategies has been more tentative and hence progress much slower. Generally these are long-established towns whose cores form strategic junctions in the national road system. Pedestrianizing streets would mean having to find alternative routes to accommodate through flows of vehicular traffic. This may be a daunting prospect. Nonetheless Aylesbury, Perth, Shrewsbury and Worcester have begun to deflect through traffic away from their traditional high streets.

Unfortunately in such cases one-way traffic schemes are often introduced to reduce journey times for motorists without considering the impact on the foot network and its users. Having gone to all the bureaucratic trouble entailed in making orders for one-way schemes, professionals may be reluctant to rescind or modify them later. Indeed there is always a risk that they later opt to entrench further the vehicular system as in Glasgow city centre.

From the pedestrian's viewpoint, a much better interim solution is the zonal access system adopted in several European Cities. Examples can be found in Göteborg (Blide and Teasdale, 1979) Kraków and Manchester. Such a system is based on the principle of preventing vehicles from crossing from one side to another of the central area while allowing access to all points from the peripheral route by loop roads, and culs-de-sac sometimes with one-way working.

Occasionally, the situation for pedestrians has been compromised by a decision to allow buses and perhaps also taxis and cycles to continue using a pedestrianized street as a through route — the American 'transit mall' syndrome. Only in very special circumstances can this be satisfactory for the pedestrian. For example, the Sixteenth Street Mall in Denver, Colorado (featured in the run-in to the TV series *Dynasty*) has a free shuttle service using vehicles capable of taking chairbound persons on board easily. Furthermore, the street is wide enough for a promenade to have been provided in the median strip, simulating the Rambla in Barcelona in that respect.

More often the public become disenchanted with such hybrid systems after a while: the minibus services in Leeds which ran through pedestrianized streets were withdrawn after an experimental period, and there is now pressure to close Cornmarket in Oxford to buses. In such a situation, naturally the bus operators will strongly resist diversion however weak their case.

For the bus traveller the location of the bus stops is more critical than the routes used by the buses to travel between them. Hence the lengthy uninterrupted pedestrian streets in Copenhagen, Essen and Holstebro are acceptable to those travelling to the centre by bus because stops are provided at regular intervals within a short walking distance of the precinct.

Conversely, the frequent interruption of the malls by cross routes for vehiclar traffic at Pearl Street Mall, Boulder, Colorado and Sauchiehall Street, Glasgow detracts from their value in terms of both safety and amenity for pedestrians. If traffic must be retained on the cross routes then at least the level of the street surface at the cross-over sections should be raised.

A special problem presents itself in relation to seaside towns because of their broadly semicircular geometry. There is often a conflict between the longitudinal flows of vehicles on roads following the line of the shore and the lateral flows of pedestrians moving to and from the seaside. The tendency has been for highway engineers to design shoreline bypasses which relieve the existing traffic routes but which fail to provide adequate facilities to accommodate the lateral flows of pedestrians. Examples are numerous, e.g. Blackpool, Colwyn Bay/Conwy, Hull and Perth (Australia). Part of the problem is undoubtedly the need to establish a drainage system which can operate successfully at high water. Nonetheless better solutions could be found if highway engineers would only treat the pedestrians as clients to be considered equally as motorists from the initial stages of planning and design.

In cities such as Chester, Nottingham, Preston and Stirling, pedestrianization has proceeded largely through the creation of off-street shopping precincts by redevelopment, combined with the conversion of some short minor links in the street system. In the 1970s, it seemed as if Chester's central area was poised to cross the threshold from having a miscellany of discrete pedestrian areas to establishing a fully integrated pedestrian-only zone. Apparently progress since then has been negligible and the centre still suffers significantly from an unnecessary degree of vehicular intrusion. Both Preston and Stirling still suffer badly from relative over-provision for through vehicular traffic at the expense of pedestrian convenience and amenity. Only Nottingham seems to be progressing to move across that threshold.

## RECREATION ROUTES

In some cities initiatives have been taken to establish:

- riverside walks either as part of valley rehabilitation schemes as in Tame Valley in Greater Manchester and Water of Leith in Edinburgh or as estuarine promenades as planned for Greenock and Gourock;
- parkland trails which link recreation attractions while providing incidentally for leisure walking and cycling e.g. Burnaby, the municipality adjoining Vancouver on its eastern flank;

- revivified towpaths as part of urban renewal programmes applied to derelict bankside sites; and
- leisure paths for cycling and walking by adapting disused railways (e.g. around Airdrie and Coatbridge).

While such projects improve the urban environment they do little to accommodate the daily journeys from home to work, school and shops which constitute the bulk of strategic travel demand by pedestrians. A townwide network of utility routes is vital to the proper civic accommodation of walking. While leisure routes may offer a valuable supplement to such a network, they cannot form a substitute for it.

## PROVISION FOR THE DISABLED

The acid test for any pedestrian system is how well it meets the requirements of disabled people. Though the definition of disablement can vary, from a traffic viewpoint the very young and the very old can be considered along with the disabled as groups of pedestrians who are particularly vulnerable (Ramsay, 1988). For those who find walking difficult or impossible, particularly the chairbound, continuity of the paved surface is generally of crucial importance. This means that a ramp should be provided as an alternative to steps whenever practicable.

Near the famous Lijnbaan — a pedestrian-only shopping street in central Rotterdam's postwar reconstruction zone — a traffic street (Binnenwegplein) was later converted to pedestrian-only use. To preserve the match between pavement and threshold levels, steps were introduced into the profile, thus making it awkward for some disabled people to travel the length of the street. It might have been better to introduce stepping and/or ramps at one or two shop entrances and thus avoid steps running the whole width of the street.

Where ramps are provided the gradient needs to be gentle to reduce the gravitational pull on wheelchairs and prevent loss of control. The approach ramp to the footbridge at Centre des Sept Mares, Saint Quentin-en-Yvelines, a new town outside Paris, has a moderate gradient for this reason. The generous headroom provided there for vehicles passing under the footbridge combined with this gentle gradient has meant that the pedestrian ramp is very long and tortuous. One way of dealing with this problem is by providing several tails for footbridge ramps as at Hadley centre in

Telford New Town and at the link to Warrington's Golden Square shopping centre.

There are practical limits to how far existing environments can be modified to achieve such aims. Where city centres are built on very steep hillsides like Edinburgh's Old Town, steps were usually seen to be necessary at the time of their original development and the level of each entrance had to correspond to that of the abutting step (Johnston, 1986). Hence it becomes impracticable to insert gently sloping ramps of flats and escalators throughout the area generally. Nevertheless the authorities are currently preparing schemes to overcome the steep ascents for the pedestrian visitor to Edinburgh and Stirling Castles, both of which sit on clifftops.

At the suburban centre of Angered, outside Göteborg, opened in 1978, a wire navigation system, developed originally for shipping, has been installed experimentally as a guidance system for the visually handicapped. The 500m-long wire is laid 0.2 − 0.5m below ground from the bus and tram station along the main pedestrian axes in the centre.

An AC circuit is used to generate a magnetic field around the wire as a basis for transmitting radio signals. The visually handicapped person carries a small receiver and can tell where he or she is by the clicking rate and pitch. Fast clicking means in contact, slow means no contact; high means veer right, low means veer left. In practice sharp changes in direction present difficulty for users and the feasibility of adding synthetic speech signals at critical points is being explored (Grauers, 1982).

Investigations are continuing into the feasibility of devising a system with a similar purpose for the central precinct in Sheffield. This has been described as a magic carpet from which persons with impaired vision will be able to deduce information about the position of various kinds of shop.

The orange badge scheme, which exempts motor vehicles carrying disabled drivers from some waiting restrictions, has been much abused and has been the subject of critical review (see Salmon, 1986, for example). In Durham and Huddersfield the central precincts or adjacent parking spaces reserved for the disabled are congested by cars sporting orange badges. But a significant proportion of these badge holders are people who do not require access at such close quarters. Many towns are introducing secondary permit systems which will give access only on a much more selective basis.

In principle the fewer ordinary road vehicles that enter a pedestrian precinct, the less complicated life will be for all pedestrians, particularly the disabled. Where conventional motor traffic is totally excluded alternative low-speed means of mobility such as wheelchairs and small 'Rambler'-type electrically-driven pavement vehicles should be available to people requiring such assistance. This is proposed for West Bromwich High Street (Anon, 1987).

## SUMMARY

The lessons from this survey can be summarized in the following principles:

1   The quantity and categories of planting, street furniture and other facilities to be provided within pedestrianized areas should relate to local culture and circumstances. Sufficient well-designed and well-positioned seating and standing space is crucial. In the north-west European climate, shelter from wind and rain is also important.

2   The characteristics of pedestrian traffic are very different from those of vehicular traffic: this must be recognized and reflected in the layout. In particular enough width should be provided so that people travelling together are not forced constantly to separate due to congestion.

3   Road vehicles of all kinds should be excluded as far as possible. Exemptions should be seen as an interim measure before establishing a pedestrian-only regime in the not too distant future.

4   Pedestrian routes and facilities for public use should be retained in public ownership and special street-management teams appointed for the most important zones in town centres and large district centres.

5   A layout which incorporates the principle of maximum segregation of pedestrians and vehicles is generally superior to one that does not, provided it relates well to the local landscape and patterns of land use and traffic. Especial care should be taken around the boundary of the pedestrian area and with the number of levels at which pedestrians are expected to circulate.

6   Extending the logic entails extending the system, sooner or later, beyond the high street and beyond the central area. A leisure path network can never substitute for a full-blown system of utility routes since the great majority of movements on foot is generated between home and work, school or shops.

7   Though the disabled must be provided for, it is a mistake to allow any pedestrian precinct to be transformed into a car park for vehicles sporting orange badges.

# REFERENCES

Allen, V. 1988, *The potential for pedestrian movement within city core areas* (paper to Planning Exchange Conference, 'A Better Deal for Pedestrians' Glasgow 12 – 14 May), unpublished.

Alty, R. and Darke, R. 1987, 'A city centre for people: involving the community in planning for Sheffield's central area', *Planning Practice and Research*, September, no.3.

Anon, 1987, 'Pedestrian precinct favours the disabled', *Surveyor*, vol. 15, October.

ANWB (Royal Dutch Touring Club), 1977, *Woonerf (residential precinct): a different approach to environmental management in residential areas and the related traffic legislation*, ANWB, the Hague.

Blide, B. and Teesdale, D., 1979, *Case study on extension of cell system in Gothenburg*, OECD, Group on the Urban Environment.

Boyer, M.A. 1973, *Armature piétonnière et paysage urbain: le cas de Munich comparé à Oldenburg, Brème, Sienne, Bologne et Amsterdam* (Pedestrian-related equipment and urban landscaping: the case of München compared with . . ), Ministère de l'Aménagement du Territoire, de l'Equipment, du Logement et du Tourisme (Direction de l'Aménagement Foncier et de l'Urbanisme, Groupe d'Etude et de Recherche), Paris.

Buchanan, C.D. 1958, *Mixed blessing: the motor in Britain*, Leonard Hill.

Fujiki, T. 1984, 'Streetscape for pedestrians in Japan', in *The City on its Feet* (proc. 5th annual Pedestrian Conf. Boulder City, Co., 20–21 September 1984) City of Boulder, Transportation Division.

Gehl, J. et al, 1968, 'Mennesker til fods' (People on foot), *Arkitekten* no.20.

Grauers, S. 1981, *Guide wire for visually disabled* (paper to International Federation of Pedestrians conference 'Handicapped in the City' Göteborg 5 – 7 May), unpublished.

Johnston, E. 1986 'Wyndy city', *Building Design* vol.14, November.

Kwiatkowski, D. 1985, 'Streetscape in the Woonerf', *Landscape Design*, October, no.157.

Lemberg, K. rev. 1973, *Pedestrian streets and other motor vehicle traffic constraints in central Copenhagen*, Københavns Kommune, Generalplanlaegnings Afdeling.

Luikens, H. et al, 1981, *New concepts in the layout of urban districts and the design and management of traffic therein*, (Dutch) National Physical Planning Agency, Government Publishing Office, The Hague.

Lyon, R.R. 1983, 'Providing for the disabled highway user', *Municipal Engineer*, vol.111, no.4.

McMillen, A. 1976, 'Pedestrian movement in a local plan', *The Planner* January, vol.62, no.1.

Matson, T.M. et al, 1955, *Traffic engineering*, McGraw-Hill.

OECD, 1974, *Streets for People*, Organization for Economic Co-operation and Development, Paris, *per* HMSO.

PasRicha, P.S. 1982, *Pedestrian planning in Bombay* (paper to international seminar 'World Developments in Pedestrian Planning' Glasgow 1—2 July), unpublished.

Perkin, G. 1973, 'The delight of a city', *Concrete Quarterly*, December, vol.99.

Perrott, Lyon, Timlock and Kesa 1972 *Launceston Central Area study*, PLT and K, Melbourne *pro* City of Launceston, Tasmania.

Plowden, W. 1971 and 1973, *The motor car and politics in Britain*, Bodley Head, Pelican/Peguin.

Ramsay, A., 2nd Edn 1986, 'Planning for pedestrians' (Topicguide 3), *Capital Planning Information*, Stamford, Lincolnshire.

Ramsay, A. and Stevenson, W.G. 1976, 'Pedestrian networks in Danish towns, *Highway Engineer*, August/September, vol.23(8/9).

Ritter, P. 1964, *Planning for man and motor*, Pergamon.

Roberts, J. 1981, *Pedestrian precincts in Britain*, TEST, London.

Smith, J. 1985, 'Pedestrianisation, shopping streets in Scotland', *Planner*, May, vol.71 (5).

Wood, A.A. 1970, 'Foot-streets: managing the environment' *Traffic Engineering and Control*, February, vol.11, no.2.

# APPENDIX: WOONERF (PLURAL WOONERVEN)

In its original conception (c.1970), woonerf was a technique for controlling driver behaviour in older residential streets, to make life more tolerable for the residents whether inside or outside the house. Since the initial experiment at Delft, woonerf has been formally incorporated (1976) into the Dutch traffic regulations ('Verkeersregels en verkeerstekens'). The characteristics are broadly as outlined below:

1 planting etc. to enhance streetscape and symbolize predominance of residential function over traffic function; ends defined with planters and the like;

2 car parking only where not a nuisance, such places clearly demarcated in paving, with any deficit in parking supply being compensated nearby;

3 children's play zones, cycle racks etc. incorporated in the layout;

4 continuous surface, with vehicular accesses constructed in width and by humps etc. at intervals of 50m maximum to limit speed;

5 vehicles obstructed from approaching any closer than 0.6m to house frontages;

6 good standard of street lighting, e.g. mounted at 3.5m with 25m spacing.

The basic woonerf approach has been extended in several ways. First, it has been applied to some modern housing layouts as well as to older residential areas. Experiments have also been made at district shopping centres with a view to creating a similar traffic regime — here the term 'winkelerf' ('shopping yard') is used. More recently (c.1986), the Dutch traffic law has been elaborated to enable municipalities to reduce the speed limit from 50 km/hour on any or all minor roads in built-up areas. This power has been used in relation to Gouda and to several districts of other towns.

# PART II
# JOBS FOR THE INNER CITIES

# Introduction

*Sylvia Trench*

The inner cities are one of the most depressing features of the UK today and at the same time they are a focus of an unprecedented amount of well-intentioned public intervention and expenditure of public money.

Few aspects of the economy have spawned more initials, more different names for central and local government grants, more 'initiatives' and 'special projects'. It sometimes seems as if there are so many people working in job creation that this activity itself must be a sizeable contribution to the problem it is trying to solve. It would be easy to come to the facile conclusion that because unemployment, social deprivation and physical dereliction persist despite all these many efforts, there is no point in trying to do anything about the problems.

This would be a serious mistake. A study of what has been happening shows that a great many of the projects which have been attempted have been fruitful and have managed not only to create employment but also to make some impact on the physical environment or the conditions of socially disadvantaged groups.

This section is therefore devoted to an examination of a number of different kinds of efforts being made by various local authorities and other bodies in various parts of the country. It cannot pretend to be fully comprehensive, but it ranges from the Greater London Council at one end of the spectrum to small schemes in Middlesbrough and community businesses in Glasgow and Liverpool; it looks at the work of Metropolitan and district councils and also at what is being done by some of the specialized 'not for profit' organizations like the Centre for Economic Initiatives and the Centre for Local Economic Strategies which are now working in this field.

Since all these various bodies are mainly concerned with promoting and maintaining small businesses in one form or another, it was decided that the economic basis of this strategy ought to be examined to put the case study material which was to follow in perspective. This section therefore begins with a contribution by Martin Binks, Director of the Nottingham University Small Business Research Unit, in which he examines the issue 'Can Small Businesses Solve the Job Problem?'

He demonstrates how the raw figures of numbers employed by small business give a misleading impression of their net contribution to job creation. The statistics must in effect be deflated to account for displacement from other jobs, other areas, and for the short life of many new small businesses. Moreover, people starting up businesses in areas of unemployment are often drawn into the most difficult end of the market. They are often in declining industries or marginal sectors of the economy, or in derelict areas which give their product a bad image, and they operate there with second-hand equipment and often out-of-date skills. 'The question is whether we can get more small firms of a different type.'

What clearly follows from his analysis is that if small businesses are to make a contribution to the inner city job problem it will require some outside intervention. Some agency has to try to influence the choice of activity, and to counteract some of the natural problems of lack of skills especially in management techniques, lack of capital and the hostility of the local environment. It is against this background that the case studies presented in the following chapters can be reviewed.

David Miller writes about the Centre for Local Economic Strategies (CLES), an organization to which 50 local authorities belong as well as bodies like trade unions and some of the enterprise boards.

Many local authorities created enterprise boards in the early 1980s beginning with the Greater London Council, and the other metropolitan counties. Almost all of the boards now have a wider range of functions and have become local economic development agencies. The five enterprise boards have invested about £40m in over 200 companies employing 14 000 people. Funds are raised from public and private sector institutions after an initial payment from local authority funds, and the enterprise boards have also done deals with financial institutions.

Miller describes some of the projects which CLES has been involved in. In the West Midlands a special project to encourage cooperatives through a separate finance organization has managed to fund about 70 new ventures. Although the aggregate number of jobs created was not large they were created at a relatively low cost per job and the survival rate for firms was better than for standard commercial firms. He also describes a quite different project involving seven district councils, the Lancashire Enterprise

Board and the British Waterways Board which was designed to revitalize the canal and combine physical and economic development. The area accounts for half of all the derelict land in Lancashire.

The importance of management skills is a clear theme in the work of both CLES and of the Centre for Economic Initiatives (CEI), another relatively new organization which works with and through local authorities.

Brian Dabson writes about the work of the Centre for Employment Initiatives. He describes collaboration with local residents' associations in promoting community business like the Eldonians Residents' Association in Liverpool. They have gone from setting up a housing cooperative to the formation of a garden centre and landscape maintenance service. It is also, through a subsidiary company, involved in what he calls 'enterprise training' in Cleveland, to help young unemployed people to design and manage projects within their own community.

The organization is very much concerned with developing the skills of local people in areas where unemployment is high and people's morale and opinion of themselves may be low. The activities described may not account for large numbers of the unemployed, but they have successfully led to the formation of viable businesses. These businesses have also produced physical improvements and developed the skills and abilities of local people. They provide an exciting model which should be considered for emulation elsewhere.

Frederick Davies's contribution is also concerned with community businesses and he writes about Scotland where this kind of enterprise has been in existence for a relatively long time and where some support structures have developed. He draws on the experience in Scotland to show that even after all the necessary adjustments to the statistics to take account of displacement effects and other negative repercussions of job creation, the community businesses there really have produced a worthwhile net increase in jobs, and have done so at a cost per job figure which compares well with costs of other kinds of official programmes. At the same time they have done so through activities which have enhanced their local communities and provided work for people who were otherwise at the bottom of the pile.

He describes a success story from a run-down housing estate in the East End of Glasgow, where around one-sixth of the houses were unoccupied and vandalized and where unemployment reached 80 per cent in the late 1970s. The area has been transformed by Barrowfield Community Business Ltd, employing 300 local people and paying £800 000 per annum in wages in an area previously heavily dependent on social security and welfare benefits. It is now forming subsidiaries with welding, landscaping and painting divisions and a security company and has several District Council contracts. It is a large local employer of long-term unemployed people and has a grant from the European Social Fund.

Studies show that around half of the jobs created in Scotland by community businesses are already viable and over 80 per cent are expected to become so in the long term. The research demonstrates clearly that this kind of activity can be a fruitful method of both economic and social regeneration. But these kinds of business are fragile and need public sector support in a number of ways, and at national and regional as well as local level. Many public sector programmes, like the Manpower Services Commission's community programme, are designed in a way that makes it difficult for community business to take advantage of them, and public sector support often requires a heavy burden of accounting and paperwork. Moreover now that the MSC's community programme has been superseded no one seems to know if community businesses will continue to receive funding as before. Frederick Davies argues that public authorities could and should do more to support community businesses so that their potential for helping local communities to regenerate themselves can be realized.

Peter Austin contributes an account of the policies of one local authority, Middlesbrough, in relation to the support of small business. His is a study of the effect of a mixture of policies which a number of local authorities have been trying out: special grants for small firms, exemption for rent and rates, provision of an enterprise centre with accommodation and common services, and management training for young entrepreneurs. Each of these policies is costed and evaluated, and compared with the results of local authority schemes in the rest of the country, found in the recent joint study by the three main associations of local authorities. A number of them are shown to have been cost-effective, and the Middlesbrough experience shows how small firms can become vehicles to create not only new jobs but some positive changes within the organization of work. Peter Austin ends by suggesting that their key feature is their potential flexibility.

Of all the enterprise boards set up in the 1980s, the Greater London Enterprise Board had the largest budget and the most publicity. Since the abolition of the GLC it has been restructured into an organization owned and controlled by 12 London boroughs, and with substantial changes in the arrangements for funding and reduction in the amount of local authority grant available. It began with substantial funding of around £20m a year.

Its aims were not only to create employment but also to improve the quality of the jobs and to help disadvantaged groups and promote social ownership through cooperatives. It was also concerned to establish good employment practice in the jobs that it created and to foster employment support functions such as training. However the projects funded had a very high failure rate and at the end of three years of high level spending only 41 out of over 200 investments costing nearly £15m had survived and only 465 people were employed by these projects.

GLEB was also concerned to establish good employment practice in the jobs that it created and to foster employment support functions such as training. However it was said in the discussion that GLEB businesses tended to pay very low wages, have menial tasks performed by women, and many firms did not even have contracts of employment. This would suggest a serious gap between very fine intentions and their execution.

One of the most interesting contributions to the Institute of Planning Studies seminar was given by David Walburn of GLEB, now re-named Greater London Enterprise. Unfortunately, it was not possible to prepare a transcript of his talk for this publication but some of the main points of his paper are summarized here.

The reorganization of GLEB has resulted in a significant change in direction for the organization. One very important change was the separation of social objectives and commercial business objectives and the separate financing and monitoring of them. The relatively high failure rate of many of the early GLEB investments was chiefly due to the fact that the businesses supported were already very weak commercially. As a result, neither the commercial nor the social objectives of the organization were achieved. GLEB's new organization has had to give priority to the commercial viability of investment, and to establish a practical balance between the social and commercial aspirations of the organization. The GLEB management believes that social objectives can only be met when a company is operating on a secure commercial base. This means that funding is first designed to meet the commercial objectives with hands on support from GLEB staff to ensure that these are met.

Close involvement by GLEB staff also ensures the implementation of social goals, particularly in the areas of equal opportunities and training. The other important reason for the high failure rate of the early GLEB enterprises was insufficient regard to the importance of management. The new regime places a good deal of emphasis on providing new start-up companies with assistance in managerial functions. An organization which is looking to increase secure jobs in the inner cities has to find successful companies which are growing and offer them the required finance to make that growth continue.

The Enterprise Board is established as a holding company with representatives from each of the member boroughs. The main policy board is not involved in day-to-day investment matters. This is done by subsidiary boards on which the only political representative is the Chair and the remaining members are commercial experts. In March 1986 GLEB had a net worth of about £20m consisting of property holdings, cash and investments. It uses this asset base as a security for borrowing to finance the future development of its business.

It is now able to stand alone commercially without any public sector grants. Under the GLC, the organization was almost entirely financed by GLC grants. It is now setting up a property management activity in joint venture with a merchant bank buying into industrial estates which will bring in about £7.5m of private sector money. There has been an initial funding of about £1.2m of public sector revenue from the boroughs which will be used to set up the social operations of the organization. The problem which faces the organization now is not one of funding: it is one of finding new profitable investments.

The quantitative contribution of the projects described in this section to the unemployment problem in the inner cities is very small. What is important and exciting about them however is not their number but their existence. It is now clear that there are some schemes which do work, whose cost is reasonable, and which can in the right circumstances fulfil social and environmental objectives as well. It is also clear that the lessons from the efforts of an earlier and more naive period of job creation are gradually being learnt. Local authorities which are willing and able to devote some staff and cash to job creation need not be short of ideas which have passed the test of practicality and viability in other parts of the country.

# 7

# Can small businesses solve the job problem?

*Martin Binks*

This question can be examined on three levels: the general the regional and the inner city. There is a different set of problems at each of these levels. First we must clear up the use of the term 'small'. Most of the figures in this chapter will follow the Bolton definition, which refers to different types of industrial structure and defines firms accordingly. Broadly speaking, 'small' manufacturing firms employ less than 200 workers and services are defined in terms of turnover. However, much of what follows concerns firms employing less than 20 people, so although data tend to be defined by the Bolton definition, we can consider small businesses as those which employ very few people.

The second problem arising from the question is 'What is the job problem?' If you ask the unemployed they will say it is lack of jobs. If you ask small businesses they will say it is a lack of labour. So the nature of the job problem is by no means clear. If small firms are to help with job creation we are either talking about having many more small firms or about having much more growth within the small firms sector or a bit of both.

## BIRTHS AND DEATHS OF SMALL FIRMS

If the stock of small firms is to grow, that implies that the number of births exceeds the number of deaths. Table 7.1 shows the number of firms registered for VAT. There is a steady growth in the stock group of registrations in 1974 through to 1982 and that has continued since. The

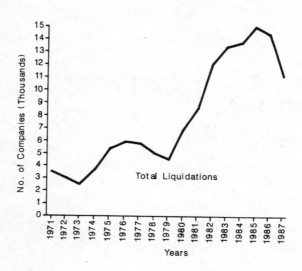

**Figure 7.1   Total voluntary and compulsary liquidations 1971 – 87**

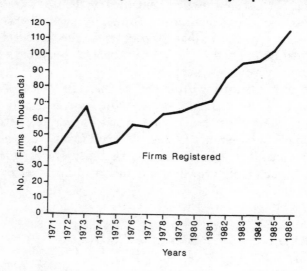

Source: Department of Trade & Industry British Business.

**Figure 7.2   New company registrations 1971 – 86**

average number of registrations exceeds the number of de-registrations. In terms of the stock of businesses there are certainly signs of a steady increase throughout the 1970s.

### Table 7.1   Number of firms registered for VAT

|  | '000s |
|---|---|
| 1974 | 1 202 |
| 1976 | 1 248 |
| 1979 | 1 287 |
| 1982 | 1 375 |
| Average registrations | 155 641 |
| Average de-registrations | 131 |
|  | 451 |

*Source*: Ganguly, 1985.

### Table 7.2   Loans guaranteed 1981 – 83

| Region | No. of firms '000s | No. of loans | Value of loans £m |
|---|---|---|---|
| S.East | 449 | 5790 | 209.2 |
| S.West | 129 | 1364 | 42.6 |
| W.Mids | 120 | 1327 | 42.3 |
| E.Mids | 93 | 964 | 32.2 |
| Yorks & Humb. | 108 | 1213 | 34.7 |
| N.West | 133 | 2004 | 61.8 |
| N.East | 57 | 649 | 19.8 |
| Wales | 75 | 700 | 21.1 |
| Scotland | 104 | 1076 | 31.3 |
| N.Ireland | — | 166 | 6.5 |
| Total UK |  | 15253 | 501.5 |

*Source*: Department of Trade & Industry

It is not just the stock that is growing but also the churning of that stock – the proportion which is entering and leaving the sector (Figure 7.1). This shows the trend in the number of new company registrations as an indication of the underlying trend of new firm formations through to 1982.

Since 1979 there has been quite a sharp increase in the number of births of firms. But this is just the trend; there has been a sharp increase in the number of births and also a very sharp increase in the number of deaths (see figure 7.2). Compulsory and voluntary liquidations give an indication of the underlying trend. The number of deaths rose to a substantially high level before they too levelled off. So the number of firms entering the stock and the number of firms leaving it increased dramatically after 1979.

There was a big increase in the 'churning effect' of businesses as well as some gradual increase in the stock itself. It is important to consider two alternative explanations of that story. The first view can be linked to what Schumpeter called 'competitive destruction' and would be interpreted here after 1979 as the less efficient firms being thrown out and replaced by more efficient firms. According to this view, there is a reallocation of resources from the less efficient to the more efficient.

The second view is that the death rate rose because of a reduction in demand: markets were in recession and therefore the number of firms serving them went down, explaining the sharp increase in the mortality rate of firms. The birth rate went up because many more people were either vulnerable in their employment or were actually made redundant and as a result were pushed into starting up in business. This implies a very different story because it is not necessarily the more efficient replacing the less efficient: it is just that some firms die and other people — who may have come from those dying firms — start up new firms. Evidence collected by Nottingham University and elsewhere tends to support this view. Many new small businesses start up in traditional and often declining industries and particularly in those areas most hit by recession. Such 'pushed' firms are less likely to start in the new high-tech innovative and more efficient 'desirable' industries.

The growth in the birth rate occurs in part because of Government schemes themselves. One reason for increases in 'small businesses' is policies such as the Enterprise Allowance Scheme which has encouraged thousands of people to set up in business on £40 a week given that they can provide about £1000 security. The question however is that, notwithstanding this considerable growth in the stock, are small firms actually creating jobs? Obviously much is happening, but whether the growth in the stock implies an actual growth in the number of employees is much more debatable.

# MEASURING NET JOB CREATION

Evaluating or assessing how much employment is created in a general context is very difficult. The main problem is to identify net job creation or additionality. It is extremely difficult to specify how many extra people are employed in the small firm sector and what that change actually represents. Economists are divided about whether or not the amount is growing. The general consensus appears to be that large firms have been shedding labour in recent years and therefore while the small firms'sector stays roughly constant or increases slightly, then the proportion of employment in small firms will rise. This appears to have been happening towards the end of the 1970s before 1979. But there are problems in terms of measuring additionality and interpreting the growth in the number of jobs.

The first point is the problem of displacement — many businesses which start up serve to displace existing firms or simply cause existing firms to shrink. The market has not grown any larger — it is just that with new entry there is also either the exit of other firms or the shrinkage of those firms within the stock. This is extremely difficult to measure.

Displacement is normally caused primarily by policies which have the effect of subsidizing Peter to put Paul out of a job; some firms receive subsidies and can use this advantage to undercut other firms which do not qualify for the subsidy. Another cause of displacement is that many new firms set up on the basis of extremely cheap second-hand capital in traditional industries. They will often have much lower fixed costs than those firms who set up before that particular market declined. When firms close, releasing second-hand capital, new firms will find they can buy it very cheaply at auction and their cost structure is therefore different from firms who started with much higher and more realistic or typical levels of costs.

A second problem in terms of measuring additionality is the role of part-time job creation. The Government claim that small businesses created about 1.1 million jobs between 1983 – 1986 (*Employment Gazette*, April 1987). However, analysis also shows that unemployment rose by around 250 000 over the same period. Many of those employed by small firms were part-time so it is difficult to transform the figure into a measure of additional 'real' full-time jobs. (See for example Storey and Johnson, 1987b.)

A third problem is the fact that Government schemes, like YTS, the Enterprise Allowance scheme and various others make the interpretation of job creation in the small firms sector much more difficult at an aggregate level.

Other difficulties in the interpretation of statistics arise because many firms that register as companies do not actually trade, so the number of registrations goes up faster than the number of trading firms. Also many firms which may appear to start up have actually previously been trading in the black economy. The situation has changed so they have now decided to admit their trading position, or they have grown to the point where it has not been feasible to stay hidden any longer.

## THE JOB CREATION DEBATE

The job creation debate has been summed up recently in a number of articles by a group of academics at Newcastle University: the proposers of the job creation thesis are Doyle and Gallagher and Gallagher and Stewart (Gallagher and Stewart, 1986; Doyle and Gallagher, 1986) and those who believe that this argument is fallacious are David Storey and Stephen Johnson (Storey and Johnson, 1987a, both references). The debate is useful as an indicator of how the job creation role of small firms can be interpreted by economists and also misinterpreted by government.

Gallagher and Stewart claimed that about 31 per cent of gross new private sector jobs were created in small businesses between 1971 and 1981. These jobs arose in the small firms sector which employed at that point about 13 per cent of the UK workforce. They qualified their results with a statement that they should be interpreted with caution since no one size of firm is responsible for the majority of job creation in the UK — all size sectors make a significant contribution.

However, the Minister said he welcomed this article which 'reveals that small firms will continue to increase their share of the labour market'. That conclusion was not justified by the work of Gallagher and Stewart. David Storey, in looking at the methodology that Gallagher and Stewart used, said it produced estimates of the employment changes over the 1971–81 period upon which 'undue reliance should not be placed' (Storey and Johnson, 1987b).

So there is very little agreement among economists that the small firms sector is creating a significant number of jobs. Even Gallagher and Stewart, who give qualified support to the argument, use methodology which is open to question.

The main points of agreement among economists are first that the mortality rate of small firms is certainly highest in the newest and the youngest. At least one-third of start-ups will die within the first four or five years and over a half will have died within ten years. The firms are therefore most at risk when new and small. The second point on which there is general agreement is that most small firms stay small. It is estimated that only around 1 per cent of small businesses become rapid growth employment creators. The potential for employment creation may still be large but the proportion of small firms involved is very small. It has been estimated that employment which is created by surviving wholly new firms is unlikely to contribute more than 1.5 per cent annually to the gross stock of jobs over a decade.

## WHERE SMALL FIRMS DO WELL

Unlike the USA, small firms in the UK tend to start up more and do better in areas that are already buoyant. In the USA there is clear evidence in many areas that small firms tend to be a response to recession. It is often regions which are comparatively disadvantaged which appear to stimulate a response in setting up many small businesses and these seem to survive and grow.

Empirical evidence in the UK suggests the opposite. In particular the response to national policies is greater for small firms starting up and growing in the well-off or prosperous areas. In the UK, many national policies have a much greater impact on the South East than anywhere else, and their smallest impact in most depressed or recessed areas. For example, response to the Loan Guarantee Scheme introduced in 1981 shows an understandable skew towards the South East. It is natural, other things being equal, that firms in areas where markets are more buoyant receive loans more easily because they will appear to have a more viable case.

The picture from a regional point of view would appear to be that not only is the number of firms highly skewed towards the South East but also that the impact of any national policy will tend to be much greater in areas of relative buoyancy. Less well-off regions will often respond to national policies less than proportionately to their own stock of firms. The result is that policies end up emphasizing the regional divide rather than closing it. (See for example Mason and Harrison, 1986.)

# THE INNER CITY DEBATE

Consider finally the inner city debate. Despite the regional perspective and the apparent advantages of the South East, the inner city problem appears to proliferate in every large city, including London. Some people regard small firms as the natural solution to inner city dereliction and unemployment and their case can be summarized as follows: first, premises in inner cities are often old Victorian buildings suitable for small firms but not suitable for large ones. Second, these areas are located close to the main market outlets in the city centres and therefore transport costs for access to the market are very low. Their location is also good for suppliers because quite often they will supply a number of firms within a very small area at the same time. Third, the prevalence of similar firms may also give them better access to finance. Banks that deal with them will be used to their problems, markets and constraints and should be able to advance funds with greater confidence. Finally, small firms tend to be labour-intensive and therefore in terms of soaking up levels of unemployment they tend to be more effective than medium and larger firms which are more capital-intensive.

Alternatively, inner city dereliction can be viewed as a reflection of the fact that they no longer attract medium or small businesses of the right type. Job-creating small firms are dynamic — they usually have aspirations towards growing, so they often have within their future projections some prospect of growth. Premises in the inner city areas are least amenable to growth; it is often very difficult to expand within them due to their basic design and structure. According to this argument, the firms that would soak up unemployment in the inner city areas are probably those who will locate in rural or peripheral areas around cities rather than the inner city which they regard as undesirable or which might constrain their growth.

Parking and receiving supplies are also very difficult in inner city locations. Victorian buildings tend to have large flights of stairs and getting supplies up them can be a problem. A further point is that the level of dereliction itself, as seen in the amounts of unused land, often discourages firms from setting up. It is not the sort of image they want to show to customers; nor does it create a pleasing environment for employees and the owner manager.

It would appear that inner city area problems are unlikely to be solved by small firms. It is mistaken but natural to assume that they are the solution, however, since there have always been many small firms in inner city areas and there still are. The question is whether more small firms of a different and more dynamic type can be attracted.

## CONCLUSIONS

There are good reasons for being cautious when assessing the employment creation potential of small businesses. On a national or general level the issue is very unclear and theoretical analysis indicates it is unlikely that small businesses will cause much employment; they tend to react to demand rather than create it. At a regional level, policy needs to be very carefully designed to avoid the natural skew in the number of firms and in the buoyancy of markets, otherwise the regional divide will get larger. Finally, for the inner city areas the problem seems to be self-perpetuating to some extent, in that the small firms that set up in inner city areas are often least conducive to solving the job problem.

In a period of recession or high unemployment, trying to raise employment in certain areas may often simply be at the expense of employment in other areas. It will produce a redistribution of jobs rather than a net increase in their number. Also, people starting up businesses in a period of recession are more likely to go into traditional rather than innovative industries. If they are unemployed, or they fear unemployment, they will start a business for the first time and they will rely on their familiar skills.

They will discover that in the local labour market the main skills available are also those of the people who worked in and have been shed from declining sectors. They will go to buy machinery at auction and find they can get very cheap capital which also reflects declining industry and closures. As a result, people setting up new businesses, particularly in areas of recession, will often find that the labour market and the capital market tend to lead them into industries which are declining rather than industries which are growing and developing new techniques (see for example Binks and Jennings, 1986).

The main points are first to try to measure or at least be very aware of the additionality versus displacement problem. Second, to look at the nature and the growth potential of the firms that are setting up in inner city areas and the extent to which that can be influenced. Third, to consider the facilities that are available and the environment within which firms exist in the inner city areas.

Finally, and probably most importantly, there is a need to monitor what is actually happening because much policy with regard to small businesses is based on highly imperfect information. There is very little monitoring and coherent evaluation — much ad hocery and short-term response. We need a better information content on which to base the interventions at both a national, regional and local level.


## REFERENCES

Binks, M, and Jennings, A. 1986, 'Small Firms as a Source of Economic Regeneration' in Curran, J., Stanworth, J. and Watkins, D. *The Survival of the Small Firm*, vol. 1, Gower, Aldershot.

Doyle, J. and Gallagher, C. 1986, *The Size Distribution, Potential for Growth and Contribution to Job Generation of Firms in the UK 1982-1984*, Research report no. 7, Department of Industrial Management, University of Newcastle-upon-Tyne.

Gallagher, C. and Stewart, H. 1986, 'Jobs and the Business Cycle in the UK', *Applied Economics*, vol.18, pp.875–900.

Ganguly, P. 1985, *UK Small Business Statistics and International Comparisons*, edited by Graham Bannock, Small Business Regional Trust, Harper & Row.

Mason, C. and Harrison, R. 1986, 'The Regional Impact of Public Policy Towards Small Firms in the United Kingdom' in Keeble, D. and Wever, E. (eds.), *New Firms and Regional Development in Europe*, Croom Helm, London.

Storey, D.J. and Johnson, S. 1987a, *Job Generation and Labour Market Change*, Macmillan, London.

Storey, D.J. and Johnson, S. 1987b, *Are Small Firms the Answer to Unemployment?* Employment Institute.

# 8
# Local economic development initiatives

*David Miller*

It is now widely accepted that local economic and employment policies are both a legitimate area of local authority concern and a potentially important element in national economic policy. Local authorities are often the largest employers and biggest spenders in local areas, so it is logical for them to use their resources for employment generation. They are allowed, under section 137 of the 1972 Local Government Act, to raise a 2p levy on the local rates 'in the interests of the area and its inhabitants'. They have used money raised in this way to fund a wide range of economic development activities including training schemes, grants and loans to small businesses and cooperatives and subsidies for initially uneconomic rents.

It was partly as a response to this growing range of activities that the Centre for Local Economic Strategies (CLES) was set up at the beginning of 1986. CLES is a national organization which operates as a local government economic think-tank. It aims to link the job creation and economic planning work of local councils with that of community, trade union and voluntary organizations, and the private sector. It is supported by a wide range of local authorities and other organizations involved in locally based economic development activities. It promotes and encourages the expansion of these activities; provides information on initiatives being undertaken in all parts of the country from its extensive computerized database; undertakes research in the local economic policy field; and publishes reports and research studies on many aspects of economic policy affecting local areas.

The scale, impact and influence of local economic policies can be best illustrated by some examples. They show how policies can not only be successful in generating jobs but can also introduce new economic relationships into the local economy. The examples are also typical of the wider-ranging economic policies now adopted by local authorities.

Many local authorities created enterprise boards in the early 1980s as a response to inner city decline. The first five were established by the former Greater London Council, and the Metropolitan Counties of Merseyside, West Yorkshire, West Midlands, and Lancashire. Control has now passed into other hands, mainly district councils and some new enterprise boards have since been created. The original purpose of enterprise boards was to intervene in industry by taking a stake in local companies but almost all the boards now have a wider range of functions and have become local economic development agencies.

The five enterprise boards have managed to invest about £40m in over 200 companies, affecting about 14 000 jobs. They have used an initial investment from local authority funds as a lever to raise other finance from public and private sector institutions. The enterprise boards have also done deals with financial institutions such as West Yorkshire Enterprise Board's £10m loan from the Bank of Nova Scotia and £20m line of credit from the Yorkshire Bank; a £10m investment syndicate involving Lancashire Enterprises Ltd, the Rothchilds, Co-op and Yorkshire Banks; and the various regional venture capital funds established with Lazards and Unity Trust for the West Midlands and the North West.

All this represents investment that might not have taken place and funds which might not have become available in these locations without the existence of the enterprise boards. It is clear that a number of jobs have been retained and created, the conditions for some workers improved and the prospects for some firms increased in areas which the conventional institutions have been all but written off (Miller, 1987). However, it is also clear that the enterprise boards have not achieved the fundamental restructuring of industrial sectors which was in the the minds of some of their original creators.

This is not to say that individual enterprise boards cannot initiate ambitious projects. The Leeds–Liverpool Canal project currently being undertaken by Lancashire Enterprise Ltd (LEL) has been developed through a partnership involving seven district councils, together with Lancashire County Council, LEL, and the British Waterways Board. The aim of the project is to revitalize a length of the Leeds–Liverpool Canal corridor stretching south through the industrial heartland of South Lancashire and into Greater Manchester. The area contains half of all the derelict land in Lancashire, and nearly one-third of the derelict land in Greater Manchester. The unemployment rate over the whole area is something like 17 per cent. The area displays many of the characteristics of a classic inner city area. To achieve the regeneration of this area, it is planned that over £100m will be spent from public, private and European funds.

The project involves four main types of activity. First, the development of small and medium sized firms to help promote local enterprises, improve information and advice to firms, and increase awareness of new and existing applications of new technology, training schemes to improve management skills, and help in gaining access to finance and premises, and stimulate community businesses. Second, the development of new industry and the promotion of economic diversification to revitalize an area where most of the industries are old and obsolete. Third, the provision of training and other measures to help disadvantaged groups and to improve the skills of the area. Fourth, the provision of property for small and medium sized firms.

One of the most interesting aspects of this project is how it will be funded. Finance is being sought from a number of sources and LEL and the local authorities will be contributing only a relatively small proportion. The principal role of the public sector in this case is as a catalyst for private sector investment. It is the sort of role local authorities might need to play much more in the future.

On a smaller scale, cooperative development is another area where enterprise boards as well as many local authorities have been involved. Cooperatives have been identified as a way of introducing new forms of work organization, particularly of ownership and control, and as a means of bringing into work people who might otherwise have been unemployed. This is clearly consistent with the wider social and community interests of many local authority economic development policies. The impact of local authority finance and other resources, combined with the upsurge of activity in the cooperative movement itself, has been significant. In the mid-1970s there were only 20 cooperatives in Britain. There are now well over 1200, with nearly 10 000 full- and part-time workers.

The West Midlands provides a good illustration of how local authorities have contributed to this expansion. In 1981 there were six cooperatives registered in the whole of the former West Midlands County area; now there are over 80. To achieve this the former County Council initially established three cooperative development agencies and a support fund of £100 000. By 1982, the budget for loans and grants had expanded to

£250 000 and eventually a grant was made to Industrial Common Ownership Finance Ltd (ICOF) to establish a revolving fund for loans to
cooperatives in the West Midlands. Since 1982, £500 000 has been granted
to ICOF. In 1984, West Midlands Co-op Finance Ltd (WMCOF) was formed to manage the funds allocated to local cooperatives. WMCOF was given
an initial grant of £400 000 and received a further £778 000 during 1985
(CLES, 1986). WMCOF is now a subsidiary of the West Midlands Enterprise Board and is the largest organization of its type in the country with
assets of over £1m.

Over 70 of the 80 cooperatives established in the West Midlands have
received funding from WMCOF and most of these are new starts; 16
cooperatives have ceased trading in the last five years. Approximately 450
people are employed and about 20 per cent of these are from the ethnic
minorities. Investment costs are about £1500 per job. Nearly half the
cooperatives are in the service sector, one third in manufacturing and the
remainder in retailing.

The example of the West Midlands shows that considerable effort and
finance is needed to create relatively few jobs. However they are new jobs,
created very cheaply, and they are jobs which would not have been provided without public sector funding and support. The West Midlands have
shown that viable jobs can be created in non-traditional working
organizations.

The future development of these types of initiatives is uncertain. There
will be major changes in 1988/9 in the statutory framework which governs
local authority intervention in economic policy and more specifically in
the role played by agencies such as the enterprise boards and other local
authority companies.

Legislation is promised 'at an appropriate date' to enact a 'general but
circumscribed power' for local authorities to engage in economic development activity. This is in response to the White Paper 'The Conduct of
Local Authority Business: The government response to the Widdicombe
Committee' (see Appendix I). The legislation is to be accompanied by the
removal of the power to use section 137 for economic development
purposes. Widdicombe's research showed that in 1984−5, economic
development activities accounted for more than two-thirds of all spending
under the discretionary spending section 137, and were the largest single
use of this power (LEDIS, 1988b). Further government proposals in a
Department of the Environment Consultation paper on local authorities'
interests in companies will restrict spending of local authority enterprise

boards and local authority economic development companies, and will also restrict freedom to allocate priorities for development activites (LEDIS 1988a, see Appendix II).

The 1988 Local Government Finance Act will replace local business rates with a uniform business rate and this will change the relationship between councils and their local business communities. The Act is also likely to lead to increased pressure on local authorities' revenue budgets and limit resources for economic development. Taken together, all these legislative proposals represent the most substantial set of changes ever proposed in the sphere of economic development.

It is clear that local economic development policies can make a significant impact on the level of economic activity and employment, but the proposed legislation represents a real threat to their continuance. The example of Lancashire Enterprises is perhaps an indication of the way initiatives could be implemented in the future. The development of partnerships with the private sector may be a way for many local authorities to bring in private sector resources. It would then still be possible to have a real impact on employment at the local level.

## REFERENCES

Centre for Local Economic Strategies, 1986, *Councils Support Coops*, CLES Report no.2, Manchester

Centre for Local Economic Strategies, 1987, *Economic Sense — Local Jobs Plans*, CLES Report, Manchester.

LEDIS, 1988a, *DoE Consultation Paper: Local Authorities' Interests in Companies*, Overview B67, Local Economic Development Information Service, The Planning Exchange, Glasgow.

LEDIS, 1988b, *Government White Paper: The Conduct of Local Authority Business*, Overview B68, Local Economic Development Information Service, The Planning Exchange, Glasgow.

Mawson J. and Miller D. 1986, 'Interventionist Approaches in Local Employment and Economic Development' in Victor Hausner (ed.) *Critical Issues in Urban Economic Development*, vol.1, Oxford University Press, Oxford.

Miller D. 1987, *An Overview of Enterprise Boards* West Midlands Enterprise Board, Birmingham.

## APPENDICES

Further information on the Government White Paper 'The Conduct of Local

Authority Business' and Consultation Paper 'Local Authorities' Interests in Companies' has been provided by LEDIS, the Local Economic Development Information Service. Appendices I and II reprint LEDIS Overview sheets B68 and B67 respectively. Both sheets where published in the LEDIS issue for September 1988. LEDIS is published monthly and is available by subscription from The Planning Exchange, 186 Bath Street, Glasgow, G2 4HG.

## Appendix I

This appendix outlines the Government's proposals contained in their recent White Paper, 'The Conduct of Local Authority Business: The Government response to the Report of the Widdicombe Committee' (CM 433). The White Paper discusses providing a 'general, but circumscribed' power for local authority economic development activities and also limiting the finance available for such activities.

### Introduction – local authority discretionary spending powers

This White Paper emerged from the Widdicombe Committee's Report examining local authorities' discretionary spending powers. They considered the need to clarify the limits and conditions governing discretionary spending, including the use of sections 137 and 142 of the Local Government Act 1972 (and sections 83 and 88 of the Local Government (Scotland) Act 1973). The Committee's research showed that in 1984/85 economic development activities accounted for more than two-thirds of all spending under the discretionary spending sections 137 and 83 (£90m). This was the single largest use of this power.

Widdicombe recommended that the Government should review the proper role of local authorities in economic development with a view to identifying any areas in which new statutory powers should be introduced.

### Scale and nature of local authority involvement in economic development

The Government's response in the form of the White Paper recognizes that local authorities of all types and all political persuasions are involved in economic development activities. Estimates of revenue spending by English local authorities on economic development in 1985/86 range, depending on the definition used, from £280 to £400m. Total expenditure by English local authorities on economic development on this basis represented around 1 per cent of total local authority spending in England. This compares with central government regional assistance in England of around £396m in 1986/87.

No detailed breakdown is available of spending by local authorities on particular types of economic development. It is clear, however, that the range of activities pursued is wide. They include grants to enterprise boards and similar bodies; grants, loans and equity finance for individual firms; capital investment in starter and other industrial units; subsidy for initially uneconomic rents; provision of training schemes; general publicity and specialist advice; and organized visits to attract industry to the area.

The Government acknowledges that 'in many cases local authority economic initiatives have been an important element in the success of central government policies. For example, the Department of Employment's work in the promotion of tourism and the encouragement of small firms has relied on the active involvement of both the private sector and local authorities, particularly through local enterprise agencies. The Department of the Environment's Urban Programme and City grant schemes, which are increasingly geared towards stimulating economic activity, also required important input by local authorities'.

However, the White Paper then goes on to argue that:

the overall scale of local authority support for various kinds of economic development raises questions about its objectives and justification. There is no conclusive evidence concerning the cost effectiveness of local authority spending in this area, although in some areas local authority schemes appear to be comparable in terms of cost effectiveness to similar schemes funded by central government. It is difficult to judge whether local authority assistance results in investment that would not otherwise have taken place, or whether subsidies serve only to move investment from one area to another. It is therefore important to ensure that local authorities are not simply competing with each other to give the largest subsidies to mobile business. Equally, local authorities should be discouraged from becoming involved in activities that can more appropriately be undertaken by the private sector or other public sector agencies.

This fairly negative assessment of local authority economic development activities concentrating on the alleged displacement of private sector capital, with no supporting evidence provided, is then used to justify the future regulation of finance available for economic development. Given the widely acknowledged lower cost per job of local economic development initiatives compared to government sponsored regional assistance and enterprise zones the motivation for the Government's action seems essentially ideological.

## Powers for economic development

Local authorities have never had a general power for economic development. A number of their functional powers — notably in the planning field — permit such intervention. Section 137/83 spending represented only about 38 per cent of the total spending by English authorities on economic development in 1984/85. Specific powers available to local authorities include: sections 2 and 3 of the Local Authorities' Land Act 1963, which permit the carrying out of works on land and related grants for this purpose; section 144 and 145 of the Local Government Act 1972, which permit a wide range of activities in the tourism and entertainments fields; and section 95 of the Weights and Measures Act 1985, permitting a wide range of advisory services.

The Government challenges the assumption that section 137/83 is the main power for economic initiatives. However, many local authorities would argue that it is precisely the flexibility afforded under section 137/83 that allows them to deliver an integrated package of economic development measures.

Despite this the Government argues that 'without the availability of section 137/83 most authorities would have adequate powers to do what they do now in the economic development field, except in relation to grants for revenue support or equipment; support and publicity for some business activities in which the local authority has no interest; and the provision of equity capital'. The fact that the Government does not consider these functions central to the work of local economic development is reflected in their subsequent proposals on the scope of the statutory economic development function. Even the Government concedes that some local authorities are more dependent on section 137/83 monies because they lack some of the other relevant powers cited above which provide for certain types of economic development spending. For example shire districts lack the relevant powers available to other authorities, in the advice and information, education and social services fields. Inner London boroughs also currently lack education powers.

## Conclusions and proposals

The Government accepts that the current situation where spending on economic development is governed by the detailed interpretation of an assortment of powers rather than what is needed is not conducive to sensible decision making. Most commentators will welcome the consolidation of the existing powers into a defined statutory power. However, the Government's commitment to a statutory framework is immediately qualified by the narrow drawing of the proposed definition, as part of a move to curtail economic development activities that the Government does not approve of.

The particular problems the Government wishes to rectify are the absence of any 'financial limit on the costly land acquisition schemes that feature largely in some local authorities' economic development activities; nor is there any incentive to dispose of assets consisting of land and buildings where local authority management has no useful role to play'. Conversely, the other areas of local authority economic development activity which the Government approves of and wishes to free up are 'small scale pump-priming initiatives in the community, social and advice fields for which local authorities are well placed, and in which they frequently co-operate with other initiatives in both the public and private sectors'. For many economic development units, this strategy involves a diminution in their powers with a forced re-orientation towards social rather than economic activities.

The government will now bring forward legislation to give local authorities a new specific power to carry out economic development to rationalize the present legislative framework, and to remove the current anomalies between what different types of authority may do in the economic development field. But the power will be circumscribed. The power to use other specific powers for economic development will be removed, as will the power to use section 137/83 for this purpose.

The government has not yet decided the precise form of the legislation. They argue that there is a case for some financially based controls, especially to make clear that some activities are not appropriate to local government. These activities include some commercial trading activities and equity participation in commercial companies, other than through the normal management of the superannuation funds or under specific legislative provisions. As indicated above, this would have profound implications for many economic development companies and enterprise boards. Because the Government's proposals in its recent DoE consultation Document on local authorities' interest in companies (LEDIS, B67) will make local authority-controlled companies (most enterprise boards and many economic development companies) subject to any capital and revenue expenditure controls imposed on the local authority.

The tendency towards even greater central government control inherent in these changes is reinforced by the Government's promise to introduce new procedural requirements 'to ensure proper consideration of priorities across the whole field of economic development; co-ordination with other activities by the authority and with other agencies in the public and private sectors; and proper scrutiny. Special provision will be made for consultation with the business community'. The precise terms of this consultation and scrutiny have yet to be laid out.

## Appendix II

This appendix provides a summary of the Department of the Environment's Consultation Paper on local authorities' interests in companies and outlines its implications for local economic development. (This appendix should be read in conjunction with LEDIS B68 on that section of the Government's Widdicombe White Paper which deals with local authority economic development activities Cd 433.)

### Introduction

The Government fear that local authorities are doing things they shouldn't, including avoiding spending controls, *ultra vires*, and activities, outwith the rules governing conduct of local authority business. However, the Government also recognize the value of local authority companies for joint ventures with private sector and in pursuing 'sound management practice'.

### Categorization of local authority interest or involvement in companies

The DoE put forward three categories of local authority interest or involvement in companies:

1    Local authority-controlled companies: 'where a local authority is formally in a position to require the company to behave as it wishes' –
through, for example, being a majority shareholder, or controlling the
composition of the board of directors.

A distinction is drawn 'between companies conducting local authority
business in much the same way as the authority itself, and companies
which are run more or less as commercial undertakings, at arms' length
...' (para.43). An 'arms' length company' is one where:

- local authority members or officers are not directors;
- transactions between the local authority and the company are fully
commercial;
- the company has declared financial objectives (rate of return on
assets);
- the LA should not cover company losses, providing finance only
for investment in fixed assets or for working capital;
- contracts over £10 000 may only be awarded to the company after
competitive tender.

2    Local authority-influenced companies: where 'a local authority has
informal links, or in which it has a signficant minority interest, and
(in either case) where an overlap of personnel and association of
business between the authority and the company are such that the local
authority has a dominant influence on the company'.
3    Other minority interests: 'where the local authority is formally involved
in the company, but does not have control or dominant influence'.

## Proposals for local authority-controlled companies

'Local authorities would be required to use their control over local authority-
controlled companies to ensure that the company did nothing the controlling authority could not do' (paras 26–8). One exception to this would
be activities in preparation for privatisation, where approved by Secretary
of State.

Capital transactions of a local authority-controlled company would be
treated as capital transactions of the local authority itself (thus reducing
its own capital expenditure ceiling)(paras 35–7). Expenditure where the
only statutory authority is section 137 would be matched by a

parallel reduction in the authority's s137 spending limits (para. 42h). The capital expenditure control would also apply to local authority-influenced companies (para.50). In the case of joint local authority companies such controls would be divided in proportion to their share of total local authority interest (para.63).

Statutory rules concerning the personnel involved in local authorities would be applied to local authority-controlled companies. For example, rules concerning the exclusion of those disqualified from council member-ship, councillors' remuneration, preventing employees sitting on their employing body, pecuniary interests, and corruption offences. Likewise other rules on the proper conduct of business (including non-commercial contract conditions, compulsory competition, access to information) (para. 41−2). Arms' length companies would be excluded from the requirements on contracts' procedures, compulsory competition, the local ombudsman and access to information (paras. 43−5).

## Proposals – local authority-influenced companies

Local authority-influenced companies would be subject to the capital ex-penditure controls noted above, and also

- be required to provide access to the authority's auditor (para.51);
- where appropriate, propriety controls on personnel and the con-duct of business (including a requirement that any councillor should be provided with any information he or she needs 'for the discharge of his functions') (para.52).

## Minority interests

Minority interests in companies would only be allowed 'for defined pur-poses' (paras. 30−2). These include:
- Public transport.
- Public airports.
- 1985 Further Education Act companies.
- Housing associations approved under 1988 Local Government Act; 'a non-profit making company which provides a facility used by, or which is for the benefit of, residents in the local authority's area, and to which the local authority gives, or has given, finan-cial assistance under a power other than section 137 of the Local

Government Act 1972'.
- An enterprise agency; 'company in which local commercial and industrial undertakings participate, which does not trade with the public (except to provide goods and services to local commercial and industrial firms) and the main purpose of which is to promote the economic development of all or part of an area of the local authority'.
- Joint ventures for the management of land buildings and structures (residential, industrial, commercial).
- Joint ventures for land development (either where the authority has sold land to the developer or has entered into a planning agreement).
- A professional association ('a company limited by guarantee concerned solely with the promotion of commerce, art, science, education, religion, charity or any profession').

In the case of these permitted minority interests, requirements would be introduced to ensure proper accounting for the local authority's interest, exclusion of persons disqualified from council membership, and the application of controls on councillor's remuneration, pecuniary interest and the provision of information (paras. 53−7).

The proposals would be extended to cover other types of corporate body such as industrial and provident societies and non-charitable trusts. The new rules would not apply to the investment of superannuation funds, but it is proposed to develop a code of practice concerning the investment in companies of charitable funds of which the local authority is a trustee.

## Possible implications for enterprise boards and economic development companies

1   There is a requirement on the boards (if they remain local authority-controlled) to do nothing that the local authority cannot do. This is likely to preclude any equity investments as s44 of Local Government (Miscellaneous Provisions) Act 1982 defines acceptable forms of financial assistance as grants, loans or guarantees.
2   The boards will be subject to statutory rules on the personnel involved and other rules on the proper conduct of business (in effect, the enterprise board would be treated as a local authority).
3   All capital expenditure if board or company is local authority-

controlled or local authority-influenced will count against the parent authority's allocation. For local authority-controlled companies, revenue expenditure whose only statutory authority is s137 would be matched by a parallel reduction in the s137 limit, although this is already generally the case for enterprise boards.

One option for enterprise boards wishing to retain the scope for commercial operations is for them to become defined as arms' length companies. However, this would still involve adhering to the conditions laid out previously for such companies including the requirement that neither members nor officers were board directors. An alternative option which would involve even further diluting local authority control would be for the boards or companies to move towards the enterprise agency model, with the local authority holding only a minority interest through a minority shareholding. A further option is to try to persuade the Secretary of State to make a special case for enterprise boards.

# 9

# Community enterprise development

*Brian Dabson*

This chapter is concerned with describing some aspects of enterprise in community economic development, a topic about which the Centre for Employment Initiatives (CEI) has had considerable practical experience in recent years. CEI was established in 1981 as an independent company. It provides a range of consultancy, evaluation and information services in areas such as economic development, labour market and employment affairs, training and responses to unemployment. Its clients now include international agencies, government departments and agencies, local authorities, private companies and voluntary and community-based organizations, which are served from CEI's offices in Liverpool, Edinburgh and London and through a subsidiary company in the USA.

## COMMUNITY ENTERPRISE

An important element of CEI's work, particularly in the context of inner city and peripheral housing estate regeneration, is with organizations and groups seeking to develop community enterprise. Both the words 'community' and 'enterprise' need to be defined and explained.

There used to be much debate among planners about the meaning of community, and the distinction between physical and perceptual communities. It is now accepted that communities of interest can be defined in all sorts of ways — they can be geographical, they can be motivated by language or cultural traditions or colour, or perhaps most importantly in the context of the inner city problem, they can be communities of disadvantage or suffering. The concept tends to embrace 'grass-roots' 'bottom-up' approaches and is clearly separate from any formal system or organization of government.

Enterprise must be one of the most overworked terms in the English language at the moment. It has become synonymous with entrepreneurship — the creation of jobs and wealth through initiatives which make or sell goods or services. While entrepreneurship is certainly part of being enterprising there are other aspects which are equally important. The point is well made by the quotation from an Entrain[1] publication:

> Enterprising people have particular skills and qualities. They have the imagination and initiative to create ideas. They have the judgement, drive, determination and organising abilities to carry their ideas into action. People need to be and are enterprising in a great variety of circumstances. Enterprise isn't the specialist preserve of entrepreneurs by any means. Any problem which needs resolving, any challenge which needs meeting, responsibility which needs discharging or idea or opportunity which needs exploiting, requires enterprise. The more individuals, groups, communities and the nation as whole have the skills and quality of enterprise, the more flexible and creative they are.

When community and enterprise are put together the concept, in its broadest sense, describes communities with common problems or aspirations. In a narrower sense it describes a form of entrepreneurial activity which can be placed on a spectrum of enterprise ranging from private companies to public ownership. At one end of the spectrum are the majority of privately owned businesses, owned and run for the benefit of the proprietor. Then there are worker cooperatives and co-ownerships in which ownership and benefit can be broader, but still rests with the cooperating group of workers. Then further along the spectrum are the community enterprises where ownership and benefit are broader still. These include the community companies and cooperatives as found in significant numbers in Scotland, and also trading subsidiaries of voluntary and community organizations. To complete the picture, on the far end of the spectrum are, for instance, municipal enterprises, owned and controlled by a local authority for general public benefit. These would include Enterprise Boards which provide investment capital for local businesses which meet defined economic and social criteria.

It is with the activities on the community enterprise part of this spectrum that the main hope for inner city regeneration lies. It is quite obvious that even if there is a large-scale and sustained upturn in the fortunes of the British economy, the benefits are unlikely to trickle down to poor inner city areas or to peripheral housing estates. New industry, if it comes at all, will demand skilled, experienced and flexible workers; people with a limited range of working experience, very few marketable skills and a history of long-term unemployment will not be in demand. Therefore different approaches are needed for what some have called the 'no-economy areas'.

## COMMUNITY BUSINESS

One approach, which developed rapidly in Scotland as a process of fostering economic regeneration from the bottom up, is the community business. The standard definition of a community business as applied in Scotland is a trading organization which is set up, owned and controlled by the local community, and which aims to create ultimately self-supporting jobs for local people, and to be a focus for local development. Any profits which are made from the business go to create more employment, or to provide local services or to assist other schemes of local benefit (see also Chapter 10).

There are four main arguments for supporting community business: first, it allows communities to create jobs to tackle local needs and provide local services; second, it enables communities to exert more influence over their own destiny; third, it provides a local and accessible route into training and skill development for people who feel distanced from formal education and training opportunities; and fourth it provides a channel for drawing external resources into an area to tackle local problems and create jobs.

Community enterprises are not soft options — they are extremely high-risk ventures which have to face all the hazards faced by traditional small businesses run by private entrepreneurs but they also have additional factors which count against them. They have little or no financial track record; they have little or nothing by way of equity or available capital; they have unconventional management structures, if they have any management at all; and they have systems of control exercised by people with little or no previous experience of business management. In addition to all these problems, they combine economic and social objectives in a way which makes them totally unacceptable in terms of risk and return to conventional financial institutions. These are the very real and practical difficulties which face a community which is thinking of going into community business. But many local areas think it is worth fighting these difficulties in order to try to create work when no-one else is doing it for them.

The contribution of enterprise in community economic development can be demonstrated by the following examples from Liverpool and Cleveland, the first of which describes the evaluation of a community business, and the second, a broadly based training project designed to develop enterprising behaviour in the wider community.

## COMMUNITY ECONOMIC DEVELOPMENT IN LIVERPOOL

The Liverpool example is located in an area, just to the north of the city centre, known as Vauxhall. Physically it is depressingly like the media image of Liverpool — tenement housing, mean streets, derelict industrial sites. People who are in work are very much in the minority and those who used to have a job have few marketable skills. Out of this very unpromising landscape has emerged something rather special called the Eldonian Community Association. The Association had its origins in 1978 when Liverpool City Council announced its plans to demolish a large number of prewar tenements which would directly affect 500 families. Unfortunately, the City Council did not go about it as they perhaps ought to have done, and gave very little information about the disruption their plans would cause, nor about their intentions for rehousing. The local community came together to form a committee to try to find out what the local people wanted to do, where they would like to live, and to prepare some alternative ideas for what should happen to their area of Vauxhall.

The Eldonian Community Association is a voluntary community organization whose members include local residents, representatives of tenants' groups and the Church. It has no staff of its own, and a very small budget, but it has learned how to work with professionals and to deal with officials and politicians. It has now become involved in an increasingly ambitious programme of community-based initiatives. It has put forward and undertaken a scheme to decapitate the tenement blocks and convert them into two-storey houses; it has also set up housing cooperatives to build 100 new houses on five small local sites.

When Tate and Lyle closed its Love Lane sugar refinery in 1981 right next door to this housing area, there was a loss of 1800 jobs. Tate and Lyle had been a source of employment for four generations. The factory passed into Government hands, and Michael Heseltine, the then Minister for Merseyside, called for ideas as to how the site might be redeveloped. An open competition was held and the Eldonians submitted their own proposals for the use of the site for housing. Although they did not actually win the competition, the Eldonians managed to convince English Estates (to whom the site had by then passed), the Department of the Environment and the Housing Corporation that their scheme deserved support and should proceed. As a result the refinery was demolished, the site reclaimed, and now an estate of 140 houses each individually designed with the prospective tenant is under construction.

The Association has also set up a Neighbourhood Watch Scheme, in conjunction with the Police, the Probation Service and the schools, which has resulted in this area having the lowest crime rate in Liverpool in spite of its location. It has also pursued many other activities in the field of adult education, and developed links between the schools and the community.

## AN ENTERPRISING COMMUNITY

This story has important implications for job creation in the inner cities, because it is about the emergence of an enterprising community. The Association's ability to act as an engine for promoting local initiatives has become increasingly recognized by politicians and funders of all sorts. Its fund-raising ability has become quite phenomenal — funds have come from local individuals, charitable trusts and private companies. Although the initiatives have mainly focused on housing and social support services, the Association has also turned its attention to exploring ways in which it can act as a vehicle for economic regeneration.

Its first venture has been the establishment of the Eldonian Garden Market, a community business producing and selling garden and house plants, and providing landscape maintenance services. Ideas for an urban horticulture project were subjected to a detailed feasibility study by CEI, which was then used to present the case for funding from a variety of public and private sources. Urban Programme funding was obtained through the Merseyside Task Force to lay out the site, and to construct and equip glasshouses; European Social Fund finance was secured to pay for the training of local people in basic horticultural skills; Northern Foods provided money to recruit and pay the salary costs of a manager, and they have also continued to provide expertise from within their own company; and other resources in cash and kind have been forthcoming from private companies and from trusts. In addition there have been many professional people and organizations, particularly the Liverpool Housing Trust, which have been willing to supply a wide range of essential support services and advice.

The Association insisted that the site for the Garden Market should be close to the new homes so that they could be looked after and linked directly into the community, both through the jobs it would offer and through the services and products they would buy. In spite of a very large number of vacant sites in the area, high land costs reduced the choice to parts of old railway yards, dockside sites, and other unattractive pieces of land. In the end, a site over one of the Mersey tunnels was found immediately adjacent to the Eldonians' Village.

The Garden Market was officially opened by a Government minister in June 1988, although it had begun trading several months before then. The Eldonians are now turning their attention to their next ventures including a managed workspace development with the theme of healthy living and eating. In addition they have been registered as a local enterprise agency so that they can provide advice and support to local people wishing to set up businesses in their area. Thus this has become a self-sustaining process of community economic development — enterprise out of adversity.

## ENTERPRISE TRAINING IN CLEVELAND

A different approach to enterprise development in the community can be found in the county of Cleveland in the north of England. Cleveland county with a population of some 565 000, mainly in the four towns of Middlesbrough, Stockton, Hartlepool and Billingham, is not a conventional inner city area but has suffered traumatic industrial decline over a very short period. When the oil, chemical and shipbuilding industries were at their peak activity in the county in the 1960s and early 1970s the area had some of the country's highest per capita incomes. Now some of the towns and outlying districts have the highest unemployment rates in the UK outside Northern Ireland.

The county has been forced to cope with major changes and uncertainty concerning its industrial and commercial future. As part of the response, a partnership of private and public sector bodies has focused on the need to foster a cultural shift throughout Cleveland towards greater personal and community enterprise initiative. To do this, it was seen as important to assist people of all ages actually facing change in their employment, training and work prospects to develop the skills of enterprise in social and economic wealth creation. CREATE Development Trust Ltd was established in September 1987 to support innovatory forms of enterprise skills training, and link together the resources and experience of the education, training and voluntary sectors with private and public sector organizations. CREATE is a company limited by guarantee and constructed as a not-for-profit organization. It has a Board of Directors drawn from the various sectors of activity which it links together, and a staff of 13. Funding of £1.4m for three years has been provided by the Training Agency (formerly Manpower Services Commission), and by Tioxide UK plc and Cleveland County Council with additional backing from local enterprise agencies in the county.

The origins of the initial proposals for CREATE did not come from the local authority; nor did they come from the then Manpower Services Commission. They emerged from Tioxide UK plc, a multinational company based in Billingham which manufactures pigments and other specialist chemicals. Over many years the company had developed innovatory approaches to employee training and development, and considered that some of the lessons from these were worth exploring in the wider community of Cleveland. In putting their proposals together and assembling local cross-sectoral support for them, the company was assisted by Dave Turner, who had for ten years worked in an enterprise skills development initiative aimed at young people in South Australia.

Over three years the aim of CREATE is to work with small groups of individuals totalling some 3000 throughout the county. Half will be unemployed and the rest at school, in YTS, in college, working in local companies and on government 'adult training' programmes. CREATE offers each group a package of resources to enable them to design and manage a project. In the case of non-business groups, this must be not for profit and of community benefit. The purpose is to encourage people to identify new ideas and opportunities within the community and at work that will lead to a project, the success of which will depend on their exercise and development of enterprise skills.

The resources CREATE offers are twofold: a grant towards the project, and a facilitator to work alongside the group to help them identify the skills of enterprise they are developing, and to identify with the group the transferability of those skills. An important part of CREATE's work also involves on-the-job training for teachers, trainers, work experience supervisors, community workers and business start-up advisers. This training is designed to encourage and help those involved in education and training to develop forms of learning and training that promote enterprise skills development within their own organizations.

By November 1988 CREATE had assisted 76 projects involving over 600 participants throughout the county. Each project lasted on average 14 weeks. A major programme of evaluation of the outcomes of the CREATE projects and of the overall impact of this form of enterprise skills development is underway. The philosophy and objectives of CREATE have attracted widespread interest throughout the UK. Not least this is because they offer a model for enterprise and enterprise skills development which has relevance for the *whole* community: those in school, in employment, not in work and in training.

## EMPOWERING THE COMMUNITY

Both the examples are about community empowerment — enabling people to develop and control their own resources. This is a theme which CEI is particularly interested in for integrating impoverished communities into the mainstream economy. It is not enough to hope that the problems will be solved by building factories, by introducing companies like Nissan, or by waiting for the small business economy to turn the country round. Unless they are given the resources to help themselves whole generations are going to be sacrificed in poor inner city communities.

Jimmy Reid, convenor of the shop stewards at the Upper Clyde Shipbuilders, described the situation when he said 'I am convinced that the great mass of people go through life without realizing a glimmer of their true potential'. That is what creating jobs in the inner cities is about.

## NOTE

1   Entrain was an organization contracted by the former Manpower Services Commission to introduce enterprise learning approaches into the Youth Training Scheme, but was disbanded in mid-1988.

# 10
# Community businesses

*Frederick Davies*

This chapter examines the extent to which community business can contribute to local economic development and help to ease the hardships faced by communities in poor socio-economic environments. It draws on the evidence of community businesses in Scotland, represented by a federal organization, Community Business Scotland (CBS), established in 1981.

A community business can be described as:

> a trading organisation which is set up, owned and controlled by the local community and which aims to create ultimately self-supporting jobs for local people, and to be a focus for local development. Any profits made from its business activities go either to create more employment, or to provide local services or to assist other schemes of community benefit. (Robinson and Wren, 1985)

## SPECIAL FEATURES

There are four main characteristics of a community business. First, unlike other community organizations it is a trading business with conventional company objectives. Second, it is owned by the community on open membership and one-person-one-vote principles. Any resident is entitled to become a member on payment of a nominal annual subscription. The business is then controlled by the community, in the sense that members elect a board of directors who are accountable to them. External professional expertise can also be co-opted on to the Board, for example, bank managers, local councillors and specialist advisers.

Third, there is no distribution of profit to individuals. Trading profits are either reinvested in the business, paid as a bonus to employees, or used in some way for general community benefit.

Finally, it is a characteristic of a community business that it incorporates social as well as economic objectives. The aim is to generate employment for local people, particularly the long-term unemployed, by matching local skills to local needs.

Community businesses are mainly located in three types of deprived neighbourhoods, namely local authority estates, inner city areas and one-company towns. It is possible to identify two main models of community business development: the 'professional' and the 'grass roots'. The professional model applies when the initiative for establishing the company is taken by professional workers, usually from local government, as a method of alleviating problems of local poverty and unemployment. However professionally developed businesses tend to remain in the hands of their initiators who find it difficult to hand over control to local residents.

The grass roots model applies when the initiative comes from members of the local community, and the business is controlled and led by them from the outset. Typically these businesses call on professionals from outside agencies for support and to provide specialist advice on matters such as company structure and finance.

## LOCAL DEVELOPMENTS

The recent growth of community business activity in Scotland dates from the late 1970s. At that time a small number of *ad hoc* and relatively isolated employment initiatives were undertaken in deprived localities in urban central Scotland.

The number of businesses had increased from 20 in July 1982 to approximately 85 at the end of 1986. A number of voluntary support structures has developed; at the national level, Community Business Scotland has operated since 1981 as a broad forum for community groups; at the regional level, Strathclyde Community Business was established in April 1984.

Recently local and central government have taken an interest in the sector. Several local authorities have included it in their local economic development strategies and allocated professional staff to community business development work. For example, in November 1982 Cleveland County Council appointed several community employment development officers (CEDOs) to support local employment schemes (Richardson, 1985).

## FINANCIAL SUPPORT

In Scotland, a principal form of public sector financial support has been the Urban Aid Programme. During 1985 – 86, 17 per cent of the income of community businesses came from Urban Aid funds and as much as 28 per cent from the Manpower Services Commission. This money went into a relatively small number of community businesses which acted as managing agents for the Community Programme. The EEC's European Social Fund provided approximately 13 per cent of total income, albeit to a relatively small number of community businesses. However community businesses themselves generated over a third of their income through trading activities. Indeed during 1985 – 86, Scottish Community Businesses generated a trading income well in excess of £2.25m.

Urban Aid revenue support is intended to meet the salary costs of key managerial and supervisory positions and some overheads. It is not provided to meet employees' wages. To qualify for grant support, community businesses must have their membership open to the local community and be non-(private) profit distributing. Furthermore the grant cannot be used to support unfair competition with other enterprises by charging artificially low prices for goods and services. Only those community businesses operating in designated areas of multiple deprivation are eligible for support which can last for a maximum of seven years.

## THE CASE OF BARROWFIELD

The way in which community business works in practice is best illustrated by looking at an example of a successful development. Barrowfield is a peripheral public sector housing estate in the East End of Glasgow, with a population of approximately 2500. At the turn of the decade there were over 100 unoccupied houses out of a stock of 614. The vacant properties were quickly vandalized, contributing to the rundown appearance of the area and making it more difficult to relet houses to new tenants. Unemployment reached 80 per cent in the late 1970s and the Barrowfield community was heavily dependent on social security and welfare benefits.

The local community decided to take matters into its own hands and, in 1981, a local tenants' association was established. In 1983, a joint initiative by the Glasgow District Council and the Strathclyde Regional Council brought together in one building all the important services which affected local people: social work, housing, community development, welfare rights and financial advice. An employment group was established by the tenants' association to see what could be done by the local people to help themselves. They decided that the concept of a community business both suited their ideas of community control and offered the structure for promoting a range of economic projects and activities. By August 1985, Barrowfield Community Business Ltd, a charitable company limited by guarantee, received a Strathclyde Community Business Management Grant enabling the group to employ professionals. By the autumn of 1987, the company had built up a turnover of £1.2m, employed 300 local people of whom 250 were on MSC-funded community programmes, and was paying £800 000 per annum in wages.

Moreover it now controls subsidiary commercial ventures, for example Field Security Ltd. This is a trading subsidiary of Barrowfield Community Business which provides a 24-hour security patrol within the estate to deter vandals. It has a Glasgow District Council contract worth £84 000 and it is estimated that in 1986 it saved the Council £200 000 in damage prevented. The company has also built up other security contracts with local private companies and now employs 28 full-time guards. In the first six months of its operation, the security patrol assisted almost 200 individuals with calls to emergency services and other authorities. Further, Field Security Ltd runs a janitor service looking after the security and cleanliness of the back court yards of blocks of flats for the District Council.

Barrowfield Landscapes Ltd is the other trading subsidiary of Barrowfield Community Business and includes the company's welding, landscaping and painting divisions. Barrowfield Landscapes now has several District Council contracts and also won some of the environmental contracts in Glasgow in the run-up to the 1988 Garden Festival.

These ventures are distinguished from conventional small business and worker cooperatives by the restriction on those who work in them from keeping any profits, or determining the long-term business goals. The principal benefit of Barrowfield Community Business to the community is the fact that it employs local people and pays them wages. Barrowfield Community Business Ltd is now a major local employer of long-term unemployed people. The company has also won a grant from the European Social Fund and will be providing 40 vocational training places for local people in conjunction with Strathclyde Community Business and the Strathclyde Regional Council Department of Further Education.

The benefits of community business however are not merely economic. The appearance of Barrowfield has changed for the better, as has the atmosphere. The community business has also contributed donations to the local family support unit, to the parents' support group and to the Barrowfield Project Fund. Further they have recently made a start-up loan to a food cooperative and also help run the community transport network.

Community business provides a structure which, once established, enables local government to contract services to local people in a way which would be impossible to do efficiently without that structure. The experiences of Barrowfield Community Business illustrate the advantages of this type of organization over conventional forms of economic development.

## MEASURING EMPLOYMENT CREATION

Before employment creation can be measured, several adjustments have to be made to the raw employment statistics. First, the distinction between direct and indirect employment must be considered. That is between employment generated directly through a community business's trading activities and employment generated in conjunction with the MSC's community programme or through workshops managed by community businesses.

Second, it is necessary to differentiate between additional and non-additional employment. In evaluating the effectiveness of public sector grants supporting the employment-creating activities of community businesses, it is necessary to determine what would have been the employment situation had no public support been forthcoming. Projects may well have proceeded regardless of public sector support, so that assistance was not 'additional' but instead represented 'deadweight spending'.

Third, it is important to calculate the displacement factor when evaluating the employment impact of community businesses. To the degree that a community business takes business away from other local employers, the overall gain to the local economy will tend to be eroded.

Fourth, in evaluating the employment impact of community businesses it is necessary to determine any multiplier effects. Community business activities are likely to raise local disposable incomes and generate demand for local goods and services thereby inducing beneficial impacts on employment opportunities in the locality.

The total employment impact of a given community business will depend on the net effect of these four factors.

## EMPLOYMENT CREATION IN SCOTLAND

Community business in Scotland has a good record of achievement in creating employment. This is demonstrated by a study of 15 community businesses which measured employment growth over the period 1981 – 86. It was found that a total of 296 person-years of employment had been generated in the 15 community businesses since 1981 (McGregor, McArthur and Noone, 1988). The main findings of the study are summarized and discussed below.

## ADDITIONALITY

In 11 of the 15 case studies, employment-generating activities would not have been initiated in the absence of public sector support so that the additionality factor, approximately 90 per cent, is very high.

A study of the impact and effectiveness of financial assistance policies in the Newcastle Metropolitan Region (Robinson and Wren, 1985) computed additionality factors of 47 per cent and 42 per cent for the Regional Development Grant and local authority assisted projects respectively. The additionality factor for Regional Selective Assistance and National Selective Assistance projects is 77 per cent. The figures therefore show that community businesses with an additionality factor of 90 per cent are an important source of employment in depressed areas.

## DISPLACEMENT EFFECTS

Removing the jobs lost through local displacement produced an estimate for net local employment creation of 91 jobs over all the case studies (McGregor, McArthur and Noone, 1988).

# MULTIPLIER EFFECTS

Net additions to economic activity in an area may have multiplier impacts on the locality in two ways. First, the community business may purchase goods and services from local suppliers. Second, the net increase in disposable income of the community business employees may increase demand for local goods and services. Local employment multipliers of 1.12 were calculated in a study of the impact of the Glasgow Eastern Area Renewal (GEAR) Project (Nairn and Swales, 1987).

Community businesses tend to have a comparatively high propensity to hire local labour which tends to raise the size of the local employment multiplier. Additionally many community businesses adopt a purchasing policy which favours local suppliers and this will increase the amount of income ploughed back into the local economy.

The number of secondary jobs created was estimated at between 5 and 23, giving estimates for net employment gains of between 96 and 114 jobs (McGregor, McArthur and Noone, 1988).

# COMMUNITY PROGRAMME SCHEMES

Until 1988, the Manpower Services Commission was funding Community Programme Schemes which were then run by local managing agencies like Barrowfield Community Business Ltd. This section evaluates the impact of community businesses through their management of Community Programme Schemes.

Of the 15 cases studied, four had a significant involvement in community programme schemes and four were primarily concerned with workshop management. In October 1986, these businesses employed 481 workers of which 160 could be directly attributed to the presence of the community businesses.

The workshops employed 456 people and this was estimated to have generated 260 net additional jobs after allowing for displacement and multiplier effects.[1]

Table 10.1 summarizes the total number of jobs created by October 1986 in the 15 case studies. (Employment created through capital works is omitted.)

### Table 10.1 Total number of jobs created in the 15 case studies, October 1986

| | | |
|---|---|---|
| 1 | Permanent jobs in community businesses | 134 |
| | Additional jobs out of above | 121 |
| | Net of displacement | 92 |
| | Incorporating multipliers (1.05) | 96 (low) |
| | Incorporating multipliers (1.25) | 114 (high) |
| 2 | Community Programme jobs | 296.5 |
| | Additional jobs out of above | 160 |
| 3 | Jobs in managed workshops | 456 |
| | Additional jobs out of above | 298 |
| | Incorporating displacement (20%) + multiplier (1.1) | 260 (low) |
| | Incorporating displacement (10%) + multiplier (1.1) | 295 (high) |
| 4 | Home producers | 6 |
| | Low estimate of total net job creation | 522 |
| | High estimate of total net job creation | 575 |

*Source:* McGregor, McArthur and Noone, 1988.

## Cost per job

The next issue to be considered is the amount of public expenditure required to generate employment in the community businesses. The principal source of funding support is Urban Aid which totalled £1.6m by 1986–87. Other sources of grant support included £63 000 from local authorities and community development agencies.

Taking the 15 case studies as a whole, the average cost per net job[2] varied between £3200 and £5100. This compares favourably with conventional Urban Aid employment generation schemes. It also compares well with the £4350 cost at 1985–86 prices, of a placement under the community programme (Manpower Services Commission, 1986) especially since the community businesses attempt to generate permanent jobs. This average conceals a wide spread of costs, e.g. from £1300 to £31 000 for

Urban Aid businesses. Costs per net job tend to be low for community businesses located in public sector housing estates because of the relatively low local displacement factors.

## Reaching the disadvantaged

A common criticism of conventional local and urban economic development programmes is their failure to reach the most disadvantaged groups in the community. The community business sector generally has a good record with respect to employing local unemployed people — 78 per cent of all the CP employees were resident in the locality, 69 per cent were previously unemployed and 47 per cent had been unemployed for over a year (McGregor, McArthur and Noone, 1988). This should be compared with, for example, the results of a recent study of the employment effect of small factory provision by the public sector in Greater Glasgow which showed that only around 12 per cent of the unemployed hired by the small private firms were previously unemployed for six months or more. The proportion of local people hired by the small private firms was only 42 per cent.

Clearly the community businesses are achieving a high degree of success in providing jobs for unemployed residents without increasing cost per job. However the managed workshops do not employ a larger proportion of unemployed and local people than conventional normal firms.

## Commercial viability

The evidence does seem to support the view that community businesses can provide long-term security of employment.

Approximately half of all the goods and services produced by community business were found to be covering their costs without the need for outside financial support. Indeed only 10 per cent were unlikely to attain long-run viability. In terms of jobs, in 1986 approximately 84 per cent were in sustainable commercial ventures (McGregor, McArthur and Noone, 1988).

## Regional and national organization

There appears too be a need for community business support at regional and national as well as at local level. A national forum exists under the

117

auspices of Community Business Scotland and it may now be appropriate to consider whether links at national level should be further developed. The sharing of experiences between groups and lobbying on behalf of community business is probably best achieved at the national level. Community business development at the regional level allows other organizations like colleges of further education and enterprise trusts to provide support.

## Role of public sector agencies

The injection of public sector funds at the embryonic stage has been vital to the development of community business activity. Eleven of the 15 businesses studied stated that they would not have started up without public sector support. Eight of them were funded by Urban Aid and received a total of £120 000 in capital and £257 000 in revenue grant in the course of their first year.

Small amounts of public support are often a critical element in a joint funding package because the private sector's contribution is often dependent on a public sector loan being made available. Enterprises which are unable to offer satisfactory security themselves need a method of providing guarantees for loan finances and businesses that cannot pay the current market rates need subsidized interest rates.

A withdrawal of public sector support would probably result in contraction of the non-commercial activities and in the development of new commercial activities. Community businesses are able to engage in a wide range of cost-effective development work because public support gives them the breathing space to do so. For example identifying local market opportunities is a time-consuming task; so is accommodating the view of the community. Community businesses need time to establish their credibility and to train their largely unskilled labour force.

Finally, and perhaps most important, it takes time for staff to develop the management and organizational skills needed for these participative and unconventional organizational structures. Community businesses need sources of finance that allow them to buy in expert support especialy during the start-up phase and public sector professionals are beginning to realize this. New groups also need advice on legal and constitutional matters and on what funds are available from central and local government or from Scottish Community Business for things like feasibility studies or start-up grants. They also need to be able to establish custom-built training courses.

There are however some problems associated with public sector support. There are delays in making decisions which slow down progress and can affect competitive ability. There may be gaps in the public sector bodies' knowledge of business practice and development finance or there may be inadequate market research support.

Private investment in local enterprise may increase. A growing number of social investment funds is now being set up; for example, The Mercury Provident Society and Financial Initiative Ltd.

There are also limitations in the way community businesses can use particular public sector programmes. For example the MSC's Community Programme was not designed to accommodate community businesses. Consequently it has proved difficult to use such programmes in developing sustainable economic activity and jobs. Further, government-sponsored industrial training programmes target resources towards the employed and to the more buoyant local economies where there are skill shortages.

Possibly the greatest criticism stems from the high costs of accounting for any public sector support received, which means that hard-pressed community business workers face pressures that their competitors do not. Finally, few public authorities have used their purchasing power to support community businesses in a systematic way.

## CONCLUSIONS

The success of community business needs to be put into perspective. The modest employment objectives of these initiatives and the present level of funding are little match for the severe problems facing some of the worst areas of unemployment. It is therefore important that the expectations about the potential of community businesses are kept realistic.

They cannot be expected to generate profits, create viable jobs and simultaneously be community-controlled on a shoestring budget when it costs on average £17 658 to create one job under regional aid (Robinson and Wren, 1985).

However because community businesses are a hybrid between conventional economic development initiatives and more traditional forms of community development work, it is inappropriate to assess them by strictly orthodox financial criteria. Appraisal methods should be developed which recognize the complexity of the objectives they achieve.

In 1988 the Community Programme was discontinued and replaced by the Adult Training Programme (ATP). The implications of this change for community businesses are not clear. There is at present no indication as to whether community businesses which have Manpower Services Commission managing agency status will meet ATP criteria in terms of staff resources for training and required throughput of trainees.

Community business initiatives can help alleviate the sense of hopelessness caused by long-term unemployment. But the potential for local communities to regenerate themselves will remain largely untapped unless Government, local authorities and other bodies like Business in the Community commit themselves to supporting community businesses by making them a focal point for community development.

## NOTES

1    Net job creation is estimated using displacement factors as low as 10 or 20 per cent. This is because there was very little economic activity in these areas before the workshops were established. A comparatively low multiplier effect is assumed here because, unlike the case study community businesses, the tenants of the workshops are normally conventional firms with little commitment to purchase or hire locally.

2    These are adjusted for additionality, displacement and multiplier effects. The gross estimates are derived by dividing aggregate grant expenditure for the period up to and including 1986−87, by total full-time equivalent jobs in place at October 1986. The cost per job figures so derived could understate the long-run costs when a community business has finally received all its Urban Aid monies. However such businesses may experience further employment growth thereby reducing cost per job estimates.

## REFERENCES

McGregor, A., McArthur, A., Noone, V. 1988, *Evaluation of Community Business in Scotland*, Central Unit Research Papers, Scottish Office.

Nairn, A. and Swales, J. 1987, 'Area Policy Impacts: A Multiplier Analysis of GEAR', *Urban Studies*, vol.24, pp.31−45.

Richardson, A. 1985, 'Promoting Economic Development: an assessment of an experimental scheme in Cleveland', *Planning Outlook*, vol.28, no.2.

Robinson, F. and Wren, C. 1985, *Survey of 201 Establishments*.

# 11

# Small businesses and local government – a view of the experience in Middlesbrough

*Peter Austin*

Middlesbrough Borough Council has built up a range of conventional industrial and economic policies through the past decade and has recently moved into new areas of small business policies. This chapter will examine their experience and evaluate the results of their policies. The main focus will be on policies of assistance for small businesses.

## INDUSTRIAL BACKGROUND

Historically, the town has always been dependent on capital-intensive industries and a relatively small number of large employers. Middlesbrough's main industry was originally the shipping of coal. Steel production and fabrication later took over, with bridge construction and shipyards being particularly prominent. In boom years the working population has enjoyed well paid, skilled, male-dominated employment. During recent periods of economic depression, however, plant closures and reinvestment in plant and processes have been as drastic as in the 1930s. High levels of unemployment are a feature of life in Middlesbrough, as they are in other parts of the North-East.

The role of smaller firms in providing jobs in Middlesbrough has changed, especially in the past 50 years and following the nationalization of the steel and shipbuilding industries. Most small firms had either become directly linked to the large employers as regular suppliers and sub contractors, or depended on producing and trading for local consumers. The Middlesbrough docks were finally abandoned in the mid-1970s. British Steel closed its mills in favour of the new Redcar works down the river, and the last shipyard on the Tees was wound up in 1986. The effects on small businesses in Middlesbrough were catastrophic.

## JOB LOSSES

Sub-contracting firms lost their regular orders and local trade slumped as incomes fell. Table 11.1 shows that over 8600 jobs were lost in the ten years 1974−84 as major plants went out of business. The knock-on effects on smaller firms pushed the official unemployment rate to its peak at over 21 per cent in 1986.

**Table 11.1   Jobs lost as a result of major plant closures in Teesside 1974 − 86**

| Firm | No. of jobs |
| --- | --- |
| Swan Hunter | 1900 |
| John Collier, Middlesbrough | 900 |
| BSC Britannia Works, Middlesbrough | 630 |
| GEC, Middlesbrough | 630 |
| Shell Refinery, Teesport | 500 |
| Paton and Baldwin, Billingham | 500 |
| Whessoe, Stockton | 500 |
| BSC, Cargo Fleet Works | 430 |
| BTP Tioxide, Billingham | 370 |
| RHN Sparks Bakery, Stockton | 350 |
| Head Wrighton, Stockton | 330 |
| Hardy Spicer, Eaglescliffe | 300 |
| Smith's Dock, South Bank | 1300 |
| Total jobs lost from major closures | 8640 |

*Source:* Middlesbrough Council

Another trend, however, has been substantial new investment in automation and in the restructuring of major local industries in the last decade, in particular British Steel, chemicals and the offshore oil fabrication industries. Table 11.2 shows clearly how, despite the new investment, there have nevertheless been job losses of 36 600 between 1974 and 1984 in the large industries. The restructuring that has taken place has led to many functions being transferred from permanent, in-house groups of employees to external sub-contractors. The recent birth of the offshore fabrication sector in Teesside has similarly been achieved by linking local firms and producers as sub-contractors in the yards. This has led to the recruitment of large numbers of redundant shipbuilders who are employed on temporary contracts rather than on a permanent basis.

## ASSISTANCE FOR SMALL FIRMS

Middlesbrough has been a priority area for central government support for many years and is well established as a development area. Large-scale funding has been available through the Department of Trade and Industry, particularly Regional Development Grants, grants from the EEC Investment Bank and Steel and Coal Community as well as from the large employers remaining in the area. Not all of this assistance has been designed to encourage small businesses; some has been used on speculative developments, large industrial training centres or redeveloping former sites. The main support for small businesses has come from the Department of Trade and Industry, in support of the central government 'seedbed' philosophy of small firms, and from experienced managers seconded from local employers to support public sector initiatives.

**Table 11.2   Industrial restructuring − job losses and investment in Cleveland**

| Major employers/industries | Jobs lost 1974 − 84 | Investment 1974 − 84 |
| --- | --- | --- |
| Steel | 17 000 | £  631 million |
| ICI | 9 000 | £1,681 million |
| Construction | 10 600 | — |
| Shipbuilding − industry now extinct | | |
| Total | 36 600 | £2,312 million |

Source: Foord, Robinson and Sadler, 1985.

Middlesbrough Council's action in support of small firms has evolved principally under the powers provided in the Inner Urban Areas Act 1978 as an urban programme authority[1]. This has given Middlesbrough Council powers to make loans and grants for the creation of jobs in local industries. The overall budget allocation and general criteria are determined by the Department of the Environment but the 1978 Act clearly leaves it to local government to choose specific projects and decide how to implement and fund them. In Middlesbrough, urban programme funds have been used to create a global budget for financial assistance to firms and specific allocations for individual projects.

The policy has developed in a largely reactive way; as major plant closures followed each other from the mid-1970s into the 1980s, it was clear that local government could do very little to create or preserve jobs as most closure decisions were not made locally. The Council's policies for business assistance have been in response to the investment decisions of local industry and also to the regional assistance offered by the Department of Trade and Industry and the County Council. There has never been a specific coordinated strategy.

## PROVISION OF ACCOMMODATION

Provision of small business premises is an important part of Middlesbrough Council's attempts to encourage new employment. The Council had originally considered offering rent guarantees or head leases to speculative developers of industrial units. But this policy ran into trouble with central government capital allocation conditions and was abandoned.[2] Instead, both the District and County Council opted for direct capital expenditure on conversions and new development schemes. About 80 small industrial units have been built in Middlesbrough since 1976 by the Council, and others were developed with Council encouragement by Cleveland County, English Estates or by the Private sector.

In addition the Council has developed an enterprise centre. This is a network of serviced business accommodation, currently providing 61 separate units at several locations around the town centre. The enterprise centre accommodation is designed to meet a range of particular needs or *new* small businesses. These include manufacturing, office, retail and crafts. As well as offering 12 months' accommodation at an average of half the level of commercial rents, the enterprise centre network provides services such as shared office and prototype development facilities, together with management advice and training. Businesses therefore have the opportunity to develop and learn new business skills in a relatively sheltered environment.

In the past two years there have been other new initiatives to encourage small firms. The first of these was the conversion of an old warehouse into small units for starter cooperatives. Like the enterprise centre, this accommodation provides shared common services like building security and maintenance, and reception; it also provides teaching facilities. The second was the conversion of a school, part of which will be a community employment centre with similar shared services and teaching facilities. Third, a youth business centre has recently been set up in an old office to provide continuous training and back-up facilities for young entrepreneurs to develop business skills. Lastly, the Council has supported proposals for local community businesses, based in areas of council housing with high unemployment.

The Council has not yet undertaken a detailed review of the effects of its small industrial units. One indicator is the high level of demand for them though this is also linked to a high turnover rate, suggesting an unstable market. The industrial units are felt to serve a range of uses with differing layouts, access and general design. They are mostly in the redeveloped, northern parts of the town and are segregated from most residential areas. This is more a result of the development style and potential of the sites themselves rather than of deliberate zoning policy. However it has the effect of isolating many of those working in small businesses.

A recent review of the enterprise centres was undertaken by the Council (Middlesbrough Council, 1988). The public sector cost per new job at the enterprise centres in the longer term was found to be around £4000, of which about half is paid by the Council.[3]

## COUNCIL GRANTS

The Council also provides a grant to pay 50 per cent rent and rates for two to three years for firms with less than 20 employees. It used also to provide a grant for market research but has now phased this out in favour of a broader business improvement scheme. The rent and rates grant was very popular and was widely taken up. It has however been twice reduced in scope in 1983 and 1985. In 1983, when an enterprise zone was declared, the Council withdrew grant assistance from firms moving into the zone which had access to other support. In 1985 the Department of the Environment ruled that urban programme funds were not to be used for rate rebates outside enterprise zones, so the grant became a rent grant only.

At present the rent grant is available for up to two years. An additional grant was recently introduced by the Council for the establishment of cooperative enterprises. This grant is limited to £1000 (under the Inner Urban Areas Act 1978) and its size will mean that it will only be of interest to small firms.

## RENT AND RATES GRANTS FOR SMALL FIRMS IN MIDDLESBROUGH

Since 1983 Middlesbrough Council has paid out about £250 000 in rent and rates grants. Allocation criteria have been adopted which limit the firm size to 20 employees and are only available for a planned move into larger premises. These grants have been very useful to those small firms who are ready to grow. But the rent grants, which encourage expansion and presumably risk taking, may not be best designed for the longer-term needs of most smaller firms which have a lower resource base and often have enough problems in simply keeping a stable position.

Council criteria for rent grants explicitly exclude retail firms and branches of larger concerns, as well as firms who only trade locally. This is to prevent unnecessary payments to firms with their own resource base and to avoid the risk of displacing local traders through assisting a competitor.

The 61 firms who had received grants in respect of rent and rates from Middlesbrough Council and had now stopped receiving their grant were surveyed by telephone. It was found that about two-thirds of the firms still operated in Middlesbrough or neighbouring districts, and one-third had either ceased trading or left the area. Of the firms remaining in Middlesbrough, half had expanded their workforce, and the other half had either maintained the same level or reduced it.

There was a total of 56 new jobs in the surviving firms. The firms that had left or ceased trading, however, had a total of 62 jobs when they started to receive their grant from the Council so there was an overall *loss* of six jobs in the area amongst firms that had received grant assistance. About two-thirds of the jobs in the firms still in Middlesbrough were thus unchanged and may be considered to have been promoted to some extent by the financial assistance.

## VALUE FOR MONEY

However, it is very important to select firms for this form of assistance that are likely to succeed and remain in the area. The survey showed that 5 per cent of the firms accounted for about half of all the new jobs created and 7 per cent of the firms accounted for half of all the jobs lost. Each firm which left the area or ceased trading accounted for an average loss of the equivalent of 3.1 full-time jobs. On this basis a ratio of 2.2 successful firms to every one which failed or left would be required to maintain a stable level of employment among the Council-assisted firms.

There was also a net increase in the number of trainees funded by the Manpower Services Commission (MSC) within the firms still in the Middlesbrough area. MSC-funded trainees represented 9 per cent of the current workforce of all the firms surveyed. Some firms were likely to offer them future employment and in one case an arrangement had been reached to secure a long-term traineeship to learn a specialized craft. In successful firms, MSC training schemes represented a means of achieving permanent employment for eligible, unemployed people. In other cases, however, the large number and high turnover suggested that MSC funding was being used to subsidize part of the labour costs for firms.

Middlesbrough Council paid out £152 110 between 1983 and 1988 in rent and rates grants for the firms in the survey. Of this total, 29 per cent was paid to firms that subsequently either failed or left the area. The average cost to the Council for each new job created in the firms remaining in Middlesbrough after receiving Council grants was £1929. (See Appendix II for calculations.) The £152 000 spent did not result in overall expansion in employment but it could be argued that it helped prevent a greater loss of jobs.

Some of the firms (23 per cent) also received a further £55 000 in grants from other sources like the Department of Trade and Industry's regional development grants, or from the Manpower Services Commission or the County Council. These other grants are obtainable directly from the organizations providing them, and cover items such as capital for new equipment or general financial assistance, as well as a specific premium to meet the cost of new employees. The overall picture is that total public sector payments of £200 000 were made to the firms surveyed. The total public sector cost per new job created in the firms remaining in Middlesbrough after receiving the rent and rates grant was thus £2906, of which two-thirds was from the Council's scheme.

## PROBLEMS FACED BY SMALL FIRMS

The main employment sectors represented by small firms in Middlesbrough are engineering, manufacturing, construction and services, each in similar proportions. Within each sector there is also a variety of sub-sectors. In construction, for example, the firms ranged from small builders' yards or specialist craftsmen, producers and suppliers of construction materials, to agencies recruiting and contracting other firms for specific jobs. Other sectors include supply and servicing of both hardward and software for new technology and specialist crafts. The more successful firms have tended to be in the service sectors, particularly those involving sales and supplies, mostly to the local market. Firms based in the engineering sector, in either production or servicing other producers, have tended to have most problems, especially where they depend on a larger firm. Some small businesses left the region or collapsed after major heavy engineering plant closures.

Another problem is that their small resource base makes them less able to withstand large financial pressures, however temporary. Flexibility in a fluctuating market may be a relative advantage for some small firms but cash flow is a common problem. Sub-contracting often leads to cash flow difficulties and small businesses usually have restricted access to credit. In general small firms suffer from a lack of resources, and insufficient capital and managerial skills.

## POLICY EVALUATION

Middlesbrough's approach, based on premises and finance, is perhaps typical of local authority economic development initiatives. A recent study of authorities involved in economic development has shown how most initiatives are on a relatively minor scale and directed at gaps in the market not otherwise reached by other public sector initiatives (Association of

County Councils, Association of District Councils and Association of Metropolitan Authorities, 1988). The Middlesbrough Council initiatives are reasonably cost-effective compared with the results of this study, which estimated the average current cost per job created by local authorities at between £3000 and £5000, and this in turn is lower than the average for central government regional policies.

There is no conclusive evidence for or against the view that supporting small firms is an effective way of creating employment. In some cases it is quite clear that supporting small firms may achieve short-term growth or stability, but there is little overall long-term change. Experience in Middlesbrough supports the findings of a national study (Storey and Johnson, 1987) that the success or failure of a scheme depends on the fortunes of a very small proportion of the firms supported.

In Middlesbrough, small firms can be expected to play an increasing role, both in the expanding service sector and in the new patterns of sub-contracting, but this may lead to decreasing job stability for many of those employed in small firms.

The policy of encouraging immediate expansion is not necessarily helpful for long-term growth or job creation in small firms as it encourages them to take relatively large risks in an unstable and competitive environment. A more flexible scheme of grant allocation might be better. Horne, Lloyd, Pay and Roe (1988) have suggested a method for selecting potentially successful firms based on their capital base, ability to identify and develop new openings in the market and ability to adjust internally to meet new demands.

The provision of sheltered or managed accommodation should certainly continue under the present enterprise centre network and it could be extended to concentrate on developing more training and cooperation between firms. Closer follow-up support might be provided by an outreach management counsellor who could visit local firms.

The idea of encouraging trading between small firms has already been developed within the enterprise centre network. This concept could be extended to involve small firms trading elsewhere in the town through a joint trading structure which could be linked to criteria for financial assistance. The Council could help reduce cash flow problems through a local small firms bank which could meet short-term demands or delayed payments.

A joint funding structure or trading organization would make it possible to combine the skills and market knowledge of small firms and their managers. This could be based on a sector as in the case of agricultural trading cooperatives, providing that member firms were not in direct competition. Alternatively it could be area-based starting in an existing block of new industrial units, for example, and modelled on the Modena experience in northern Italy (Shuttleworth, 1987). In Modena, the Council has played a key role in servicing local networks of small firms. These firms are then able to support each other without losing their separate identity.

Small firms are also ideally placed to develop new employment opportunities such as jobs for women in non-traditional occupations. Similarly where community-led enterprises succeed, the enterprise centre network might be extended or use made of small firms' outreach counsellor.

## GENERAL CONCLUSIONS

There appear to be two views on small firm support. The first is to assume that certain enterprises are destined to succeed if offered the right help in a competitive market. The main aim of policies then will be to select the potentially successful firms and meet their specific needs. The second policy view is to reject the competitive market in its present form as an inefficient and unjust mechanism and devise policies to improve the relative position of the majority of small firms in the market as well as to encourage community or municipal enterprises.

The evidence in Middlesbrough shows not only the problems faced by small firms but also their strengths. Small firms can be helped to provide limited numbers of new jobs at low cost although the selection of firms for assistance is critical to the overall success. Small firms are well placed to develop changes in how work is organized and how profits are distributed. Middlesbrough Council has recognized some of this potential in its policies by supporting cooperatives and community enterprise.

The evidence in Middlesbrough supports the view that local authorities can respond to the needs of small firms even though their resources are limited. The key feature of small firms is their potential flexibility, both in terms of their internal organization and in relation to the local market. Though the numbers of jobs created may be small, the effect on the quality of local employment is potentially significant.

# NOTES

1   Cleveland County Council is also an urban programme authority and has developed policies mostly offering grant assistance to small firms, in parallel with Middlesbrough's policies.
2   One of the first applicants proposed to develop small industrial units but required further public sector support — in this case an urban development grant. The central government saw the Council's policy as unnecessary intervention leading to double public sector funding, and threatened to withdraw part of the Council's capital allocation.
3   Analysis showed that the Council was supporting each job at the centres at an annual, average running cost of £1000. About half of the licensees were subsequently successful and received additional public sector support at an average of £1000 per job while at the centres. Initial estimates suggest that about £2000 per job is received by firms after leaving the enterprise centres, including Council rent grants.

# REFERENCES

Association of County Councils, Association of District Councils and Association of Metropolitan Authorities, 1988, *Stimulating Local Enterprise — The Local Authority Role*, London.

Central Office of Information, 1986, *Small Firms Service. Annual Report 1985—86*, Department of Employment, HMSO.

Foord, J., Robinson, F. and Sadler, D. 1985, 'The Quiet Revolution — Social and Economic Change on Teesside, 1965—1985', Special Report for *BBC North East*.

Horne, M., Lloyd, P., Pay, J. and Roe, P. 1988, *Structuring Knowledge of the Small Firm: A Framework for Informing Local Authority Intervention within the Private Sector*, School of Geography, University of Manchester.

Middlesbrough Borough Council, 1988, *Enterprise Centres — A Review*, Report to the Council.

Shuttleworth, D. 1987, 'The Entrepreneurial City', *Initiatives*, August.

Storey, D.J. and Johnson, S. 1987, *Are Small Firms the Answer to Unemployment?* Employment Institute.

## APPENDIX I

## Financial assistance available to firms in Middlesbrough

| Middlesbrough Borough Council | Grants and loans<br>Rent grants | Rent-free Fitting out periods; flexible lease terms; Provision of common services |
| --- | --- | --- |
| Enterprise zone | Corporation and income tax relief<br>Rates relief | |
| Cleveland County Council | Flexible assistance schemes<br>Small business grants<br>Recruitment premium scheme<br>Business services grants<br>Marketing/sales training grant | |
| Central government | Development area support<br>Selection assistance | |
| EEC | European Coal and Steel Community loans<br>European Investment Bank loan | |
| Other | British Steel Corporation (Industries) Ltd<br>British Shipbuilders' Enterprise | |

## APPENDIX II

## Cost analysis of completed rent and rates grants, 1983 – 1988

Total payments to firms     £152 110
Payments to firms which ceased trading or moved     £ 44 074
Payments to firms remaining in Middlesbrough     £108 036
(of which: − expanded firms     £ 67 142
− stable firms     £ 25 894
− contracted firms     £ 15 000)

Total number of jobs in firms     162
New jobs in remaining firms     56
Jobs in firms which ceased trading or moved     62
Net overall increase in jobs     −6

Average payment per net new job in firms remaining
in Middlesbrough     £108 036/56 or
£ 1929
per job

Average payment per job lost through firms ceased
trading or moved     £ 44 074/62 or
£ 710
per job

# PART III
# HOUSING THE HOMELESS

# Introduction

*Taner Oc*

Homelessness is a very great problem in the UK as it is in many countries. Although the numbers of homeless people sleeping on the pavements in the UK are nothing like the numbers in India and some other poor countries, there are about 120 000 families housed as homeless nationally. This is a clear indication that the UK has an acute housing problem even before considering unfit housing and the probable £50m it would cost to bring private and public sector housing to a minimum state of repair. This section studies the acute problem of homelessness because it needs immediate attention.

As argued in the previous section, the current problems of the UK's cities and their residents have less to do with land uses, zoning or issues of urban design — the outdated and constraining domain of town and country planning as it used to be taught and practised — and more to do with personal poverty and local authority poverty, unemployment, homelessness, neighbourhood deterioration, crime, inadequate mobility and so forth (Krumholz, 1975). Traditional local authority planning departments are increasingly being involved in what could be termed equity solutions for the unemployed and the homeless. More significantly, over the past decade increasing numbers of planners employed in local authority chief executives' departments have been involved in devising policies for the unemployed and the homeless as well as other disadvantaged groups in our cities. Therefore it was no surprise that this seminar attracted a large number of planners from a wide area from Northampton to Leeds.

This section covers the legal aspects of homelessness, the problems of inadequate statistics and the difficulty of proper planning in their absence, and the way in which the policies of a number of central and local government departments contribute to the numbers of homeless people. One problem for planners is that responsibility for homeless people has been shifted between government departments.

After 1948, with the introduction of the National Assistance Act, the local authorities had a duty to provide temporary accommodation for persons in urgent need arising from circumstances which could not reasonably have been foreseen. People were entitled to assistance if made homeless as a result of fire, flood or other disaster. The legislation also said 'or in such other circumstances as the authority may in any particular case determine', the interpretation of this being the political decision of those who had to raise the necessary finance (Chapman, 1987). As circumstances other than disasters increasingly became major factors leading to homelessness in the 1960s and 1970s, it became necessary to introduce a new legal framework. Already in 1974, a circular issued by government had tried to transfer the responsibility for homelessness to the housing departments.

The 1977 Housing (Homeless Persons) Act was enacted as a response to an acute and increasing problem. The chapter by David Hoath shows with clear detail that this is a sloppy, ill prepared bill which fails to solve homelessness. He claims that its primary beneficiaries are lawyers. The Act does not address the hidden homelessness arising from poor housing conditions and it also fails people who are homeless as a result of family break-ups. Yet another shortcoming of the Act surfaces as problems relating to 'priority need'. Very often councils do not have the resources or the will to take adequate care of their homeless, and this is illustrated by their failure to offer suitable accommodation, efforts to rehouse homeless through general housing waiting lists, the single offer syndrome and especially bed and breakfast dumping. The chapter deals with the problems concerning legal challenge to councils' decisions in some detail and argues that there is a need for reform of the rules regulating challenge.

Nottingham set up a service for the homeless as early as 1974. Until then the Salvation Army were acting as agents for the City Council, exercising the right to select and reject. As a result of a report by Geoffrey Chapman, the city decided to build a purpose-built hostel, which was opened in 1978, for emergency accommodation. This 27-unit building provides self-contained accommodation for families. Although the city hoped with this provision they would never have to use bed and breakfast accommodation, the increasing number of homeless people has forced the authority to use this facility as well as women's aid refuges. No eviction takes place in Nottingham from a council property, or a property mortgaged from the council, without the close scrutiny of a sub-committee. Thus in 1987 only 7 per cent of the homeless were families evicted for a rent or mortgage default. In 1986 the housing department interviewed 1961 people. Of these, 806 were in priority groups, 416 mainly young persons were provided with non-priority housing and the rest were given advice (Chapman, 1987). The decision of intentional homelessness is made by the housing finance sub-committee and not by a bureaucrat.

The chapter by John Ferris and David Whynes looks at the current problem in Nottingham and the response of the City Council. Ferris and Whynes describe their studies of the problem based on data collected from various hostels and shelters in the city. They show that the majority of homeless people are younger, single, unemployed men. They note that women more often tend to be among the hidden homeless. There is also more hidden homelessness amongst the ethnic minorities. Their data lead them to conclude that there is no typical cause of homelessness among single people. Various factors singly or in various combinations may result in homelessness.

The final chapter in this section by Patricia Mounser and Philip Bean looks at 'Homelessness and the Mentally Disordered'. This is a special case of homelessness and possibly the most difficult to tackle. The current problem of homelessness for the mentally ill is exacerbated by the policy of closing down mental hospitals and the lack of adequate provision of housing to accommodate them. Large numbers of mentally ill people are discharged and spend short periods in various types of emergency accommodation before being re-admitted.

Homelessness among mentally ill people is very much tied to the policy of replacing hospital care with care in the community. On the face of it this would seem to be a more humane approach. However without adequate provision in the community, this policy turns into callousness, and becomes nothing more than a simple attempt to save money which causes further misery to the mentally ill. Discharged patients need housing that would give them the opportunity to live free and independent lives.

Mounser and Bean hope that the 'social fund', introduced in April 1988, will create opportunities for community care through the use of the community care grant. It is too early to assess whether the community care grant is working and whether it will alleviate some of the misery of the mentally ill homeless.

As the chapters in this section show, the Housing (Homeless Persons) Act has failed to address the problems faced by a large number of people. Local authorities, which have a duty under the Act, choose to discharge their duties in different ways, the costliest and most unpopular solution being bed and breakfast accommodation. Figures for 1987 show that in London about 8000 homeless families were accommodated in bed and breakfast at a cost of over £100m (Fox and Steam, 1987). In round figures this gives £12 500 per year per family which would pay the mortgage of a property worth about £125 000. The economics of bed and breakfast accommodation are indefensible.

Apart from being a wasteful use of ratepayers' money, bed and breakfast is a socially unacceptable solution. Families with young children, young and old single people, have to endure totally unhygienic conditions, and live in overcrowded accommodation without cooking or proper washing facilities. In most cases they have to leave the premises during the day and try to keep warm in day centres or pass the day in parks. Most live on take-away food. Children suffer particularly because they have no play facilities and parents, crumbling under the strain, subject them to physical abuse. Marriages break down, health problems increase; in short, the long-term homeless in bed and breakfast accommodation feel they are being punished for being homeless.

Recently, some local authorities have been experimenting with private leasing schemes. There are several different arrangements. Some local authorities place the homeless with private landlords at hotel rates. Other local authorities enter into arrangements with housing associations on an agency basis. It is argued that if a complete management scheme is offered to property owners they are more likely to find the scheme attractive (Williams, 1988). The real solution for a local authority is for a developer to provide a large number of units. This of course depends on the satisfactory return on their investment and guarantee of vacant possession. The parallel with the current housing bill proposals for private sector renting shows government support for this development (Williams, 1988).

This is an improvement on bed and breakfast for the families and significantly cheaper for the local authorities at about £140−£200 per week. However this is not an adequate solution either because people are still housed in insecure and relatively expensive accommodation. Like the bed and breakfast accommodation it replaces, the only winners will be the private landlords who will enter into lucrative deals at public expense. Councils being cash-strapped and unable to build houses will not be able to find permanent homes, so large numbers of people will spend years in temporary accommodation. As Williams points out, this is 'complete privatisation of homelessness, with the extra advantage that homeless people will no longer be seen as a particular problem' (Williams, 1988).

The Government is being pressed to allow councils to spend money to bring empty council houses back into use. So far, the money allowed on such expenditure is too little and too late. Although the Government promises a review of homelessness law, the Secretary of State refuses to recognize the real causes of homelessness and sees it as a result of young people trying to leave home earlier, and certain people making themselves homeless to jump council house waiting lists. Unless local authorities are allowed to spend their own cash to build more housing, homelessness will remain as a major problem, resulting in large sums being spent on inadequate temporary accommodation. We must also note that the new social security system introduced in April 1988 'abolished urgent need payments which enabled homeless people to book into cheap bed and breakfast hotels'. Also supplementary benefit payable in advance was replaced with income support paid in arrears. There is now strong evidence that these changes are 'causing poverty among the homeless of a type virtually unknown for 20 years' (*The Guardian* 28 November 1988).

Thus central government, instead of providing local authorities with enabling policies and designated cash so that they can house homeless people, seems to be contributing to the increase of homelessness.

## REFERENCES

Chapman, G. 1987, 'Housing the Homeless in Nottingham', talk given at the Institute of Planning Studies, 21 May.

Fox, J. and Steam, J. 1987, 'Bed and Breakfast Breaks all Records', *Roof*, July – August, pp.12 – 13.

Krumholz, N. et al, 1975, 'The Cleveland Policy Planning Report', *Journal of the American Institute of Planners*, vol.1, no.5.

*The Guardian*, 1988, 'Homeless Hardship Worst for 20 Years', 28 November.

Williams, B. 1988, 'Private Leasing Schemes Lurch Ahead', *Roof*, March – April, p.13.

# 12

# The law and homelessness

*David Hoath*

This chapter is about the legal provisions governing councils' responsibilities towards homeless people, and some of the issues dealt with are
of necessity rather complex. The discussion is not meant to be comprehensive (for example, there is no attempt to provide detailed coverage of all
the difficult issues concerning 'intentional' homelessness). The purpose
of the chapter is merely to explain some of the problems created by the
present state of homelessness law, and to make some modest suggestions
for reform.

The Housing (Homeless Persons) Act of 1977 was very poorly drafted.
Indeed the Act was described by one MP when it was still a Bill, as a
'sloppy, ill-prepared Bill which could have been drafted on the back of
an envelope during an evening while watching television'. Despite the
potential for litigation created by the poor draftsmanship, the sheer volume
of case-law actually generated has been more than may have been expected
bearing in mind that the legislation confers wide discretion on councils
and there is no straightforward method of appeal. The House of Lords
has recently taken steps to try to reduce the amount of homelessness litigation, but the law on this subject remains a happy hunting-ground both for
academic and practising lawyers. This in itself is a good indication of the
deficiencies of the legislation, for social welfare law of this sort should
not operate so that its primary beneficiaries are the lawyers. Although the
provisions of the 1977 Act have since been consolidated in Part III of the
Housing Act 1985, the fundamental problems of interpretation remain.

# THE STATUS OF THE CODE OF GUIDANCE

The precise status of the Ministerial Code of Guidance (the second edition of which was issued in 1983) is uncertain. Under s.71 of the Housing Act 1985, councils must have regard in the exercise of their homelessness functions to such guidance as may be given by the Minister. It seemed to be Parliament's intention that the Code should have a rather more exalted status than a mere Ministerial circular, particularly because the Act merely gives the bare bones of the legal duties and there is thus a need for more specific guidance. It is clear that councils must not systematically disregard the Code as a matter of policy, a point emphasized in, for example, *R. v. Police Complaints Board, ex p. Madden* [1983] 2 All E.R. 353, which was concerned with Codes under the Police Act 1976.

However, councils are free to refuse to follow the guidance in any particular case, as in *De Falco v. Crawley Borough Council* [1980] 1 All E.R. 913, where the Court of Appeal said that the Code is not part of the statute, and that a council is not bound to follow it in any particular case.

Lord Denning went further, and said that the paragraph of the Code in question was all very well for people coming from Yorkshire, but it need not apply to people coming from Italy. So it appeared that he thought that councils could be permitted to indulge in xenophobia when deciding whether or not to follow the Code! Similar remarks about the non-binding nature of the Code have been made in several other cases. Of course the Code does contain very important guidance, and there is little point in having a Code at all if councils can disregard its provisions. At present, the judges tend to apply the Code if it happens to fit in with their own particular views, and to disregard it where it does not.

It would seem sensible to clarify the law by firmly placing upon councils the burden of justifying their refusal to follow relevant guidance as given in the Code.

# HIDDEN HOMELESSNESS: POOR HOUSING CONDITIONS

Homelessness is not just a matter of being literally without a roof. The problem may be hidden in various ways, and this means that legal definitions of homelessness have to be applied to a variety of factual situations.

One example of hidden homelessness is homelessness arising from poor housing conditions. A difficult problem which has emerged in interpreting the definition of homelessness in the Act concerns the situation where the applicant has a right to occupy accommodation (within s.58(2)), but the accommodation is in a very bad state. Before the reforms introduced by the Housing and Planning Act 1986 discussed below, there was no general suggestion from the cases that accommodation did not 'count' (and therefore the applicant was legally homeless) just because it might not be reasonable to continue to occupy the accommodation. There was some suggestion, however, that the accommodation did not 'count' if it was in a really bad state: in that situation, the applicant was deemed to be legally homeless.

The cases originally drew a distinction between s.58 (the definition of homelessness) and s.60 (the definition of intentional homelessness) as regards this issue of poor quality accommodation: it was thought that there were important differences of degree between the two sections, in that accommodation might be of a sufficiently poor standard to entitle the applicant to *leave* it, thereby becoming clearly *homeless*, and he would be unintentionally homeless because it would not have been reasonable for him to stay; yet such accommodation might not have been of a sufficiently bad standard to mean that he was legally homeless while he was actually living in it.

Nevertheless, there were several cases (prior to the harsh decision of the House of Lords in *Puhlhofer v. Hillingdon London Borough Council*, discussed below) where it was recognized that sometimes accommodation could be of such poor quality that it would not even rank as accommodation under s.58, so that the applicant was homeless even while actually living in it: see, for example, *R. v. South Herefordshire District Council, ex p. Miles* [1984] 17 H.L.R. 82, where a hop-picking hut measuring 20 feet by 10 feet, infested with rats and with no mains services, was held *not* to constitute 'accommodation' within s.58 for a family including two young girls and a new baby.

This basically sensible line of reasoning was reversed by the harsh decision of the House of Lords in *Puhlhofer v. Hillingdon London Borough Council* [1986] 1 All E.R. 467. The case involved a husband and wife and their two children, who were living in a single bedroom at a guest house. The room contained a double bed and a single bed; there were no cooking or washing facilities in the room. The council decided that the family was not homeless, and the House of Lords upheld this decision. Lord Brightman said that issues of the appropriateness or reasonableness of the applicant's current accommodation were irrelevant for s.58 purposes, and it was normally irrelevant that the accommodation might be statutorily unfit or statutorily overcrowded. The test was simply whether the accommodation could properly be described as accommodation within the ordinary meaning of that word. Section 60 was considered irrelevant to this issue.

Although Lord Brightman thought that the statutory definition of over-crowding was irrelevant, he nevertheless added that 'accommodation must, by definition, be capable of accommodating', so that, for example, Diogenes (an ancient Greek who lived in a barrel) would be 'homeless'! Lord Brightman said that the question was one of fact to be decided by the council, adding unhelpfully that 'there are no rules'. It is arguable that if the Puhlhofers had left the guest house, thereby clearly becoming homeless, they would *not* have been *intentionally* homeless, because the accommodation was not 'available for their occupation' within ss.60 and 75, but the case did not actually concern the intentionality issue.

Section 58 has now been amended by the Housing and Planning Act 1986. The new s.58 states (in s.58(2A)-(2B)) that a person shall not be treated as having accommodation unless it is accommodation which it would be reasonable[1] for him to continue to occupy; and in determining whether it would be reasonable  for a person to continue to occupy accommodation, regard may be had to the general housing circumstances in the district of the local housing authority to which he has applied for accommodation or for assistance in obtaining accommodation.

However it would be wrong to imagine that the 1986 Act's amendments (by way of introducing the new s.58(2A)-(2B) into the 1985 Act) have reversed the effects of *Puhlhofer*. Section 58(2B) gives the council a wide discretion to say that so many people in its area live in poor conditions that the applicant's own conditions should not be enough to deem him to be homeless. Thus if the facts of *Puhlhofer* recurred, councils like Hillingdon could still try to rely on the local housing conditions as a reason for not accepting people as homeless, and it is not clear to what extent the courts would allow councils to wriggle out under the cover of this s.58(2B) argument.

There are some encouraging decisions on intentionality which could be relevant, such as *R. v. Westminster City Council, ex p. Ali* [1983] 11 H.L.R. 83. This case concerned gross overcrowding, and basically the judge said that no evidence had been placed before him that accommodation in the area of Westminster was in such desperately short supply that it was reasonable to accept overcrowding of the degree present on the facts.[2]

Another problem with s.58(2A)-(2B) is that Parliament unfortunately used the words 'which it would be reasonable for him to continue to occupy'. These are virtually the same words as those used in s.60, a section which, according to the House of Lords in *Puhlhofer*, had nothing to do with the inherent quality of the accommodation. Presumably Parliament in passing the Housing and Planning Act 1986 intended to achieve some improvement here so it seems that these comments in *Puhlhofer* about the reasonableness criterion cannot now stand as regards s.58(2A)-(2B). In other words, the poor quality of the accommodation should now be recognized *for s.58 purposes*, regardless of the former position concerning s.60. It cannot be said that the present position is wholly satisfactory, however, and the statute needs a clarifying amendment.

## HIDDEN HOMELESSNESS: SPLIT FAMILIES

Hidden homelessness can also arise in the case of split families. For example, take a man and woman (married or unmarried) who have children but who do not have any accommodation in which they can live together, so that each partner is forced to live with his or her respective parents. The couple can argue that, as well as being in priority need, they are legally 'homeless' even though they are each separately accommodated, and even though they have never yet been able to reside together. That view is supported by passages in the judgements in *R. v. Westminster City Council, ex p. Chambers* [1982] 6 H.L.R. 24 and *R. v. Preseli District Council, ex p. Fisher* [1984] 17 H.L.R. 147.

This argument depends on establishing the correct interpretation of s.58(2), which says that a person should be treated as having no accommodation if there is no accommodation which he, together with any other person who normally resides with him as a member of his family or in circumstances in which it is reasonable for that person to reside with him, is entitled to occupy or is occupying in one of the prescribed ways. Section 58(2) is ambiguous on this point, but it does seem that the family unit could include either people who *normally reside* with the applicant as members of his family, or *any* other person in circumstances in which it is reasonable for that person to reside with him; this latter limb could include those who have *never* resided with the applicant, but whose immediate residence with him is considered to be reasonable. This is an important issue, given the incidence of split families, and the ambiguity in s.58(2) needs clearing up.

## PRIORITY NEED

Councils owe no duties to accommodate homeless people who are not in priority need. People are in priority need, within the definition in s.59 if, they are pregnant, or they have dependent children, or they are vulnerable, or they are homeless as a result of an emergency. This concept of priority need has led to many problems. In the particular case of homeless young single people without children, if there is no pregnancy, then the only possible priority need is normally by way of 'vulnerability' as a result of 'special reason' (s.59(1)(c)). According to the Code of Guidance (para. 2.12), this category should include 'homeless young people who are at risk of sexual or financial exploitation'.

However, the courts have varied in their application of the 'vulnerability' criterion to homeless young people. In *Crichton v. Harrogate Borough Council* [1980, unreported] a 17-year-old girl living in a tent claimed to be vulnerable on account of sexual and financial exploitation, but the council refused to accept that she was in priority need. The county court judge dismissed her action, brought in order to establish that she was in priority need and was therefore owed a housing duty. The judge said that the council had properly taken the possibility of sexual and financial exploitation into account, and was entitled to find that she was not in priority need. This seems a tough decision. However, the judge added that in certain large cities it was possible that young people could be at risk of exploitation, although he thought this was unlikely in a town like Harrogate!

The case of *Kelly v. Monklands District Council* [1986] S.L.T. 169 can be usefully contrasted with the *Crichton* decision. Ms Kelly was aged 16, and she had left home because of assaults by her father. She had no capital. The council nevertheless decided that she was not 'vulnerable' and therefore was not in priority need. She relied, in the court proceedings, on the passage in the Code about risk of exploitation, and was held to have demonstrated vulnerability: the court said that it was enought to show that the girl was less able to fend for herself, thus giving rise to a *risk* of harm and exploitation; it was not necessary to show *actual* exploitation. The court decided that no reasonable council could have concluded that she was not vulnerable. The court also held that the council had failed to pay proper regard to the Code, and had failed to take account of the views of the relevant social work department. The court here actually ordered the council to find accommodation for the girl, but added that not all 16-year-olds were 'vulnerable' in terms of the Act, and that the accommodation secured did not have to be a house of her own.

Some councils have taken a more generous approach to the question of the vulnerability of young people than that adopted by the Code. For example in 1982 Newcastle-upon-Tyne City Council began implementing a policy effectively accepting all homeless people under 18 as in priority need. Further, in 1983 Glasgow District Council adopted a policy of treating all 16 to 21-year-olds as vulnerable and therefore in priority need, but due to limited staffing resources this policy was initially only implemented for 16 and 17-year-olds.

There is a strong case for the extension and clarification of the various priority need categories, on which the right to housing depends. This is particularly important in relation to vulnerability as a result of 'other special reason', which as it stands in the Act is a very vague expression. Changes to the priority need categories can be introduced quite easily by statutory instrument under s.59(2), but successive Ministers have not chosen to exercise this power.


## COMPETITION WITH THE GENERAL WAITING LIST

The claims of the homeless to be rehoused as against those on the general housing waiting list is a perennially thorny issue. Homeless people who are owed rehousing obligations by councils under Part III of the 1985 Act do not of course have any right to *council* housing as such. What the 1985 Act says (in s.22) is that councils are merely obliged to ensure that in selecting their tenants they give a 'reasonable preference' to people found to be homeless; while s.69 states that accommodation for the homeless can be provided either by way of council housing, or by the council securing that the accommodation is obtained from 'some other person', for example in a guest house.

At one stage it was thought that the obligation in s.22 to give a 'reasonable preference' to the homeless in allocating council housing was too vague to be enforceable. However, it is now clear from the decision in *R. v. Canterbury City Council, ex p. Gillespie* [1987] 19 H.L.R. 7 that councils cannot operate their waiting lists in such a way as to impose blanket fetters which prejudice the homeless (for example by a general resolution only to offer them flats rather than houses, whatever their individual circumstances might be). Similar condemnation of blanket fetters on council house allocation schemes can be found in several decisions of the local government ombudsmen.

## SUITABLE ACCOMMODATION

Another issue concerning the accommodation offered to the homeless relates to its suitability. There is some doubt as to what are the relevant standards with which the accommodation must comply. Under the new s.69 of the 1985 Act (as amended by the Housing and Planning Act 1986), the accommodation secured for the applicant must be 'suitable'. Originally, according to *Puhlhofer v. Hillingdon London Borough Council* [1986] 1 All E.R. 467 (H.L.), no adjective such as 'appropriate' or 'reasonable' was to be read into the statutory accommodation duties, nor did accommodation fail to count as such because it might be unfit or overcrowded. The House of Lords in *Puhlhofer* said that the statutory unfitness and overcrowding criteria were not to be imported into the homelessness provisions for any purpose. However the amendment of s.69 by the Housing and Planning Act makes it clear that the accommodation secured for the applicant under s.65 or s.68 must be 'suitable', and that in determining whether it is suitable the council must have regard to those parts of the 1985 Act relating to slum clearance, overcrowding, and houses in multiple occupation (i.e. Parts IX–XI).

The requirements of the Public Health Act[3] can also be relevant in assessing suitability in an appropriate case. There still seems to be a need for more detailed criteria concerning the 'suitability' of the accommodation, although the English 'suitability' amendment to the 1985 Act has been more sensibly drafted than the relevant amendment to the Scottish legislation.

## THE 'SINGLE OFFER' SYNDROME

According to the case-law, a single offer (provided, now, that it is of 'suitable' accommodation) is a discharge of the council's duty even if the offer is refused (see: *R. v. Westminster City Council, ex p. Chambers* [1982] 6 H.L.R. 24; *R. v. London Borough of Wandsworth, ex p. Lindsay* [1986] 18 H.L.R. 502). It is important that homeless people should not feel pressured into accepting the first offer which is made. To this end, it should be made mandatory for them to be given the same number of offers by councils as applicants for 'normal' council housing receive, which is in fact a recommendation contained in the Scottish Code of Guidance.

## BED AND BREAKFAST ACCOMMODATION

The 'purgatorial stint' in bed and breakfast accommodation (whether in hostels or hotels), which many homeless people have been forced to endure following a successful application to the council, has received the stamp of judicial approval. There is no legal objection to a council offering an applicant a period in such accommodation (even initially, where the applicant has been found unintentionally homeless, provided he is moved on to more permanent accommodation in due course): see *R. v. East Hertfordshire District Council, ex p. Hunt* [1985] 18 H.L.R. 51. However there is much to be said for the introduction of a clear obligation on councils to rehouse in permanent accommodation as soon as possible people who are unintentionally homeless and in priority need. Further, the 'reasonable charges' imposed by councils under s.69(2) on homeless families for bed and breakfast accommodation should take account of the fact that this form of housing is far less suitable than a permanent home, even though, of course, the charges actually levied by those providing such accommodation may be very high.

The considerable use hitherto made by some councils of bed and breakfast accommodation for the homeless is likely to slacken off following the action taken by central government in July 1988 to block all further subsidies in relation to the use by councils of accommodation in bed and breakfast hostels and hotels. Councils are now being encouraged to provide alternative forms of housing for the homeless, for example through the allocation by central government of additional grant aid for the refurbishment of empty council dwellings.

## LEGAL CHALLENGES

Various difficulties confront an applicant who seeks to challenge a council's homelessness decision in the courts. One such difficulty can be described as the 'remoulded reasons' syndrome. Under s.64(4), councils must give reasons in writing where they decide that anything less than the full rehousing duty is owed. However judges have sometimes been prepared to redraft the stated reasons of the council in order to mould them into a form which accords with the wording of the Act (see, for example, *De Falco v. Crawley B.C.* [1980] 1 All E.R. 913 (C.A.)). The better view is surely that the council's reasons should be adequate, dealing with all the substantial points raised, and if inadequate reasons are given, the court should require the council to provide adequate ones (as in *R. v. Reigate and Banstead Borough Council, ex p. Paris* [1984] 17 H.L.R. 103). Councils should themselves provide proper reasons without expecting a judge to do the job for them.

A further problem facing the applicant is that he cannot normally challenge the decision before a county court judge. Instead, he has to take complicated and expensive proceedings by way of 'judicial review' in the High Court (see *Cocks v. Thanet District Council* [1982] 3 All E.R. 1135 (H.L.)). This procedure, which is laid down by Order 53 of the Rules of the Supreme Court, is somewhat akin in the present context to using a sledgehammer to crack a walnut. Moreover, under this jurisdiction the judge cannot interfere with a council's decision merely because he disagrees with it. He has to be satisfied, before he can upset the decision, that there has been an 'administrative law breach', in that the council has taken into account irrelevant considerations, or has failed to take into account relevant considerations, or has arrived at a decision which no reasonable council could reach.

There is also a heavy burden of proof imposed on an applicant who seeks to show that the council has contravened any of these administrative law principles. In *Puhlhofer v. Hillingdon London Borough Council* [1986] 1 All E.R. 467, the House of Lords stated that the homelessness decisions of councils should only be open to challenge where the circumstances are 'exceptional'. Furthermore it is getting more difficult to obtain legal aid for judicial review applications in homelessness cases. Although the Court of Appeal has recently permitted a slight relaxation in the burden of proof here (see *West Glamorgan County Council v. Rafferty* [1987] 1 All E.R. 1005), there is a need for reform of the rules regulating the means whereby the applicant can challenge these important decisions of local authorities.

There ought to be a swift, cheap, effective, independent, 'user-friendly' and locally based appeal mechanism for homelessness cases. This has been recommended several times by the Council on Tribunals. It does seem strange that if a private tenant thinks his rent is too high, then he can go to the local rent officer and/or to the local Rent Assessment Committee (depending on the type of tenancy he holds), but if a homeless person has been turned away by a council, he has no such independent method of local redress at all.

Pending the introduction of effective means of challenging the council's decision, the disappointed applicant should at least be made aware of such remedies as do already exist. There should be a requirement for the decision letter under s.64 to inform him of his legal remedies and of the availability of local advice and assistance. A useful precedent is provided by the information requirements for notices to quit and notices of intended proceedings which have to be sent to certain private and public sector tenants under the Notices to Quit (Prescribed Information) Regulations 1980 and the Secure Tenancies (Notices) Regulations 1980 and 1984.

## CONCLUSIONS

The judges have been hampered in their policing of the homelessness functions of councils by the strict principles governing the judicial review procedure, although that does not excuse some of the extremely strange decisions like *De Falco* and *Puhlhofer*. However the present highly confusing state of homelessness law is largely the responsibility of Parliament, because of the poor drafting of the relevant statutory provisions. The amendments made by the Housing and Planning Act 1986, effective from January 1987, have by no means solved all the problems.

Part III of the Housing Act 1985 represents crucial social legislation: it deals with the fundamental human need for a roof over one's head, a need which was recognized by the United Nations when it designated 1987 as the International Year of Shelter for the Homeless. It is reasonable to expect that this would be an area above all others which Parliament would have taken pains to get absolutely right, and it is a great pity that it does not yet appear to have done so.

## NOTES

1    Thus cases decided under s.60, on the issue of intentional homelessness and

whether it would be reasonable to continue to occupy, are clearly now relevant to s.58(2A)-(2B) on the issue of whether somebody is homeless at all.
2   The case involved the reasonableness criterion with regard to intentionality, and the judge refused to allow the council to escape under the intentionality equivalent of s.58(2B). It is difficult to know which way the courts are going to jump in dealing with such arguments.
3   The amended s.69 does not specifically refer to matters like the statutory nuisance provisions in the Public Health Act 1936, but the criteria which are expressly set out in s.69 are in any event merely examples.

## FURTHER READING

Arden, A. 1986, *Manual of Housing Law*, 3rd ed., chap. 10.
Hoath, D.C. 1989, *Public Housing Law*, chapters 4–6, Sweet and Maxwell, London.
In addition the monthly journal *Legal Action* (published by the Legal Action Group) regularly contains articles and notes discussing current issues concerning homelessness law.

# 13

# Homelessness — facing the facts

*John Ferris and David Whynes*

For citizens of countries subject to all but the most hospitable of climates a satisfactory standard of accommodation represents a pressing human need. Nevertheless, it is clear that this need remains far from fulfilled even in a country such as the UK which can boast a 40-year history of state provision of comprehensive welfare services.

Homelessness in the UK and in capitalist economies generally is historically associated with poverty. The eighteenth century Poor Law, for example, recognized the existence of vagrancy resulting from destitution and charged parishes with the resonsibility for shelter of, and assistance to, those without accommodation. In common with most areas of pre-war welfare legislation, policies directed at the homelessness problem became formalized in the post-1945 welfare state; the 1948 National Assistance Act gave local authorities the power (if not the obligation) to offer shelter to all those in need.

If the architects of the welfare state genuinely believed that growing economic prosperity would alleviate poverty problems within a short period of time they were to be disappointed. Even in the 1960s, before the economic chaos engendered by the oil crisis, public awareness of shortfall was growing; two examples in the case of homelessness were the formation of the housing pressure group, *Shelter*, in 1967 and the televising of the now-famous BBC drama documentary *Cathy Come Home* in 1968. Stronger policies were evidently required.

## CATEGORIES OF NEED

Following local government reorganization in 1974, social services departments within local authorities were created and the responsibilities for homelessness were transferred to specialist housing departments. As a result of the 1977 Housing (Homeless Persons) Act, consolidated in the 1985 Housing Act, local authorities presently have an obligation to prevent homelessness amongst specified 'priority need' groups. For the purposes of the Act the following are deemed to exhibit priority need:

- pregnant women, and those normally residing with them;
- persons with dependent children;
- vulnerable persons like the elderly, the sick, the handicapped, victims of domestic violence and minors open to sexual exploitation;
- persons homeless as a result of a disaster such as fire or flood.

Persons outside such categories must be offered advice and assistance, and temporary accommodation if it is deemed necessary. Homeless individuals without local connections must be referred to the relevant local authority. Note that in the last two cases the precise housing obligations of local authorities are not clearly circumscribed and much therefore depends on the attitudes and resources of particular housing departments.

## STATISTICS ON HOMELESSNESS

Those in priority need have become the responsibility of local authorities. Their numbers are relatively well documented and local authority returns are regularly consolidated to produce the central government's annual *Homelessness Statistics* (Department of the Environment).

It is evident immediately, however, that such data are bound to understate the true homelessness position for two principal reasons. First, there will exist a class of homeless persons who do not qualify for accommodation by virtue of being considered outside the statutory priority need categories. The most obvious representatives of this class are able-bodied single adults with no special circumstances. Such persons may be disinclined to use the official channels in the knowledge that the authorities have no necessary obligation to house them.

Second, there will exist a class of persons presently occupying accommodation which they consider unsatisfactory. Such persons would willingly move into alternative accommodation were it to become available; these people are generally termed the 'hidden homeless'. Examples of this class might include couples presently living with parents, children coming of age and anxious to leave the parental home, and individuals staying with friends.

In comparison with those in priority need very much less is known about these other homeless persons. The reason for this is not difficult to understand – the data are difficult to obtain. In the first place, individuals are only likely to report themselves as homeless if they feel assistance will be forthcoming. Many people, aware of the pressure under which most housing departments currently operate, do not report themselves.

Second, the majority of formal data recording systems presently in operation, such as census or tax returns, make the implicit assumption that the individuals concerned have fixed places of residence. Migrants very obviously run the risk of frequent periods of homelessness yet the very fact of their migration confuses the issue of responsibility for recording. Third, many homeless persons seem to exist at the margin of the economy proper, receiving little from, and asking little of, the society in which they function. Accordingly they have little interest in identifying themselves as homeless.

Finally, a good deal of accommodation for homeless persons in non-priority categories is provided by the voluntary sector, in the form of shelters and hostels. These hostels are quite heterogeneous – some are run by religious charities, some only deal with applicants of specific genders or ethnic origins and some aim to house ex-offenders or those formerly in care. Given such diversity of needs there might not be a common interest in homelessness as such. Indeed, voluntary agencies could conceivably be seen as atomistic, even in competition with each other, and the spirit of cooperation necessary for the establishment of a general data recording system might not prevail within a given locality.

The true picture of homelessness in the UK accordingly remains opaque and as long as this situation persists, the interests of homeless persons are unlikely to be well served. The collection of basic data on the nature and characteristics of the homeless population within a given locality is vital to inform fundamental policy arguments directed towards improving the circumstances of the homeless. Even a simple estimate of numbers, for example, would help to establish whether care provision both government and voluntary in a particular area could be deemed adequate.

## CHARACTERISTICS OF HOMELESS PEOPLE

The identification of characteristics of homeless people would be even more valuable in indicating, for instance, which types of accommodation ought to be provided — for single unemployed males as opposed to, say, families.

Important as such findings would be they would remain essentially static, in that they would describe a situation at a given point in time. Of perhaps more consequence would be two dynamic considerations. First, a knowledge of the characteristics of homeless persons opens the way for an analysis of causes which is necessary if the problem is to be properly understood and dealt with. Second, a characteristics analysis would provide a rational basis for both public and private future funding in support of homeless persons, by identifying areas of special need or problems requiring urgent solution. While data of this kind are difficult to collect, the expected pay-off merits the attempt.

In October 1987 a homelessness research programme was instituted at the University of Nottingham with the specific intention of learning more about the nature and characteristics of homelessness in the locality. The long-term goal of the research is to collect and analyse data on all aspects of the homelessness issue but the initial study involves an enquiry into the characteristics of the population using the various shelters and hostels in the city. The next section of this chapter describes the setting up of the study and presents its preliminary findings.

## THE NOTTINGHAM HOSTELS STUDY

In addition to accommodation provided by official agencies, including the housing department and the probation service, there are some 25 voluntary sector hostels in the City of Nottingham. This voluntary sector provides in excess of 600 places for homeless persons. The hostels make available a wide range of facilities and cater for an equally wide range of clients. The two largest are the Salvation Army hostel and the Macedon Trust, both offering approximately 150 places, with the Macedon Trust providing round-the-clock refreshment facilities. The Night Shelter offers 30 places and maintains a very open admissions policy. Amongst the smaller hostels are the Addison Street (10 places) and the Croft (5 places) hostels, specializing in accommodation for recovering male alcoholics and young single mothers respectively. Around half of the Nottingham hostels offer

10 or less places each.

The Nottingham Hostels Liaison Group has been in existence for some six years and acts as a forum for the voluntary sector hostels. One result of its activities has been the development of a common referral and monitoring system, an extended version of which has been used by the research team as the basis for its questionnaire (the principal data-gathering technique). This questionnaire is distributed to the participating hostels and is completed by hostel workers for each applicant on arrival. Records are subsequently forwarded to the research team for processing and analysis.

## WHO ARE THE HOMELESS?

To date, the database consists of completed records of 850 individuals who have applied for accommodation as non-priority need cases. This sample displays the following characteristics:

1. *Age.* All ages are represented in the sample, from children in their early teens (and thus technically ineligible for assistance) to persons in their 70s. The younger age groups appear to predominate however. The proportions of the sample in each age range are:

|  |  |
|---|---|
| 16–19 | 23.5% |
| 20–24 | 22.5% |
| 25–39 | 22.5% |
| 40–50 | 15.9% |
| 51 and over | 15.6% |

The median age of the sample is 26 years.
2. *Gender.* 79.9 per cent of the sample is male, 20.1 per cent female.
3. *Marital status.* The vast majority of individuals in the sample are single (82.0 per cent); 4.7 per cent are married and 7.8 per cent divorced; 5.5 per cent are widowed or separated.
4. *Employment.* 10.9 per cent of the sample were in employment at the time of their application for accommodation. Of those not in employment 35.1 per cent had only recently become unemployed (within the preceding 12 months). A further 10.1 per cent had been unemployed for between one and two years while at the other extreme, 18.1 per cent had been out of work for at least ten years. 10.9 per cent of those

unemployed reported that they had never worked.

An analysis by social class from data of present and previous occupations has been made using the standard criteria. Based on a sub-sample of 530 persons generating usable data the social class breakdown is as follows:

| | |
|---|---|
| I | 0.0% |
| II | 3.5% |
| III | 30.9% |
| IV | 21.5% |
| V | 27.3% |

The residual 16.8 per cent comprises unclassifiable individuals, primarily those formerly or currently engaged in post-school work experience programmes. Occupation data were also classified into socio-economic groupings; for those individuals so classifiable the following principal categories emerge:

| | |
|---|---|
| Unskilled manual | 27.1% |
| Skilled manual | 17.1% |
| Semi-skilled manual | 16.1% |
| Personal service workers | 12.4% |
| Junior non-manual | 6.9% |

5. *Ethnicity*. Applicants are invited to classify themselves by ethnic origins. The vast majority in the sample are UK or Irish Caucasians (92.3 per cent), Afro-Caribbeans making up 5.2 per cent and Asians 1.8 per cent.

6. *Last permanent address*. Table 13.1 indicates the geographical region in which applicants last resided on a permanent basis. It also includes data on the location of present/previous employment for the relevant sub-sample.

7. *Homelessness situation*. On arriving at a hostel applicants are invited to report their own perceived housing needs. Of the sample nearly two-thirds (63.4 per cent) reported that they were actually homeless at the time of application, 16.5 per cent said they expected to be homeless in the very near future, and 13.7 per cent reported difficulties with respect to their current accommodation.

**Table 13.1  Geographical region and present/previous employment**

|  | Last permanent address | Location of employment |
|---|---|---|
|  | % | % |
| Nottingham City | 56.4 | 52.2 |
| Nottinghamshire | 8.8 | 4.0 |
| Other Midlands | 11.5 | 9.7 |
| Southern England | 10.8 | 16.6 |
| Northern England | 6.3 | 6.6 |
| Other UK | 4.7 | 5.8 |
| Outside UK | 1.5 | 5.1 |
|  | 100.0 | 100.0 |

When asked about the nature of the previous night's accommodation the sample replied as follows:

|  | % |
|---|---|
| In a hostel | 10.4% |
| With a friend | 17.4% |
| With a relative | 15.6% |
| In lodgings | 13.3% |
| In prison or police cells | 10.8% |
| In emergency accommodation | 12.9% |
| Other | 19.6% |

Not surprisingly the location of the previous night's address was more centred on Nottingham than the location of the last permanent address. 65.3 per cent spent the previous night in Nottingham, 8.1 per cent in the county and 14.7 elsewhere in the Midlands region. Nearly 90 per cent, therefore, had come into Nottingham from within an approximately 50-mile radius. Those from the South and North of England numbered 3.9 and 5.2 per cent respectively.

The most common reason given by applicants for their current accommodation problems was the inability of friends or relatives to continue to house them (27.0 per cent so replied). Other frequently cited reasons included marital breakdown (15.7 per cent), loss of tenancy (10.4 per cent), loss of bed and breakfast accommodation (7.2 per cent) and prison discharge (5.3 per cent). 11.7 per cent reported that they had never been successful in obtaining secure accommodation.

8. *Health problems*. More than half of the sample reported no particular health problems. 11.5 per cent, however, admitted to problems of physical, and 7.9 per cent to problems of mental, health. A self-perceived alcohol problem was mentioned by 17.4 per cent of the sample; by contrast, drug problems were scarcely ever mentioned.

9. *Nature of referral and action taken*. Individuals apply to a hostel either in person or by telephone — two-thirds of our sample applied in person. 32.7 per cent applied directly to the hostel of their choice (self-referral), the remainder being referred by other hostels or agencies. In the sample, 26.0 per cent of applications resulted from referrals by the probation service and 13.5 per cent from referrals by the social services and housing departments. The remaining referrals originated from the other participating agencies and hostels, the distribution of origin being approximately even.

As a result of application for an accommodation place 25.3 per cent of the sample obtained permanent accommodation and 29.7 per cent were offered temporary shelter. Of the remainder, 7.4 per cent were placed on a waiting list, and the rest were offered advice and assistance and/or referred elsewhere. The Macedon Trust and the housing department were the two agencies most widely recommended to unsuccessful applicants.

The data have already thrown up patterns pointing the way for future investigations.[1] First, the age distribution of hostel users is heavily skewed towards youth, half of the sample being in the first ten years of adult life. Youth unemployment and 'leaving home' might be important explanatory factors in this context.

Second, the homeless in Nottingham display a certain geographical mobility. Approximately one quarter of our sample last permanently resided or worked outside the Midlands region. We need to discover motives for migration to Nottingham, the possibilities being perceived improved employment opportunities, perceived quality of accommodation on offer and the proximity of family and friends.

Third, the whole structure of family and friendship relationships merits exploration; a significant proportion of the study population merits exploration; a significant proportion of the study population has recently left this 'hidden homeless' sector to demand accommodation within the voluntary sector. One possible explanation would be economic pressure on households causing the forcing out of marginal members.

## RESEARCH INTO SINGLE HOMELESSNESS

Before the 1977 Housing (Homeless Persons) Act administrative responsibility for the single homeless had, since 1948, resided primarily with the Department of Health and Social Security (DHSS) and its predecessors. The DHSS provided reception and resettlement centres for 'people without a settled way of life', as the official jargon had it, and also financial support for voluntary agencies providing for specific need groups of single homeless persons such as alcoholics, drug addicts and those accustomed to 'sleeping rough'.

The DHSS also provided guidance and advice to local authorities through circulars. Within this administrative context the forms of voluntary and statutory provision and the social perception of single homelessness were reciprocally reinforcing. The category 'single homeless' in both popular and official usage meant vagrants — in more popular stereotypical imagery, drunks, dossers and tramps.

Research up to the early 1970s tacitly accepted this definition of the situation and the implied boundaries of concern. Investigations were carried out in specific agencies such as reception centres, night shelters and large voluntary hostels[2]. This research effort was directed towards the high proportion of disturbed individuals with personality and behavioural disorders, often with alcohol and mental health complications, amongst the homeless population.

In the main, this research emphasized the behavioural problems of hostel clients additional to their accommodation problems. Social policy in the area had a distinctly therapeutic flavour. More pragmatically, it was concerned with managing the segment of the population perceived to have behavioural problems. As such it was not much concerned with housing provision or access to mainstream tenures. Even at the time such perspectives were far too narrow. In central London alone for example, during the period 1971–73, there were at least 25 000 squatters unable to find adequate housing in either the private or public sector. Many, if not the majority, were young persons under the age of 25 with no particular 'behavioural problems' of the types mentioned (Wates and Wolmar, 1981).

Around the time of the 1977 Act perceptions of single homelessness began to change. There was a growing awareness, led by campaigning groups such as CHAR and Shelter, that the problem involved larger numbers and a far greater diversity of needs than either local or central government had been prepared to acknowledge. Homelessness was a problem not only of the behavioural disorders of a minority but, more fundamentally, one of access to housing for single persons generally, and particularly those on low incomes. Since the late 1970s research and campaigning activity has been much more orientated towards the demarcation of housing and income needs and demands on support services such as health care and forms of social work.

The preliminary analysis of the Nottingham survey, as presented above, seems generally consistent with the findings of the more recent research. Two particular investigations in this area can be fruitfully compared with the Nottingham results. First, there exists the Drake (1982) study, a national survey and the most comprehensive to date, and second, the Henry and Gallagher (1984) study, one sponsored by the Single Homeless Advisory Service and specific to Nottingham. Points of comparison are as follows:

1. *Age*. In the Drake study it was found that, whilst the age of homeless men mirrored the population distribution generally, that of women did not. Women who became homeless were, on average, far younger than men. Henry and Gallagher confirm this finding for Nottingham. It is too soon to perform an age/gender analysis for the Nottingham University data but one important difference between these findings and those of the earlier studies can already be detected. The homeless population is markedly younger. The sample displays a 5 per cent rise in cases under 19 years of age compared to other studies, although fairly consistent in respect of higher age cohorts. This lends some support to the emerging view that more teenagers are becoming homeless.

2. *Gender*. The male/female ratio is currently higher than Drake's (4:1 as opposed to 3:1), although the research is not sufficiently advanced to interpret the significance of this result. No evidence of an increase in homelessness amongst women has been found but studies have shown that this group tends to display a higher degree of 'hidden homelessness'

(Austerberry and Watson, 1984).

3. *Ethnicity*. Although Drake provides no data on ethnicity, the Caucasian/non-Caucasian ratio identified by Henry and Gallagher (9:1) is very similar to the Nottingham results. Non-Caucasians are accordingly 'under-represented' in the local homeless population, compared to the local population as a whole. This ratio might reflect for example, a higher degree of hidden homelessness amongst non-Caucasians or, alternatively, a higher degree of communal support. Such a finding points the way for further investigation.

4. *Addiction*. Here detailed comparison is impossible although it can be said that drug abuse is not a major homelessness issue according to any of the studies. Of the Drake sample, some 4 per cent had used Class A drugs, although Nottingham's 'drug problem' is very minor when compared to other regions of the country. Heavy drinking seems to be associated with around 15 per cent of the homeless population both nationally and locally (implying that, in spite of the earlier stereotype, 85 per cent of the homeless do not see themselves as drinkers).

5. *Employment*. Both the Nottingham surveys point to a significant proportion of employed and recently unemployed in the homeless population. Over and above this, the Drake study discovered a 15−20 per cent proportion of 'unemployables' in that sample, consisting of the sick, the disabled and those close to or above retirement age and it is expected that such a group will be identified in the Nottingham Study. None of these data support the stereotype of the homeless person as a 'workshy vagrant'.

6. *Health*. In all studies, a proportion of respondents reported physical and mental health problems. Aggregating the data with those of the other studies suggests that at least 20 per cent of homeless persons are incapacitated in some degree by health problems. Drake demonstrates that the severity of such problems increases with the length of time spent in unsettled living conditions, as do alcohol-related problems.

## CONCLUSIONS

The preliminary analysis of the Nottingham study raises some disturbing questions about the numbers of people now becoming homeless and rootless.

It is clear that there is no 'typical' single homeless person. As a category the term 'single homeless' only arises because of political and administrative priorities reflected in legislation and government circulars to local authorities. If there is a common factor it is surely low income, either because of low wages or because of dependence on income support and board and lodging allowances.

The manner in which income support is provided is itself an important variable influencing the ability of benefit recipients to achieve a settled existence and a stable home. This may explain the noticeable geographical mobility of many in the sample although such a question is beyond the scope of the present study. The DHSS 'four-week' rule for persons under 25 years of age is likely to have some effect on the relatively high numbers of young persons now using direct access hostels such as the Nottingham Night Shelter. Drake clearly demonstrated that employment opportunities increased with settled residential existence and it would be a perverse outcome indeed if contemporary DHSS policies intended to get young people into work have had the unintended effect of creating a new generation of vagrants by pushing them into hostel sub-cultures.

It is also evident that many of the sample might legitimately be deemed to be in 'priority need' on vulnerability grounds − sickness, disability, youth − yet they appear not to have been treated as such. Clearly the policy for homelessness requires not only clearly articulated legislation but, perhaps more crucially, adequate resources. In this respect, the public, the private and the voluntary sectors all have roles to play.

## NOTES

1   It must be stressed that the study, running as it has for only a matter of months, remains very much at the pilot stage. After so little time the sample is not yet truly representative of the homelessness agencies in the city as a whole. Questionnaire responses have been processed as and when they have come in with the result that, at this stage, some hostels are, strictly speaking over-represented in our sample. The passage of time will resolve this problem although at present, the larger hostels are slightly under-represented.

2    See, for example, the bibliography in Drake et al, 1982.

## REFERENCES

Austerberry, H.C. and Watson, S. 1984, *Women and Homelessness*, London, Routledge.
Drake, M. et al 1982, *Single and Homeless*, London, HMSO.
Henry, D. and Gallagher, J. 1984, *Single Homelessness in Nottingham*, Nottingham, Single Homeless Advisory Service.
Wates, N. and Wolmar, C. 1981, *The Squatters*, London, Bay Leaf Books.

# 14

# Homelessness and the mentally disordered

*Patricia Mounser and Philip Bean*

'Homelessness' to most people means 'houselessness', but over the years it has become used to include bad housing conditions. Shelter, for example argued that people were not only homeless who were houseless, but were homeless where the conditions in which they lived simply could not be termed 'homes' (Shelter, 1969).

Homelessness is inevitably linked to poverty as examplified by the 1911 Census which recorded 258 000 people in Poor Law Institutions: this incidentally included 5 per cent of all single women and 25 per cent of all single men aged 65 and over (Donnison and Ungerson, 1968).

There was a decline in numbers after the introduction of pension schemes and the 1948 National Assistance Act which entrusted local authorities under Part III Section 21 (1) with the duty of providing temporary accommodation for persons in urgent need of it (Burke, 1981). Admission to Part III accommodation, as it was known, became the measure of homelessness.

However during the 1950s and 1960s the problem of homelessness was exacerbated by slum clearance programmes and road-building schemes which effectively moved whole populations of the poor. The Rent Act of 1957 produced evictions and harassment of tenants, drawing attention to the homeless. The problem was made still worse by the shrinking of the private sector through the switching of investments to commercial development or to selling for owner occupation.

By 1966 there were 2558 households in temporary accommodation, which by 1970 had risen to 4926, and by 1976 to 10 270 amounting to some 50 000 people (Burke, 1981). Between 1980—1987 officially recorded homelessness has increased from 57 000 to 150 000 (Department of Environment Statistics).

Yet homelessness is not just about families. The 1971 Census, for example, counted 11 million single adults, but only 3 million had a place of their own (OPCS, 1976). In addition, there was a vast number of 'hidden' single homeless who were living in bed and breakfast small hotels or multi-occupation houses — these are licensees who have no security of tenure. There are also those who have live-in jobs with no other homes to go to should they lose them. Groups of single homeless, corresponding to the old idea of the vagrant, were according to the 1971 Census living in common lodging houses, hostels, night shelters and reception centres. Many also slept rough. Others were living in isolation and physical squalor which far exceeded that of most homeless families (Brandon, 1969). In 1972, one of the years where figures were available, 26 823 people lived in hostels and lodging houses, but this did not include those living in small, unlicensed lodging houses, or in the beds in mental hospitals which were occupied by potentially homeless single people.

Nor is homelessness just about poverty: it often operates alongside and is part of other social problems including mental disorder. The St Mungo Trust attempted to count the number of people sleeping rough in Inner London and in two Outer London boroughs on one night in 1972. They found 1415 people and estimated a further 1048 people in hospitals, police cells and reception centres. There were 500 inmates of Brixton prison and 9000 people in common lodging houses, making a total of 11 963 in all (Wilkinson, Galley and Dobkin, 1973). They found many people suffering from mental illness and who had been recently discharged from psychiatric hospitals or prisons, many with drink problems or who were alcoholics and who fitted the term 'social inadequates'.

## MENTAL DISORDER AND HOMELESSNESS

Similarly the Glasgow Council for the Single Homeless rated 1 per cent of their homeless sample as 'mentally ill', but over 50 per cent as having family or marital problems (Glasgow Council, 1980). Furthermore Leach and Wing found a high prevalence of mental illness and personality disorders in their sample of homeless men, although they found it difficult to quantify the exact number (Leach and Wing, 1980). Presumably many may have been the same kind of patients as reviewed by Cooper and Early when they examined a hospital population and concluded that 80.3 per cent of the male patients and 71.0 per cent of the female patients were unfit for discharge — even, it appears, to supervised hostel care (Cooper and Early, 1961).

Of course not all mentally disordered patients leaving hospital are homeless, nor are they social inadequates with family problems. But by their very nature admissions to hospitals are likely to be disruptive so that some will be homeless on discharge. In London in 1981, for example, of the 24 705 discharges from psychiatric hospitals 10 per cent were homeless and 90 per cent returned home or went to hostels and lodgings (GLC Health Panel, 1984). In Nottingham in 1985 it was found that of the 1825 discharges from mental hospitals, 82 per cent went home and 18 per cent were homeless (Bean and Mounser, 1989). Kay and Legg in a study in London took a different sample. They looked at 100 homeless mentally disordered people. They found 20 living in emergency homeless accommodation, 19 in social service hostels, 22 in group homes, 23 alone in independent housing and only 16 living with their families (Kay and Legg, 1986). Most of these were single (54 people), separated or divorced (24 people), or widowed (8 people). Out of the 100 people they looked at 91 were unemployed; this is another problem affected by hospitalization because it is not easy to hold a steady job with continual interruptions.

Yet whatever problems they may have had these patients said by far the greatest problem seemed to be housing; 80 per cent were dissatisfied with their current housing situations and 75 per cent wanted their own independent housing in the future. In contrast 25 per cent said their biggest problem was coping with their mental illness. Kay and Legg concluded that community care was not working. They added that if psychiatric hospitals continued to close at the current rate further social disasters would ensue (Kay and Legg, 1986). Moreover they felt the problems could not be overcome by the injection of more money, for many such problems they said stemmed from the organizational and administrative complexities of the various services involved, and the historic low priority accorded to mental health (Kay and Legg, 1986). Nonetheless it is worth noting that 90 per cent of expenditure on mental health goes on the 10 per cent of the mentally ill people who are in hospital and only 10 per cent is allocated to non-medical services (Kay and Legg, 1986). While this remains the case we feel that little can be achieved in the field of community care.

Changes in the patients' housing conditions were not uncommon, Kay and Legg also found in their study of 100 discharged mental patients that 64 had experienced significant changes in their housing situations at discharge, the majority going eventually to institutional or supported accommodation. Of the 22 people who had previously lived in insecure housing 18 had lost their accommodation while in hospital, their landlords having relet it in their absence.

> For the majority of those interviewed the period in hospital had dramatically altered their housing situation. An important issue is the role of their discharge in either resolving or creating housing problems. (Kay and Legg, 1986)

Clearly mentally ill people have specific problems which other homeless people do not have yet they are competing for the same housing. Many people discharged from psychiatric hospitals will be single, and therefore are likely to suffer additional discrimination. Not only this; they have to come to terms with their illnesses by themselves; and the support they have had in hospital often comes to an abrupt end (Bean and Mounser, 1989). They will usually be unemployed or unable to return to work and must live on reduced incomes. Moreover they may well not be used to handling money. They might have lost their previous homes because of their admission, or if they have been in hospital for many years may never have had a home of their own. Yet if they are to be integrated into the community their problems need to be dealt with. If not they may be unable to cope, or they may deteriorate and require readmission.

## CHANGES IN POLICY FOR THE MENTALLY DISORDERED

The modern problem of homelessness for mental patients has many origins but it is exacerbated by two features: the policy of closing down mental hospitals with the reduction of hospital beas for the mentally disordered, and the inadequate provision of housing ) accommodate them. In the first case the asylum no longer provides a refuge, and in the second cheap housing, which many patients would otherwise have used, has diminished, the emphasis now being placed on housing families.

The discharge of mental patients was a policy announced by Enoch Powell (the then Minister of Health) in 1961 at the Annual Conference of the National Association for Mental Health. The intention was to reduce the

150 000 mental hospital beds (42 per cent of all hospital beds) by half that number by 1975 and to locate those that remained in general hospitals (Jones, 1983). Following this announcement the community care 'blue book' was published in April 1963. It went to great lengths to lay down the guidelines of what community care should mean (HMSO, 1963). Lacking any rationale of community care and with the absence of any positive lead from central government, it was based on the assumption that the decline in hospital beds, already observed in the previous five years, was due to new developments in psychotropic drugs. These were introduced in the mid-1950s and had, their supporters claimed, opened the doors to the wards and removed the padded cells.

No one seemed to notice that the decline in patient numbers had begun earlier, before the introduction of these drugs. Equally, little acknowledgement is given to the fact that such a decline could not have continued unabated, for there would always be some patients required to stay in hospital.

> Much of the time, it appears as if policy makers simply do not know what will happen when their schemes are put into effect. Nor do they seem very concerned to find out. (Scull, 1973)

Certainly Sir Keith Joseph, when announcing the new policy, believed the drug evolution to have changed the treatment of psychosis, neurosis and schizophrenia. It was, he thought, able to effect real 'cures' of the mentally disordered and so effectively abolish the mental hospital system (Hansard, 1971). Enoch Powell had earlier advocated the reduction of mental illness beds from 3.4 to 1.8 per thousand population; by 1971 beds were reduced to 2.0 per thousand population (Jones, 1972). Richard Titmuss, speaking the day after Powell, doubted that the Government's intentions were other than economic and doubted that concomitant community care would be developed — in this it seems he was largely correct.

Certainly implementation of the Government's policy has been dramatic. Between 1960 and 1975 some 52 000 beds in psychiatric hospitals have closed. Yet paradoxically the hospital admission rate rose in England and Wales from 155 000 admissions in 1964 to 179 000 in 1976. How can this be? The answer lies in the length of stay of patients. Whereas in the 1950s the mean length of stay would have been about six months and 12 months or more was not unusual, in the 1980s it is between one and two months. This dramatic reduction has allowed large numbers of beds to be closed (HMSO, 1975).

However the reduction of beds would have been greater had there not been a rise in subsequent admissions. In Nottingham the data show a decline in aggregate number of admissions between 1980 and 1985 of 18.8 per cent (compared with a decline nationally of 1.4 per cent). This decline is due largely to a decline in first admissions — re-admissions have increased over this period, but not it would seem at a sufficient rate to make up the numbers (Bean and Mounser, 1989). Essentially this means that mentally ill people are spending shorter periods of time in hospital, but having more admissions — hence the reduction in the number of beds. It is interesting to note in this respect that 80 per cent of the 24 705 discharges from London hospitals in 1981 had been admitted at least once before (GLC Health panel, 1984).

## LOCAL AUTHORITY HOSTELS

The policy of removing cheap accommodation affects the mentally disordered quite dramatically. The Housing (Homeless Persons) Act 1977 (consolidated in the Housing Act 1985 Part III) was the first major change in statutory provision for the homeless for over 30 years. It was also the first to deal specifically with the 'homeless'. It acknowledged homelessness as a 'housing' problem and not a 'social' problem, and directed those people who were likely to become homeless, or who had nowhere to live, to the Local Housing Department.

But the building of hostels by local authorities for patient rehabilitation was resisted by many communities; it was expected that only a limited number would be built and that they would have a rapid turnover of people through them. However, it became clear that they were providing a permanent environment for patients who had nowhere to go. Local authorities had not realized that they would have to house a long-stay population (Durkin, 1971). This became obvious by the provision made; beds in hostels or lodging houses declined by 17 per cent between 1965 and 1972, at the same time that beds in psychiatric hospitals also declined.

Pressure on all housing for single people grew during this period. Single households grew by 30 per cent between 1966 and 1971, and this included a 20 per cent growth in flat sharing largely due to the number of people under 30 years of age in the population generally (Burke, 1981). Apart from Glasgow where two new hostels opened in 1970 with 240 beds and 61 beds respectively, the Office of Population and Census and Surveys found only five hostels with 58 beds between them opened in the whole of the UK in that year (Burke, 1981). These hostels were hardly lavish for the policy has always been to keep accommodation spartan so as not to encourage a rough and self-destructive way of life; such amenities were thought to be open to abuse. Yet one CHAR worker reported that the appalling low standards at the Camberwell Reception Centre, which had been an old Poor Law institution, was a major contributing factor in the 'disturbing pattern of violence' which had been reported there (Jones, Brown and Bradshaw, 1978).

## CONDITIONS IN PRIVATE HOUSING

The same conditions prevailed in common lodging houses and multi-occupation dwellings. Attempts to get landlords to improve their accommodation usually resulted in closure, or a reduction in beds. Most tenants it appears put up with poor conditions because they had nowhere else to go. The result has not just been a shortage of homes, but a shift in the perception of the homeless. Homelessness was seen as a 'social' problem due to individual personal circumstances or failings rather than as a problem of 'housing' consequent upon the decline of low-rent housing.

The lack of public awareness or interest in the problem stemmed from this. Yet redevelopment and the emphasis placed on providing family homes has drastically reduced the cheapest, albeit the most inadequate of housing.

For those people who are not doing very well, this means they may have lost their only opportunity of maintaining contact with the rest of society, and thereby the potential for self-rehabilitation. For the mentally disordered this is of critical importance.

## COMMUNITY CARE

The policy of reducing the number of hospital patients has been expected to lead to care in the community — as if it would somehow naturally follow one from the other. The asylum had stood for two centuries, a refuge for those people who could not live in the community, or who did not fit in to the socially accepted way of life. It is now to be relegated to a new place for treatment: the community itself. Yet the phrase 'community care' by itself means very little. It is a phrase used descriptively by some to outline specific services provided in certain ways at certain times. By others it is prescriptive and a principle used to judge existing services and model new ones on.

Whether so or not, community care is the new policy which accepts that these same people are fit to live in the community where once they were unable to. Yet it seems that this has been achieved by simply adding the word 'care' to 'community', and doing little else. Community care is more than minimal provision, for as Apte pointed out, hostels in the community can produce just as depersonalizing an environment as the hospitals. To spend all day in a training centre returning at night to a hostel is little more than a two-part institution (Apte 1968).

> To talk of the outside world as 'the community' is to assume a level of social support which may not in fact exist. (Jones, Brown and Bradshaw, 1978)

Community care, as MIND emphasized, is not simply the closure of hospitals with the expectation that patients will find board and lodgings or be cared for by relatives. It is about reintegrating the patient into the community and the provision of opportunities for them to lead independent and fulfilled lives. MIND argue that people should not be expected to live in an institutional environment in the community; for some accommodation is little more than 'wards in streets' or 'mini-hospitals' housing patients who are not actually ill (MIND, 1987).

Yet community care can sometimes mean swapping one institution for another. The data examined on the discharge of patients from the psychiatric hospitals in Nottingham in 1985 show that those patients came mainly from vulnerable social groups. Of the 1825 patients discharged, nearly one-third (571) were over the age of 65. Of the total discharged, 336 (18 per cent) were discharged to places other than their own homes. Sixty per cent of the 336 (or 202 patients) were over 65 years of age and 169 went to either Part III accommodation (now the name of old people's homes) or to private nursing homes. A further 54 went to hostels (Nottingham Psychiatric Case Register; Ovenstone and Bean, 1981). It was not clear, however, how many of those going home later came to be admitted to Part III accommodation or private nursing homes.

Other studies have shown the difficulty in obtaining places for older patients in Part III accommodation − in Nottingham one-third of all patients discharged were over the age of 65 and some had spent many years as in-patients and the data show they received little or no psychiatric contact after their discharges whether they went to other institutions or not. No wonder that the reduction in the number of psychiatric hospital beds is having a serious effect on the ability of Part III accommodation to provide a homelike environment for residents.

It is the burnt-out schizophrenics who are likely to be accommodated straight from hospital, sometimes after decades in care. Their strangeness makes it difficult for them to fit in easily, and this has nothing to do with the prejudice of the other residents, for they are of a generation that has little feeling or understanding of this (Kay and Legg, 1986). However the real issue is that Part III accommodation could not and was never intended to meet such needs, whether in terms of the number or quality of places available.

MIND argue that good housing creates a therapeutic environment in which people can grow and develop and overcome their illness. They cannot do this alone, for they need the same access to services that others have. They also need to have the same expectations, patterns and conditions of life made available as ordinary people (MIND, 1987). Far from being expected to live in an institutional environment in the community, new opportunities are required to give them the chance to live free and independent lives. This same point was also made in the recent Griffiths Report which said community care was aimed at ensuring an optimal quality of life for the individuals leaving hospital (Griffiths Report, 1988). This Report is a landmark as its aim is to review the way in which public funds are used to support community care policy and to advise on options which would improve the use of these funds as a contribution to more effective community care.

The Report's conclusions contained nothing that was not already known to be true, but at least it is an official recognition of the problems. The hope for the future lies in ensuring that:

- the right services are provided in good time, to people who need them most;
- the people receiving help will have a greater say in what is done to help them, and a wider choice;
- people are helped to stay in their own homes for as long as possible, or in as near a domestic environment as possible, so that residential, nursing home and hospital care is reserved for those whose needs cannot be met in any other way (Griffiths Report, 1988).

## THE SOCIAL FUND

In a more practical way the newly introduced social fund (fully implemented on 11 April 1988) might be expected to give support to the aims of community care that the Griffiths Report spoke about. The social fund, replacing the system of supplementary benefit single payments, is to help people with needs arising from exceptional expenses which are difficult to meet from regular income (Becker, Hannan and Hyde, 1988).

The community care grant is intended specifically to promote community care and to help people live as independent a life as possible. It provides certain one-off payments for people leaving institutional care, or by helping them to remain in the community. Such grants are at the discretion of the social fund officer, and are paid from a fixed monthly budget. The priority groups it is aimed to help are the elderly, mentally ill or handicapped, the physically disabled, chronically sick or terminally ill, alcohol and drug addicts, ex-offenders requiring resettlement, people without a settled way of life (i.e. the homeless), families under stress and young people leaving local authority care.

There are numerous grants available, but particularly important to mental patients is the 'start-up grant' which is allocated to enable someone to set themselves up with esssential furniture, bedding and household equipment in an independent setting upon leaving institutional care. To qualify for such a grant the patient must be receiving income support alone; this means that anyone receiving another benefit, like an invalidity allowance, is automatically disqualified. Unfortunately this will include many patients in mental hopsitals. The social fund may only be given to a small group who have need of it.

Similarly it will not help those patients who are discharged to hostels, lodging houses, staffed or group homes etc. To help people to remain in their own homes grants are available to ease exceptional pressures on families under stress. The kind of pressures anticipated may arise through the breakdown of established family relationships; or some deterioration in the home which makes it unfit or unsuitable for someone to live there; or the commencement or continuation of persistent disability or chronic sickness.

The Government claims that the social fund will process all applications within 28 days. This is important to patients discharged from psychiatric hospitals. Even the Griffiths Report pointed out that before the introduction of the social fund there was 'insufficient clarity of responsibility for the arranging of publicly provided services in line with people's needs and service priority' (Griffiths Report, 1988). Indeed, it emphasized the need 'to improve planning and communicaiton between the different bodies, so that the appropriate range of services is readily available to patients when they are discharged from hospital' (Griffiths Report, 1988). Often the procedures are haphazard yet the crucial determinant in the discharge and rehousing of patients is whether they can settle in the community; if there is no proper organization before discharge then community care will not work (Kay and Legg, 1986).

## DISCHARGE PROCEDURES

It would seem that the high re-admisison rates are a direct indication that community care is failing. One reason for failure is that there is a lack of communication between the psychiatrists discharging the patient and those bodies in the community responsible for re-establishing the patient into a community setting. The grand intentions of the social fund will fail if the mechanisms are not aligned to the discharge procedure. For example, in Nottingham 17 patients discharged in 1985 were recorded as having 'no fixed abode' at discharge (Bean and Mounser, 1989). How is it that these patients were allowed to be turned out on to the streets? Clearly there is a gap between the actual discharge and the relevant resettlement organizations providing their support. Kay and Legg are right when they say that no patient should be discharged without suitable housing having been arranged, that this should be after a thorough discussion of various options available to them with the discharging team and that it should include advice about welfare benefits and medication (Kay and Legg, 1986).

However this does not mean that it is desirable to keep patients in hospital longer than they need to be just because housing cannot be found, a situation which could and does arise. In some cases patients may secure independent housing but not have the means to furnish it. The social fund does not work for these people; they are exempt because they are receiving the wrong kind of benefit like invalidity or state pensions. In some cases this amounts to only a few pence more than income support. There has to be some middle ground where sensible decisions are made without undue stress on the patients.

Even if those operating the social fund can reach decisions within 28 days, as they claim they can, that application needs to be made well before the patient is to be discharged from hospital. There are obvious grounds for improvements to be made in the discharge procedure (very little research exists which evaluates this) and in the procedures of social service departments and other resettlement bodies, so that the patients do not have to resort to emergency measures, or find themselves on the streets because of bureaucratic mechanisms which cause delays.

This seems to be what is happening in Nottingham where the community care policy is well advanced through the sectorization of psychiatric services and a positive policy to give psychiatric care in the community. But it can only work if:

- patients have suitable housing arranged for them before discharge;
- financial matters have been discussed with the patient, especially matters related to welfare problems and entitlements, and also problems of outstanding debts;
- discussion is had about future medication and treatment (within the community) and advice is given about the approriate forms of help which are available, i.e. liaison with general practitioners or community psychiatric nurses;
- suitable arrangements for day care are discussed to enable patients to attend if they need and want to, and not be penalized if they choose not to (Kay and Legg, 1986).

Of primary importance to the discharge procedure is the input from the patient; for the patients alone will know of their social situation outside the hospital, and this surely is as important as their medical condition at discharge. Equally the preference of the patients as to the type of accommodation to be arranged for them should be a main consideration, for it is the patients who will have to try to adapt and settle there.

If the patient prefers independent housing, rather than special accommodation, as it seems from some studies to be the case, then efforts ought to be made to provide it. If the housing situation is such that accommodation is scarce, it is the responsibility of the Government to provide sufficient housing to meet the needs they have created by the closure of mental hospitals, especially if it is to foster the concepts of community care that the Griffiths Report presents.

The continued acceptance of homelessness in a prosperous society can only be regarded as a dreadful administrative failure of central and local government, for it is within their power to remedy the situation within a relatively short time. Some would argue that such remedies should have been included as part of the policy for the closure of mental hospitals in the first place.

# REFERENCES

Apte, R.Z. 1968, 'Halfway Houses', *Occasional papers in Social Administration*, Bell.

Bean, P.T. and MacPherson, S. (eds.) 1983, *Approaches to Welfare*, London, Routledge and Kegan Paul.

Bean, P.T. and Mounser, P. 1989, 'Community Care and the discharge of patients from mental hospitals', *Journal of Law, Medicine and Health Care*, vol.17, part 2, Summer.

Becker, S., Hannan, J. and Hyde, S. 1988, *Guide to the Social Fund manual*, Benefits Research Unit, Nottingham.

Brandon, D. 1969, *The Treadmill: a report on common lodging houses*, Christian Aid, London.

Burke, G. 1981, *Housing and social justice: The role of policy in British Housing*, London, Longman.

Cooper, A.B. and Early, D.F. 1961, 'Evolution in the mental hospital', *British Medical Journal*, vol.3, June pp.1600−3.

Donnison, D.V. and Ungerson, C. 1968, 'Trends in residential care 1911−1961', *Social and Economic Administration*, vol. 2, April, pp.75−91.

Durkin, E. 1971, *Hostels for the mentally disordered*, Fabian pamphlet no.24.

Etherington, S. and Bosanquet, N. 1985, *The real crisis in community care*, London, Good Practices in Mental Health.

Glasgow Council for the Single Homeless, 1980, *Homeless men speak for themselves*.

GLC Health Panel, 1984, *Mental Health Services in London*.

Griffiths Report, 1988, *Community Care: Agenda for Action*, report to the Secretary of State for Social Services by Sir Roy Griffiths, London, HMSO.

Hansard 1971, 879, 280−281, (7 December). Written in answer to a question by Dr Stuttaford.

HMSO, 1963, *Health and welfare; the development of community care*, Cmnd 1973, London, HMSO.

HMSO, 1975, *Better Services for the Mentally Ill*, Cmnd 6233, London HMSO.

Jones, K. 1972, *A history of the mental health services*, London, Routledge and Kegan Paul.

Jones, K. 1983, 'Services for the mentally ill: the death of a concept' in Bean, P.T. and MacPherson, S. (eds.), *Approaches to Welfare*, London, Routledge and Kegan Paul.

Jones, K., Brown, J. and Bradshaw J. 1978, *Issues in social Policy*, London, Routledge and Kegan Paul.

Kay, A. and Legg. C. 1986, 'Discharged to the Community; A review of housing and support in London for people leaving psychiatric care', *Good Practice in Mental Health*, February.

Leach, J. and Wing, J. 1980, *Helping destitute men*, London, Tavistock.

MIND, 1987, *Housing — the foundation of community care*, MIND publication.

Nottingham Psychiatric Case Register, 1988, in mimeo.

OPCS 1976, *Hostels and lodgings for single people*, by Wingfield-Digby, P., Office of population Census and Surveys, HMSO.

Ovenstone, I. and Bean, P.T. 1981, 'A medical social assessment of old people's homes in Nottingham', *British Journal of Psychiatry*, vol.139, pp.226—9.

Scull, A. 1973, *Decarceration; community treatment and the radical view*, New York, Prentice Hall.

Shelter, 1969, 'Who are the homeless?' *Face the Facts.*

Wilkinson, A., Galley, R. and Dobkin, L. 1973, *Down and out: problem of single homeless*, Appendix 1, National Advisory Committee of the Young Conservatives.

# PART IV
# NEW DIRECTIONS FOR PLANNERS AND DEVELOPERS

# Introduction

*Taner Oc*

Planners and developers have had difficult relations for decades. The results of a survey published in 1981 showed that 'Planners were least favourable toward development and developers'. Given planning's historical struggle against unregulated development, this was not a surprising find (Howe and Kaufman, 1981). Of course the attitude is mutual; developers have for years blamed planners for stifling development, and enterprise zones and the Government's current measures to deregulate planning stem from years of anti-planning lobbying.

Nathaniel Lichfield in his chapter, 'Dialogue in Development Planning: The Changing Dimension', charts the development of planning after the war, since the introduction of the 1947 Planning Act, which he describes as a planners' charter for creating a better Britain. However the disregard for land values in the early period, it is argued, started the inadequacy of dialogue because planners detached themselves from the things which really interested the developers. Although changes took place in the early 1950s, the gulf between the developers' attitude to planning and the planners' attitude to development has continued and planning education has done nothing to encourage a proper dialogue with developers.

The chapter continues with an outline of policy planning which further alienated developers in the 1960s. They were frustrated by lack of firm guidance when putting forward proposals, and this was compounded by the slow moving planning machinery.

The current move to market-oriented planning with enterprise zones and urban development corporations gives extraordinary freedom to developers, but it castrates planners and forces them into defensive positions. Thus today the advantage is with the developer who is much more sophisticated than his predecessors and has proper professional advice at his service. The dialogue is therefore significantly different from 1947; today there are strong developers and weak planners.

However planning gain is still an important lever available to the local authorities, and developers are willing to oblige as long as they make a reasonable profit. Thus there is a dialogue going on to secure the maximum benefit for the community and maximum profit for the developer. Lichfield proposes a kind of development impact assessment to help the developers and planners understand each other and work towards a mutual goal. This dialogue, based on a certain acceptance of the others' interests, can very often be meaningful. One of the interesting paradoxes of planning is that, just as economic planning in the 1960s was far from being an anti-industry weapon and turned out to be a way of enabling industry to avoid overproduction and supply bottlenecks, so planning at local and county level is often fulfilling the same kind of function. It helps developers avoid the undesirable long-term consequences of their cumulative actions. There will be many issues where planners and developers are in a sense on the same side.

Peter Ambrose outlines the ill effects of current land strategy and argues for a socially responsive control of land development. His strategy is for land conversion with a view to achieving socially sensitive and economically efficient development. The proposal is to designate current structure planning authorities as land and planning authorities so that capital gains by developers and community gains could be held in a certain equilibrium. The philosophy behind his arguments is that rather than control development by public ownership, incentives and conditions for provision of land could and should produce better results. This unfortunately has not happened in the London Docklands area, and as a result the community's needs are not met. Thus the chapter asserts that the future should bring a form of an effective alliance with property capital that is mutually rewarding to the developer and the community.

John Holmes, a planner who recently moved from a local authority to a development company, refers to the confrontational relationship between planners and developers. The chapter, after examining his experiences of local authority practices, outlines the importance of planning permission and guidance expected from the professional in local authorities. Developers' activities are very much constrained by the financing arrangements as well as the attitudes of councils. Current financial arrangements mean that developers work to very tight programmes to realize profits from turnover.

Developers have to take steps to ensure their supply of land and therefore look ahead with private treaty purchases — freehold purchase, conditional contract or an option. However, this involves considerable risk. If the plans produced by local authorities are properly prepared at the draft local plan stage this would reduce risks for the developer. Thus the chapter argues for a better dialogue between the planners and the developers, most of whom employ their own planners. An example is cited where the local authority cooperated to identify possible sites — a significant move from the confrontational relationship.

Currently retailing is going through a certain degree of transformation with many square metres being developed in areas which provide easy access for the car, for example super-stores, DIY stores, carpet and white goods outlets. Retailers are all competing for such sites. The Greater Nottingham Co-operative Society is a large retailer with a development programme which started at the beginning of the decade. Frank Doherty in his chapter describes the Co-operative Society's experience and questions the practices of both the developer and the planner.

If the land for sale belongs to the local authority, the developer negotiates a cash price which means the land comes with planning consent. In the cases where land is in private ownership, the deal often involves planning gain agreements in the form of roads, community buildings, housing and so on. In most British cities experiencing de-industrialization, there is an increasing amount of land available for new developments. Retailing creates the highest land values, so landowners use various ways to obtain permission for retail developments. One way of going about it is by planning applications for change of use to retail; thus in Nottingham land for other uses is not available. The chapter argues for matching the use of land with the need.

There is also a discussion of the evolution of potential sites, which is basically an evaluation of the site's ability to generate a return on capital at an acceptable level of profitability. The financing of such large developments takes many forms. The Greater Nottingham Co-operative Society, as a large retailer, has used a limited number of options open to it, some of which Mr Doherty considers questionable.

The final chapter by Douglas Wright is based on the experience of the Nationwide Housing Trust. The Housing Trust works closely with local authorities and undertakes developments in designated areas. Although, on the whole, the relationships with the planners are mutually rewarding, cases of frustration, due to change of mind on the part of the planners and local authorities, are cited as having wasted a great deal of the Housing

Trust's time. The aims of the Trust are to promote high standards of design; to act as a catalyst; to provide homes for particular sectors of the market, like first-time buyers and the elderly, and finally to achieve these aims through partnerships.

The partnerships entered are with local authorities and with contractors. Most sites are obtained from local authorities and in turn the Trust provides housing that meets the authorities' assessed housing need. In an era of rapidly shrinking local government housing investment, this is a most important partnership. The chapter includes a number of examples of housing schemes developed by the Trust and outlines the arrangements for financing and partnership with developers.

In an age of declining public sector investment in developments of any type, the partnerships between planners and developers assume a very important role. Central government, in its effort to curb local government spending, has made planning gain a more widely practised tool in planning. This is sometimes the only way local authorities can get various infrastructure improvements, or obtain certain community uses. Thus hard gains in terms of roads, buildings and so on are currently a very important factor in planning. It could be argued that this new reality is leading to a more cooperative relationship between planners and developers.

Currently an increasing number of local authorities are realizing the advantages of establishing a positive dialogue with the developers to achieve significant community gains. Enlightened developers are also entering into agreements to provide soft gains, like training facilities, funds for youth centres, increased local employment and other arrangements, for communities in various parts of the country. Since local authorities cannot sell planning permission, it is essential that the relations with developers are not confrontational and are based on good will. Likewise developers have a duty to honour their agreements although they are not legally binding. Failure to do so would mean a return to the difficult relations of the recent past.

## REFERENCE

Howe, E. and Kaufman, J. 1981, 'The Values of Contemporary American Planners', *Journal of American Planning Association*, vol.47, no.3, July.

# 15

# Dialogue in development planning: the changing dimension

*Nathaniel Lichfield*

While developers and planners appear in practice to be on opposite sides of the fence, they are wedded together, until death do them part, because they are both fundamentally engaged in development. It is the lifeblood of the developer's industry. For the planner, it is the raw material which he needs to mould, stimulate, control, encourage or discourage in making the plan for his community. In the implementation of the plan he makes his enduring impact at that moment when the development is being formulated, planned and carried out. It is for this reason that the traditional term 'town planning' is less meaningful than 'development planning' or 'planned development'.

This common bond in marriage has arisen from the facts of human evolution. In this, human settlements are relatively new, it being only some ten thousand years since the beginning of urbanization. The planning of settlements is perhaps some four thousand years old starting with the Egyptians and Greeks. But it was only in this century that the reaction to the squalor of urbanization following the industrial revolution led to the introduction of government statutory planning. This has grown to the formidable urban and regional planning system of the present day.

In this there is a well accepted logic. Faced with the continuing growth and renewal of settlements, government urban and regional planning aims to improve the quality of urban services for people beyond what would otherwise be provided by the market. It is also generally accepted that such government-led planning should be able to make an improvement over the market process but in practice it does not necessarily do so.

One of the many reasons for the failures, both in the content of plans and their implementation, stems from the difficulties of both partners in this marriage in recognizing, understanding and appreciating the role of the other. As in all marriages, coherent dialogue between the partners is essential. It is the theme of this chapter that the nature of this dialogue has been, since the Second World War, to the detriment of both development and planning.

## POST-WAR PLANNING – THE 1947 ACT

The 1947 Town and Country Planning Act addressed itself to the inadequacies of the pre-war planning system (see Lichfield and Darin-Drabkin, 1980 ch.5, and Parker, 1985). This system was regulatory and not positive. The landowner had development rights which could not be infringed without compensation. This gave rise to fears of enormous financial liability at the local level which distorted the plan-making process; there were significant difficulties in collection of offsetting betterment.

To overcome this, the 1947 Town and Country Planning Act resolved the compensation-betterment problem by the following changes:

- the negative pre-war planning scheme was replaced by the development plan; this reflected the immediate post-war preoccupation with the need for economizing and programming in a situation of limited resources;
- the landowners' development rights were compulsorily nationalized for a predetermined global sum with interest, and returned to the landowner only through a specific planning permission;
- since the rights had been nationalized, the permission was accompanied by a betterment tax which returned to the state the full development value from the permission.

It also introduced positive planning by the public sector, either direct or in partnership; since public authorities could acquire land at current use values they were able to earn the increase in development values.

This planners' charter for a transformed post-war Britain led to one undesirable consequence: the planners mistakenly thought that both actual and potential land values could be disregarded. (For a statement of what they could obtain from not doing so see Lichfield, 1956.) They thought there was no need for local authorities to compensate for restricting development rights, because Government picked up the tab for their nationalization. This disrupted the dialogue: the landowners' expectations of reaping increased development values were removed, and with them went their willingness to collaborate in the development process; the early post-war developers could see little prospect for their operations in the slack economy. Therefore the private sector played little role in immediate post-war development.

While the 1947 Town and Country Planning Act planning system persists in many of its principles, it has been subject to a variety of changes, reflecting the evolution of the social, economic and political post-war Britain (see Reade, 1987; Ambrose, 1986 and Ravetz, 1980). There have been five significant aspects of change relating to the financial system, local planning, use of discretion, the development industry and market orientation. These will be discussed below.

## THE FINANCIAL SYSTEM

The symmetry of the 1947 Act was undermined in the early 1950s at its most controversial point: development rights remained nationalized, and landowners were not given the statutory legal rights to development which they had before the War, in town planning schemes, but they did not, as under the 1947 Act, have to buy the rights by a betterment tax, and obtained them free of charge with the planning permission.[1] However a subtle compromise was reached in that the compensation provisions were not removed, so that landowners still have no rights to compensation if development permission is refused. This both reduced the financial burden of refusal on the local authorities but meant great financial windfalls for the developer on grant of permission, on which there was no betterment levy nor, to begin with, capital gains tax. A later provision, in the 1959 Town and Country Planning Act, increased the costs on local authorities over that of the 1947 Act, in that they were required to pay market price and not current use value on their land acquisition.

This situation has by and large continued despite the two short-lived Labour Government attempts at revival. In reaction, this abandonment of betterment, together with the increasing financial straits of local government, has led to growth in the practice of planning gain, which can be construed as a betterment tax in kind.

## LOCAL DEVELOPMENT PLANNING

With the growth in the private sector, and relaxation over controls on land release, the concept of local development programming of the early 1960s became more difficult to visualize and carry out. This was accompanied by the perceived need for a different form of statutory planning. In 1965 the Planning Advisory Group (PAG) recommended a new system of development planning and their views were implemented in the 1968 Town and Country Planning Act. The development plan as originally conceived was translated into an outline (structure) plan and the more action-oriented local plans.[2] But nonetheless, just as the term 'town planning' has fondly persisted so has the term 'development plan', despite the fact that neither accurately describes the activities currently carried out under their names.

A further blow to development planning was given in the playing down of physical planning in the 1960s. The Schuster Report drew attention to the limitations of physical planning dominated by the development professions. This led to increased contributions from planners from other disciplines, in particular from the social sciences. But while these considerably enriched the content of planning, they overshot in one respect. They assumed that physical and land use plans were necessarily without any socio-economic content. In consequence they undermined the physical emphasis in planning and pushed planning towards making wide-ranging proposals across the field of social and economic policies.

The culmination of this was in policy planning. This made its own kind of contribution to the breakdown in the dialogue. Developers intent on physical development would be confronted with policies, which were often mutually conflicting, capable of many interpretations and difficult to pin down in practice. This in itself was healthy, but not when policies are taken to be more than directions in which the authorities wish to go, and more than mere guidelines to the decisions they will make on application. The situation is aggravated when, as so often happens, the policy planner fails to take account of the 'other material considerations' which are required under the 1971 Town and Country Planning Act, Section 29.

## THE MISUSE OF DISCRETION

A key feature of the post-war planning system which has been retained is the great discretion given to local and central planning authorities to determine each case on its merits without being rigidly bound by the plans themselves. Administered correctly, this is a great boon to both planners and developers, for it enables each situation to be judged in the light of contemporary circumstances. This is better than having, as in pre-war Britain and in much of the world today, statutory schemes which spell out fairly rigidly restrictions in zoning for development into the distinct future.

But the system needs favourable conditions for its sensible use. These have been gradually eroded under various influences. There is a considerable time lag in the approval and review of plans, so that the guidelines to the discretion became steadily dated, and thereby all the weaker. The 'other material considerations' have become more and more politicized in local and central government, so that the 'best use of land' becomes more and more detached from the advice from the professional planning process. The discretion requires an academic and professional infrastructure for its defensible use, something which has been very slow to evolve.

## THE EVOLUTION OF A SOPHISTICATED DEVELOPMENT INDUSTRY

Before the Second World War the mature development industry of today did not exist. This industry cut its teeth in the post-war redevelopment of town centres, where it showed a tendency for innovation which led the planners. As part of the making and losing of fortunes, there was a restless, entrepreneurial innovation which has led the way in tranforming the urban environment. But being profit-oriented, the transformations have tended to be confined to the private sector's shops, offices, and commerce to the neglect of social uses and infrastructure.

But this has been changing under the impact of planning gain pressures and the frenetic competition in securing the planning permits. The weight on the dialogue has shifted in this respect towards the planners (Lichfield, 1989).

# FROM GOVERNMENT-LED TO MARKET-ORIENTED PLANNING

In the 1970s and the 1980s, the context for planning changed dramatically in at least two ways, both of which tended to give greater weight to the developers in the dialogue:

1. There was a change in the economic climate from growth and full employment to stagnation and high unemployment. Thus, in the less prosperous parts of the country at least, planning began to be employment-led.
2. There was a shift towards the market and against central intervention and control in all aspects of socio-economic life, including urban and regional planning. In place of government-led planning there emerged market-oriented planning. While this meant a healthy recognition of the important role of the development industry, and 'lifted the burden' of controls in desirable ways, it led to a weakening of some necessary controls.
3. In some quarters the reaction against the planners' control has led developers to wish for a revival of the greater certainty which existed in Britain in the inter-war planning schemes and which still prevails in most parts of the world. In certain areas simplified zoning would be laid down with the presumption, if it were followed, that permission would be granted. In this way the planners' area of discretion is reduced, although the developer loses the advantage of having his site 'taken on its merits'.

Generally speaking, the presumption has moved towards the grant of planning permission with the onus on the planners of showing sound reasons for refusal. This is as it should be, for landowners and developers have an inherent right to develop their property, provided they do so in a manner which accords with the machinery of social control created under development and planning law. In relation to development clearly come the relevant development codes for infrastructure, traffic access, and so on, and also the need to ensure minimum standards of development, layout, light and air, and landscaping. In relation to planning, there is the need to avoid externalities, namely the costs the developer does not have to bear but which fall on others. In shopping centre development, questions must be raised like whether there is adequate provision on the developer's land for car parking, and whether he should make a contribution to the cost of road improvements required off-site. In the case of new housing development, it is important to establish whether the location will give rise to public expense in the provision of roads, infrastructure and social services ahead of the local authority programme.

However it may be that the presumption has now gone too far in favour of development. A recent formula from the Department of the Environment states that permission should be granted '... unless that development would cause demonstrable harm to interests of acknowledged importance' (Planning Policy Guidance Note No.1, para 15, HMSO, 1988). This raises difficulties of interpretation. First, at what point does harm become not demonstrable? Second, at what point are interests which are harmed not of acknowledged importance? Should not the criterion instead be the balancing of the net benefit from the development itself against the net disbenefit from the external costs imposed on the community?

## DIALOGUE IN THE 1990s

While the immediate post-war development planning system was the basis for a good dialogue, the start was shaky for a number of reasons. It was undermined by subsequent events affecting both planning and development separately, which weakened mutual understanding and affected the dialogue in various often conflicting ways.

In the 1980s there is a greater recognition of the fundamental partnership of both planners and developers. Planners are reacting against policy planning and towards development planning. At the same time the developers, despite their greater muscle, are accepting the benefits of some logical planning framework as opposed to the free-run market freedoms, at least for the other developers if not themselves.

This brings out a curious dichotomy in the minds of the developers in relation to planning control. While each landowner or developer clearly seeks the maximum freedom on his own site, he is fully aware of the danger to his investment if there is insufficient control over its environment. A new shopping centre, based on careful feasibility analysis, could be undermined by permission for later shopping centres of more modern layout. A new housing development requires control of the local environment to ensure prohibition of uses which could be a potential nuisance for residential amenitites.

This aspect of the planning system became notoriously obvious in the course of the Labour Government's ban on new offices in London in the 1960s. It was introduced to control the growth of office employment, long-distance commuting and traffic congestion. Potential developers suffered, but the owners of established offices found that they had windfall gains because the limitation of supply increased the market value of their holdings.

In the dialogue the advantage is now with the developers, owing to their strength, sophistication, power, command of professional expertise, influence on economic growth and political support from the enterprise economy. By contrast the planning authorities are in a relatively poor state because they are bewildered as to their true role in government; planning officers are undermined by politics at local level and by the impatience if not hostility towards planning and local government at the central level.

## IMPACT EVALUATION AS A BASIS FOR DIALOGUE

If the dialogue is to be improved, there is clearly a need for an improved understanding on both sides of their respective roles and also of their complete mutual dependency.

Development requires a coordinated public infrastructure of utilities, roads, and so on; the maintenance of good neighbourliness to protect investment; protection from unfair competition and instability which follow unrestrained market-led planning. All are music to the planners' ears. And the planning system needs a healthy development process, of adequate quantity, of adequate quality, run professionally with competent professional advice, all music to the developers' ears. In essence, development today must be good development and also good planning. Successful development is that which scores best on both counts, and achieves neither at the unacceptable expense of the other.

A useful basis for the dialogue is the recognition that any development has to be seen not only in its conventional *on-site* context, the traditional and often the only concern of the developer himself, but also in its ramifications *off-site*. The good developer needs to know just what the impacts of his development will be on the surrounding community, whether beneficial or adverse, so that he can take them into account. An unhealthy social, economic and natural environment for his development can only be bad for his investment.

Thus the dialogue should start with an understanding of each proposal in terms of its implications for the urban and regional system. This can be done in simple terms at the everyday level of discussion. It needs to be done in more complex terms if the scale and kind of development necessitates some kind of development impact assessment. (For an illustration see Smith and Lichfield, 1987.)

But whatever the scale of the proposed development, the understanding of the implications on both sides could be increased if the documentation submitted with the planning application went beyond the minimum requirement of the statutory forms, necessary plans and perhaps the descriptive letter. There should also be a report or memorandum which both describes the development itself in terms of its content, and the change which that content will make by way of impacts on the physical, social, economic, natural and cultural environments. In addition, there could be a statement on the planning case for the development, arguing why the authority should give planning permission, even if the proposal contravenes the authority's plans or policies.

This will improve the dialogue in several ways. The developer will be stimulated to think through his proposals, in terms of both development and planning; and the documentation would make it easier for the planning authority members, officers, official consultees and neighbours to understand the proposal. It would ensure that the planning officer's report would describe the development with the benefit of the applicant's own submissions. It could be the basis for obtaining from the public informed views as opposed to possible misapprehension.

Impact assessment of this kind will receive encouragement from the 1988 Regulations relating to Environmental Assessment, originating from the Directive of the EEC (Lichfield, 1989). While these are compulsory only for the particular classes of large-scale projects (Schedule 1) they are already entering the scene for other projects with significant impact (Schedule 2), and in some cases they are being volunteered by developers who recognize the value of the dialogue which results from presenting their proposals in this way rather than waiting until they are required to do so.

## CONCLUSION

In brief, after some 40 years of post-war innovative planning, the dialogue between the planners and the developers is by no means as mature and stable as it should be.

It is recognized that part of the reason is the gulf between the developers' attitude to planning and the planners' attitude to development. It is also recognized that the weakness may be due to gaps in planning education which have failed to equip the typical planning officer to pursue dialogue with developers. Many planners still find the development game a mystery, much to the financial benefit of developers and of planning and development consultants. To many planners, developers and valuers are hostile forces to be kept at arm's length and treated with suspicion and condemnation. Typically, but not always, the planners show little tendency to collaborate with the developers to secure good development.

But the planners have the moral strength that comes from attempting to achieve for the community some of the benefits from development, and avoiding its disbenefits. With the hunger of developers for permissions, and their ability to give up part of their profits in a bull market, the planners and their authorities have secured a position of strength in terms of bargaining for permissions and achievement of planning gain.

The prospects for improved dialogue between planner and developer will be greater if it is recognized that there is no necessary identity of interest between the various components of the development industry. The development industry includes both landowners and developers in addition to contractors, financiers, and suchlike. Landowners and developers have different functions. By definition, the developer is entrepreneurial and risk-taking in large enterprises, for which he legitimately earns a developer's profit. On the other hand the landowner is comparatively passive in his contribution to the process and this is why so many doubts have been expressed over the centuries about whether the increase in land value should accrue to him or the community.

Thus the dialogue needs to differentiate between the two. The developer, in producing the goods and services which are so vital to the growth and development of the country, tends in the process of land assembly to be in friction with the landowner. It was this friction which made the Community Land Act potentially a developers' charter. It offered the prospects of the local authorities taking over the hassle of land assembly and then offering the developers the opportunity to bid for what they needed for their trade: land at the right place, right time and right price.

But that Act has gone. Will a new land policy emerge to rationalize land assembly in the interests of development?

# NOTES

1   It is a daunting thought to contemplate the following: if the rights had not been denationalized in 1952 by the Conservative administration, what would the global investment in compensation of £350 000 (capital + interest at 1948 prices) have earned for the Government since then at current prices in accrued betterment tax on permissions, and would still earn in potential tax into the indefinite future. The computation still awaits the interested researcher.

2   The original concept of development plans also had this distinction between outline and detailed development plans, which bore a striking resemblance to the structure and local plans of the 1968 Act (see Cullingworth, 1987, p.251).

# REFERENCES

Ambrose, P. 1986, *Whatever Happened to Planning?*, Methuen, London.

Cullingworth, 1987, *Environmental Planning 1939–1969*, vol.1, London, HMSO.

Lichfield, N. 1956, Economics of Planned Development, London, *The Estates Gazette*.

Lichfield, N. 1988, 'Environmental Impact Assessment and Project Appraisal in Britain', *Project Appraisal*, vol.3, no.3.

Lichfield, N. 1989, 'From Planning Gain to Community Benefit', *Journal of Planning and Environmental Law*, February pp.68–81.

Lichfield, N. and Darin-Drabkin, H. 1980, *Land Policy in Planning*, Allen & Unwin, London.

Parker, R.H. 1985, 'From Uthwatt to DLT, The end of the road?', *The Planner*, April, vol.71, no.4.

Ravetz, A. 1980, *Remaking Cities: Contributions of the Recent Urban Environment*, Croom Helm, London.

Reade, E. 1987, *British Town and Country Planning*, Open University Press, Milton Keynes.

Smith, G. and Lichfield, D. 1987, 'Large Scale Private Developments: The Role of the Development Planner', *Built Environment*, vol.12, no.4.

# 16
# An alternative land strategy

*Peter Ambrose*

The purpose of this chapter is to put forward an alternative strategy for the management of the flow of development land. The current system, dating from 1947, suffers from a number of serious defects (Ambrose, 1986). In particular, all land use control regimes implemented so far in the UK have permitted trading and speculation in land before its conversion to higher value uses. This is as detrimental to the efficient production of the new built environment as would be speculation in building materials before their use in construction. It means that intermediate interests cream off some of the initial investment, whether from public or private sources, committed to the construction of new environment with a consequent reduction in the ratio of investment to new construction. This relationship could be conceived as the investment:output conversion ratio, and it is obviously in nearly everyone's interest that it should be maximized (Ambrose and Barlow, 1986).

These weaknesses cause a number of disadvantages:

1. Windfall gains from land trading and speculation are inadequately recouped to the public purse by taxation.
2. Small capital builders and self-providers are often squeezed out by volume producers in the scramble for land in high pressure areas.
3. Local authorities have little or no control over the type of jobs attracted to an area or the price characteristics of new or converted housing because they have no leverage mechanisms to affect the social content of development.
4. Local and public authorities have to rely on *ad hoc* deals with developers and housebuilders concerning the cost of infrastructure

provision for such things as roads, sewers and schools.

5. The construction industry is chronically under-capitalized compared to other industries of similar significance here and in the rest of Europe (Ball, 1983).

6. Housing provision is not smoothly geared to employment growth. There are labour recruitment problems in some areas stemming partly from bottlenecks in housing supply, and this has held back the economic development of certain growth areas such as central Berkshire (Barlow and Savage, 1986).

## AIMS OF A REFORMED SYSTEM

The key aim should be to get land from one use into another, for example agriculture into housing, or derelict industrial into commercial use. This would be in line with socially responsible and democratically agreed principles serving as far as possible both social needs and equity on the one hand and economic and productive efficiency on the other. The object should be to do this at minimum public cost in terms of both revenue and capital expenditure, and with no scope whatsoever for speculative gain out of land itself. This should not however preclude a fair level of private sector profit and a secure investment environment for the construction industry — indeed it should be an aim of policy to produce and preserve these conditions.

Given these aims it does not follow that large-scale public ownership of land is necessary. Past experience has shown generalized public appropriation of land to be expensive, politically explosive, and in any case beset with legal and valuation problems. It is much more sensible to work within political constraints and seek for solutions that are acceptable to a wide range of interests both public and private.

## THE SOCIAL ECONOMIC AND POLITICAL CONSTRAINTS

It follows that it is pointless to draw up grand theoretical schemes for the socially responsive control of land development unless they have a realistic chance of implementation. The UK has a social, cultural and political history which is particularly 'rightist' compared with the rest of Western Europe, especially in terms of ideologies of property ownership and in relation to the jealously guarded autonomy of the City. These are both contextual factors of great importance.

In recent decades, and since 1975−76 in particular, there have been severe long-term economic difficulties and a marked retreat from Keynesian solutions. This means that it is also pointless to develop theoretical solutions that depend on large-scale increases in public expenditure because there will not be any. Solutions which appear to give a good chance of saving public money, like those advanced here, have a much better chance of success.

Nearly all the inputs of the construction process − finance, materials, plant, labour and land − are in private ownership. It is true that much land in Docklands was in the notionally public ownership of bodies such as the Port of London Authority, but this has turned out to be socially meaningless. Inevitably, therefore, new strategies for land development must take account of the opportunities for profit for private capital as well as the interests of users of the built environment.

Without a realistic prospect of profits, and in an increasingly multinational development scene, private sector interests will not cooperate in reform. Nor will they be willing to invest on the scale required both to produce new development and to update their technologies and labour practices. Given all these constraints the parrot-cry of 'nationalize it all' is a pointless self-indulgence. Any effective strategy has to involve some kind of deal.

## A LAND AND PLANNING AUTHORITY

The strategy advanced here is based on the view that public ownership is a separate issue from democratically accountable and socially sensitive control of development. Public ownership is a valuable tool to achieve control but it is required only at certain stages of the land conversion process. It is thus an error to see long-term public freeholding as an end in itself.

In essence, the proposed strategy would make it illegal to carry out any land conversion or intensification of its use on land other than that acquired from the relevant land and planning authority (LPA). The effect would be to make the LPAs the sole legal providers of development land.

Clearly much would depend on the competence and democratic legitimacy of the new LPAs and their composition and powers would need to be very fully discussed. As a starting point it would seem sensible for them to operate at the county or structure planning level and to be largely composed of elected county and district councillors, but with a strong minority presence of appropriate private sector, officer, and central government interests appointed by the Secretary of State.

Their main task would be twofold — to develop a structure planning framework and to ensure a land supply, at lowest public cost, so that plans developed within this framework could be effectively implemented. The aim should be to avoid the conflicts between levels of government which undermined former schemes and ultimately contributed to the demise of the 1968 Land Commission and the 1975 Community Land Scheme (Ambrose, 1976; Boddy, 1978).

## NEW LAND SUPPLY ARRANGEMENTS

The identification of land needs for socially sensitive and economically efficient development would rest, as now, with the two-tier, planning system. But it would need some reorganization of practices and philosophies and more capacity to carry out proper research on needs. The restoration of the Metropolitan authorities including, of course, one for London would be a prerequisite since the LPAs would need to operate on a city-wide level.

To carry out the role of sole land providers, the LPAs would need compulsory acquisition powers. These are long established, but the big problem that has not been solved is that of acquisition price. This should be existing use value, plus a sweetener — say plus 25 per cent or plus 50 per cent. The sweetener would be a recognition that unwilling vendors may have lost large-scale potential capital gains by the introduction of the scheme.

A transition stage would have to be managed to protect the interests of people holding land for which they had paid a price with built-in hope value. Incidentally, large staff resources in the Inland Revenue should be released because all the time spent trying to recoup betterment under most post-war tax regimes would be saved. Neither compensation nor betterment would arise under this system because land for planned development would be acquired by the LPAs and passed on for development at cost plus a mark up to cover administrative expenses.

Sites coming on stream for planned development would now be exclusively in the LPA's ownership. There are four main possibilities for the next step in the land conversion process:

- the LPA or a lower-tier local authority (or a district) could promote development itself;
- the land could be leased to a private sector promoter;
- the freehold could be sold to a private sector promoter;
- a long lease could be sold to a private sector promoter.

The choice of promotion mode would be made to suit the mutual convenience and financial capabilities of the partners in the development. For example, the first possibility provides only building contracts for the construction industry; the second provides contract work plus a rental share to private entrepreneurs and a ground rent for the LPA. Ideally this would be related to revenue growth from the scheme to the LPA. The third option provides a once-for-all capital sum for the LPA and all other forms of benefit to the private sector; and the last provides a similar split of benefits which are renegotiated on expiry of the loan.

Clearly in practice an almost infinitely variable combination of these modes is possible. What are crucial are the *terms* in which agreements are made and the achievement of both a sensible ratio of risk to reward opportunity for the private sector and an appropriate return to the public interest in the form of the LPA. The representation of a wide range of interests on the LPA boards should help to ensure this.

## THE NEW STRATEGY IN PRACTICE – A HOUSE BUILDING EXAMPLE

If a piece of land were being processed for private sector house building on fringe land, the site could be made available, via the LPA, at a *base price* calculated as follows:

LPA acquisition price (existing use value) say £2000 per acre
plus 50 per cent mark-up to vendor
plus cost of infrastructure for house building
plus administrative cost mark-up of, say, 50 per cent to the LPA
= base price of infrastructural land to house builder, say *£20 000 per acre*.

However, for land to be released at the base price the house builder would have to agree to being bound legally to complete the construction within a given time, say, three years, and to offer the houses for first sale in accordance with the price profile laid down by the LPA. This first sale price would be registered, and subsequent sales would be at the initial price updated by an appropriate house price inflator. Any failure to agree to these pre-specifications would not necessarily prevent the disposal, but would entail a very sharp increase in the disposal price and subsequent failure to meet the conditions would lead to either a large fine or the repossession of the completed, or part-completed, development under some appropriate legal arrangements.

The scheme could work in much the same way in the case of land disposed of for retail development by leasing according to the second or fourth options above. The base ground rent or sale price would be well below current market levels but would be conditional on some LPA control over retailing content, housing or other gain. Ground rents would be reviewed closely in relation to rack rental growth, ideally every five years or so.

If land were disposed of for industrial schemes, the base release terms would be conditional on such issues as the number of jobs to be created per acre, the skill or gender characteristics of the labour force required, and some legal commitment about the length of time the employing enterprises would remain in the area.

The whole philosophy here is not to control development processes by means of the ownership of public freehold which would be expensive, and almost certainly ineffective. The strategy is to exert control using a mixture of incentives and conditions at the crucial point of land provision by the monopoly provider. The incentives and conditions are legal and financial in nature, unlike the present crude dependence on use control. They could be infinitely calibrated to meet local needs and even to some extent the changing needs end of the construction industry itself.

## BENEFITS FOR THE PRIVATE SECTOR

These procedures would create what might be called 'an attractive planning-related investment environment' for property and finance capital. The development industry would benefit in a number of ways.

There would be an end to the costly and anarchic scramble for land in growth areas. The LPAs would be the sole agencies to approach when seeking sites for development.

seeking sites for development.

There would be a drastic reduction in land costs and ground rents for housing land in high-pressure areas. A reduction from, say, £1m or more per acre to around £20 000 per acre base price is quite plausible. Builders could avoid the conditions on resale prices, but only at the cost of paying perhaps near-current prices for land from the LPA (which would provide a healthy surplus for the body) and having their product outpriced by other builders who had acquired land at base price.

Infrastructure costs would be borne by the LPA since an element to cover these costs would be built into the LPA base price; there would therefore be no need to devote resources to negotiation over this element.

There would be a more assured market for the final product, whether it be housing, retail, or industrial space, because the development would be in accordance with LPA and district planners' calculations about needs in the area. Promoters of all kinds of development could be kept well informed of these calculations and the procedures by which development requirements in the area are assessed. To some extent, they could be invited to participate in these procedures themselves.

A fair rate of return on the capital invested in development, whether for sale or for leasing, would be assured. Private sector economic realities would be taken into account in the conditions and reflected in the base price at which land was released for development; if the potential returns to private investment in an area were perceived by the market to be too low (perhaps because very low-price housing was required in an economically depressed area) then some updated form of urban development grant should be available. But given the extremely low land costs under the proposals, a UDG should be necessary only in exceptional cases.

Another possible policy measure which could be applied, together with the LPA strategy, would be to offer the construction industry some security. This could take the form of a bipartisan commitment to, say a seven-year programme of public expenditure on infrastructure and housing renewal. It is generally agreed that this is necessary, and both the industry and academic observers are united in calling for it. However if this were introduced without the reforms under discussion in this chapter, much of the public money involved might leak away, mainly in support of land speculation. Under the new practices proposed, there is a much better chance that the investment will more effectively be turned into new construction.

## AREAS WITH SPECIAL NEEDS

Given even the radical set of reforms outlined above, some emergency powers may well be necessary for especially run-down areas. One move would be a greater use of, and therefore funding for, LPA promotion in these areas. Urban development corporations may well be useful in special cases so long as the boards have a majority presence of locally elected members on secondment. But it seems likely that any special and almost by definition externally imposed agencies are likely, sooner or later, to come into counterproductive conflict with the LPAs. Such conflicts have undermined the efforts of earlier externally imposed bodies such as new town corporations, the Land Commission, bodies associated with the Community Land Scheme and, most recently, the London Docklands Development Corporation.

By contrast, enterprise boards, largely centrally funded, might have a place in difficult areas. Their functions of providing capital and business expertise would be complementary to rather than in conflict with, the LPAs, whose efforts would be mainly directed towards the rational production of the built environment.

## GENERAL BENEFITS

If a scheme such as that outlined in this chapter were implemented it would produce a number of benefits. First, there would be an end to speculation and dealing in land itself. Second, there would be an end to the vast un-taxed windfall gains of vendors. Third, there would be integration of the present system of two-tier planning with the provision of an appropriate flow of development land. Fourth, there would be land disposals on self-financing or mildly profitable terms for the LPAs. Fifth, the construction industry would acquire land on extremely attractive terms for as long as promoters carried out the planning intentions. Sixth, public control over local housing costs and employment opportunities would be far more sensitive than at present. Urban development grants and enterprise boards could be used to provide extra incentives for promoters in areas with special problems. Seventh, given a bipartisan commitment to long-term infrastructural investment, there would be a more secure investment environment for the construction industry. In addition to all these advantages, the scheme would have much electoral mileage — very few people love land speculators.

## CONCLUSION

This general strategy might well deserve careful consideration by house builders, commercial developers, surveyors, finance and lending interests, and building contractors, as well as planners, local politicians and representatives of central government. It is very important that any such discussion should include commentators or practitioners expert in land development practices in, at least, Sweden, France and West Germany. Well informed Swedish participation would be especially necessary because the scheme described here has much in common with current practices in Sweden (Dickens et al 1985; Duncan, 1986).

The UK planning system, right from its legislative inception in 1947, has failed to implement the land nationalization strategies recommended in the wartime Uthwatt Reports (Parker, 1985). It has certainly never solved the land problem. Economic values have been publicly created and privately appropriated — mostly by vendors and dealers. Uthwatt would now be too radical for most people's taste. But a rational, social democratic solution, along the lines proposed in this chapter, is perfectly possible and it might well command a wide measure of support (see also Ambrose, 1986). In this respect as in others, the UK should begin to catch up with the better practices evident elsewhere in Europe. 1992 is not far ahead.

## REFERENCES

Ambrose, P. 1976, *The Land Market and the Housing System*, Urban and Regional Studies Working Paper no.3, University of Sussex.

Ambrose, P. 1986, *Whatever Happened to Planning?* Methuen, London.

Ambrose, P. and Barlow, J. 1986, *Housing Provision and Housebuilding in Western Europe: Increasing Expenditure, Decreasing Output*, Urban and Regional Studies Working Paper no.50, University of Sussex.

Ball, M. 1983, *Housing Policy and Economic Power*, Methuen, London.

Barlow, J. and Savage, M. 1986, 'The politics of growth: cleavage and conflict in a Tory heartland', *Capital and Class*, vol.38, Winter 1986, pp.156–182.

Boddy, M. 1978, 'Community Land Scheme is dying of neglect', *Roof*, May.

Dickens, P. et al 1985, *Housing, States and Localities*, Methuen.

Duncan, S. 1986, 'House-building, profits and social efficiency in Sweden and Britain', *Housing Studies*, vol.1, no.1, January.

Parker, H. 1985, 'From Uthwatt to DLT — the end of the road?' *The Planner*, April, vol.71, no.4.

# 17

# Housing developments and planners

*John Holmes*

This chapter presents a view of the relationship between local planning authorities and developers by someone who has worked in both sectors. Surprisingly working for a housing developer involves as much if not more town planning as working in a local government planning department although there is much less concern with procedural and administrative requirements. Many developers see the relationship between themselves and local planning authorities as confrontational and share the view of planners expressed by Tom Baron (1984) that they are obstructive, unimaginative, slow, and interested only in the administrative procedures for their own sake. Why should there be this confrontational relationship?

## VARIATION IN LOCAL AUTHORITY PRACTICES

There is a surprising variety in approaches adopted by local planning authorities both towards policy making and implementation. It cannot be assumed that there is a fairly consistent theme running through the whole planning system. Although policies applicable to green belts, to areas of outstanding natural beauty, the highest quality farmland, to conservation areas and so on, are directly related to nationally established views and policies, and local flexibility of interpretation is therefore limited, this consistency does not extend to other issues.

A few examples will illustrate the variation. One local planning authority might have a policy which requires 10 per cent of all housing sites to be reserved for open space; another might insist on there being a children's play area on every housing site; another might look for 5 per cent open space provision, and yet another will have no fixed standard at all. One structure plan will talk of quarter of an acre for every 50 dwellings for open space while another does not mention local open space provision. Some local planning authorities are quite happy to see DIY stores on industrial estates, while others will not accept them at all. One local planning authority will want all its housing developments tightly grouped around small informal access roads; another will be constantly seeking space with greater emphasis on the public garden area than on the private space of each dwelling.

Of course the last example is partly a matter of design and there is clearly a need for regional variation on design issues, but these examples can be the basis of the confrontation which so often has occurred. It is difficult to appreciate why the play and open space requirements of children in Essex should be significantly different from those living elsewhere. It is even more baffling why a particular size and design of road in say Essex can safely access up to 400 dwellings where the same road in Leicestershire is held to be capable of handling only 100 dwelling units.

So perhaps a plea for more consistency in approach is appropriate, certainly on fundamental land use issues. It seems remarkably crude to require a blanket percentage of any site to be devoted to open space. That is simply taking town planning and landscape design out of the hands of skilled professionals and handing them over to an administrator.

## VARIATIONS WITHIN A DEPARTMENT

Unfortunately an absence of consistency can exist not only from one local planning authority to another but also within one department. For example it is often important to discuss an intended project, sometimes in confidence, with the local planning authority before a planning application is submitted. However most local planning authorities have divided their departments into particular sections or divisions — policy, local plans and development control, for example.

A recent example of this concerned the possibility of building a diner or bar-grill. This proposal was on a site adjacent to a trunk road with an existing access but there was no allocation in the local plan, certainly not for a diner. This was discussed with the head of the policy team, after giving prior notice of the subject so that any internal discussion necessary could have taken place. The comments received were favourable, the application was made, there were objections from the highway authority, but no policy objections. However the recommendation to committee from the development control officer in charge was to refuse the application on grounds which related to issues of policy.

While it is understandable that an officer's initial view may be rejected by a committee, it is quite unacceptable for initial views expressed quite clearly on behalf of the planning officer to change before they reach the members. When this happens it raises doubts about the professional credibility of planners.

The ubiquitous planning brief can also be less advantageous than the guidance it should bring suggests, particularly where it arrives on the scene as part of a planning permission. Planning briefs, now widely used, often cause difficulty despite the fact that they are supposed to be a source of helpful guidance.

Some local planning authorities are more fond than others of supplementing their permissions with sometimes quite detailed interpretations as to how a particular site is to be developed. Again the principle is fine but consistency of approach is crucial. It is of no help at all to a developer if issues not covered in pre-submission discussions are suddenly introduced in a planning brief allied to a condition. Surprising as it may seem, a developer's assessment of the value of a site is reached only after an exhaustive, usually quite sophisticated, study of the various factors involved.

## ATTITUDES OF THE DEVELOPERS

The economic appraisal of any proposal at Wilson Bowden is computerized, clever and quick. The actual acquisition of a site can take place in a variety of ways — by private treaty or by tender or auction. To purchase by tender or auction the economic appraisal has to have been carried out thoroughly as there is clearly no room for manoeuvre once the transaction has been completed. In the majority of cases a planning permission will exist, conditions will be identified and the planning brief may have been prepared. In such a situation therefore, the prudent potential purchaser will build all the known constraints into his equation, but crucially he has to prepare his scheme, which for the sake of argument is assumed to be a housing project, in order to make an assessment of the likely ultimate value of the development.

The planning permission might guide the type of housing likely to be acceptable to a greater or lesser extent. But a judgement has to be taken on the marketability of a product on the site, bearing in mind location, environment, nearby competition, accessibility, and proximity to schools, shops and services. The type of development, the size, the style of the dwelling likely to prove most successful on a particular site, is therefore most strongly influenced by the sales organization of any company. They advise on dwelling mix, and the layout is therefore prepared on the basis of this advice. Most prudent developers would discuss that scheme with the local planning authority at an early stage.

Unfortunatly the importance of this element in the process is perhaps not equally recognized by both sides. The local planning authority will see it as an informal preliminary discussion subject to their consultations and their having a detailed look at the site. On the other hand, the developer is working out very carefully how he can maximize revenue in order to submit as high an offer as possible for the land. He is treating the layout as being much more permanent. Consequently the seeds of confrontation are sown early. Any reduction in dwelling numbers, any layout adjustment likely to devalue a part of the scheme, could be vital as far as its economics are concerned.

The importance of a site appraisal to the developer goes a long way to explain why there is the widespread use of the standard house type. Once a particular house type has been built, the developer knows precisely how much it costs and how much he can sell it for, which means his assessment of a future site can be that much more accurate. With individual house designs there is not that degree of accuracy and that makes accountants nervous. So pre-submission discussions are very important and both sides should always make clear to each other the basis on which that dialogue is taking place.


## FINANCIAL CONSIDERATIONS

There are three methods of financing generally employed by developers:

- the Stock Market — going 'public' to raise capital;
- loans from banks — preferably having negotiated preferential rates;
- profits from turnover.

Until October 1987 one favourite source of finance was the Stock Market.

Wilson Bowden became a plc in 1987, and by so doing raised £14m which it is using to acquire and develop sites on a wider basis. All clever developers will have secured loans from banks up to a certain level which they will be able to call on at any particular time to fund their activities. The third aspect is the profits from turnover and it is this latter point which is quite crucial and probably under estimated by local planning authorities. It helps to explain the pressure from builders to proceed with a scheme as quickly as possible, a pressure which is often the cause of confrontation.

Once a programme of construction is established, an income from sales is planned for, then speed becomes vital. All planning departments have been guilty at some time or other of sending out requests for extensions of time on applications without ever being aware of the consequences for the developer. As time slips by a developer's construction programme is threatened, his anticipated income is reducing and monies intended for further land purchase or whatever may no longer be available. Some developers work to very tight schedules from land acquisition to development and they will not entertain the purchase of sites on which development could not be guaranteed within a very short period, perhaps say only two years, where the emphasis is clearly on the most effective use and re-use of the total financial resource.

It is however possible and sensible to look much further ahead. Where land has been allocated for development, its likely disposal would be by tender, if it had not already been purchased by private treaty. A private treaty purchase can take on several guises: it can be an outright freehold purchase, a conditional contract, or an option to purchase at some future date. Perhaps this option method is the most interesting for developers because it is the most flexible and overall it has the ability within it to produce benefit for all the parties – local planning authorities, the developer and landowner. As far as the landowner is concerned it is a device whereby at some future date the value of his land would be enhanced with the grant of planning permission. It may involve farmland to housing, old industry to retail, commercial, for example.

The principles of such an agreement usually involve the initial payment of a fee to the landowner to secure the option to purchase and the granting of the planning permission, and any fee is usually related to the likelihood of obtaining planning permission within a given time. Second, the agreement involves the pursuit of a planning permission by the developer; third, the purchase of the land, perhaps at a percentage of market value to reflect time, effort and expense involved by the developer in pursuing that application; fourth, an assessment of market value which relates to net developable area and which is net of abnormal infrastructure costs. The benefit to the local planning authority, and thereby the community, can be through the legitimate incorporation of planning gain or community benefit elements in the total package of the scheme. This may involve off-site highway works, special provision of open space, perhaps a community hall, or even social housing. As prerequisites for a planning permission these features would be classed as infrastructure and normally would be a charge on the land, not on the development.

The developer may benefit on grant of planning permission by obtaining the land without further competition and perhaps at a discount value. The local planning authority may benefit because abnormal infrastructure costs can be taken out of the economic equation before market value is assessed. Much common sense is attached to this approach, but it necessarily involves considerable risk. A judgement must be made after assessing the risks involved to determine whether to enter an option agreement and if so at what price and over what period of time.

## LOCAL PLANS, DEVELOPMENT AND PLANNERS

Increasingly when planning authorities produce their local plans they publish draft plans which have evaluated a series of alternatives for development. Most professionals would agree that planning should incorporate as sophisticated as possible an approach to the evaluation of the competing demands for land. More often than not there is no clear right or wrong.

The increase in the number of planners now operating in the private sector, either directly employed by one organization or in consultancy, can only benefit both the profession and the ultimate end product. The profession as a whole will benefit as developers and public alike begin to see planners as more than administrative bureaucrats with a reputation for saying 'no' all the time. The environment will ultimately benefit through the greater involvement of planners in the development process, perhaps by introducing sometimes for the first time issues which were previously never considered by the builders.

This can be illustrated by an example of a recent scheme. This relates to a situation which is fairly common throughout southern lowland England, where a prosperous economy stimulates pressure for house building. In Ampthill in Bedfordshire, on a site promoted by Barratts, a proposal was refused because of its location in the sensitive gap between the built-up area of Ampthill and the green belt. Barratts were struggling to convince local people that it was a worthwhile scheme. They brought in Derek Lovejoy and Partners who redesigned the scheme on sound ecological principles protecting the particularly valuable parts of the site from built development. The Bedfordshire and Huntingdon Trust for Nature Conservation agreed to take over and manage the open parts of the site should it be granted planning permission. Barratts agreed that each house purchaser will become a member of the Trust and will make a financial commitment to it to guarantee the ongoing management of the important open areas. It is an example of a case where if the development does go ahead the ultimate scheme will be vastly superior to that which would have resulted without this sophisticated approach.

## CONCLUSION

In this and many other examples, 'option to purchase' agreements have allowed enough flexibility to develop the schemes which can generate significant benefits. It should be emphasized that there is everything to gain by avoiding confrontation between the public and the private sectors. This can best be achieved by the determination by local planning authorities to establish objectives for development sites early and in the appropriate detail. It will usually be possible to build reasonable and proper requirements into the financing of developments. But sometimes a bit of self-examination by local planning authorities would be useful to make sure that the highest professional standards are maintained and to guarantee a consistent approach to invididual issues. Most important of all, assessment should be done before a proposal becomes a planning application, either through the proper development brief work or local plan work or through pre-submission discussions as part of the development control process.

## REFERENCE

Baron, T. 1984, *Address to Summer School*, Royal Town Planning Institute, Exeter.

# 18

# Developments in retailing

*Frank Doherty*

This chapter will examine how a large retailer in the region, like the Greater Nottingham Co-operative Society, approaches development by addressing the following questions:

1. How do developers evaluate the potential of a site?
2. How is finance raised?
3. What is the scope for new forms of partnerships or bargaining between local authorities and developers?

## SCOPE FOR NEW FORMS OF PARTNERSHIPS

The third of these points is, of course, the most interesting. Opportunities for new forms of partnership or bargaining between local authorities and developers exist:

- where the land belongs to the local authority and they have sold it with a planning consent for cash with a payment deferred until building commenced, or until building was completed, or they have retained an equity interest in the completed development;
- where the land either did or did not belong to the local authority, and they have received payments towards roads which they *may* construct some time in the future, or they have received a library, or a community centre, or a bridge over the canal, or whatever else seems appropriate to them, and where the cost of providing such inducements is less to the developer than the added value of the land when a retail planning consent has been attached to it.

Some would argue that many if not all of such arrangements may be legally questionable, but what developer is going to test that? Of course local authority funding restrictions have made the game even more interesting. Because certain capital receipts, or a percentage thereof, cannot be used by the local authority in the way that they may wish, this has led to the reintroduction of bartering. Instead of offering to pay the local authority say £4m for a site, a developer may instead offer £3m and 50 council houses, for example. There have been examples of all of these arrangements in Nottingham and the Co-operative Society has even been involved in some.

Then of course there is the local business which has fallen on hard times, and would like to sell its old factory. This could be worth approximately nothing, but it would like to sell for say £5 million or £10 million or £15 million or maybe even more, for a retail park. This even happens in Nottingham with old colliery sites. The local business may approach the local authority and offer to take one of their bright shining new advanced factory units which the local authority cannot let, providing it is given a retail planning consent for the old semi-derelict site. The money provided by the sale of the old site for a retail park will enable the business so the story goes, to re-equip the new factory and save the jobs of its 1000 staff. Surely the local authority does not want to be responsible for closing down the business and adding to the unemployment in the area?

Such arguments of course tend to weigh rather more heavily with councillors than planners, but this argument has been known to produce a planning consent. Indeed it has produced at least two within ten miles of the centre of Nottingham.

And yet, perhaps there still are novel approaches. The tobacco company Players said they would like to put something back into the community when they closed their factory in Lenton. The something was a retail development, and an asking price for their derelict old site of around £5m. A consent for around 130 000 sq.ft was eventually given against the planners' better judgement, but they apparently felt there was a need in the area for a small food shop and a fast food restaurant, both of which were included, albeit as a small element in the eventual planning consent. It appears, however, that the development is to go ahead without either of these units, as no operators can be found for such shops in this area.

Many of the schemes thought up may be interesting — some of course are just downright cheek; perhaps there is still a novel idea to be found — but it is not planning.

The local authority may give a retail planning consent so that an eyesore may be transformed into an attractive shopping development. That is ideal if the shopping development is right for that catchment and that site. If, however, it is merely to eliminate the eyesore, then again — it is not planning.

Over the past ten years or so in Nottingham, the Co-operative Society has carried out more site assessments, pursued more sites, and built more new retail units in the area in which it trades than any other retailer. There have been disagreements with planners, but it is understood that planning is an important task. Of course, the Society is not always happy with what the planners do. A large number of cases over the years seem to have involved either obstruction or doubtful tactics. But planning — good planning — is vital. Market forces are not a satisfactory substitute for sensible planning.

## MATCHING LAND TO NEEDS

What happens if unrestricted development of so-called retail parks undermines a vibrant shopping centre such as Nottingham? What happens should overprovision of retail space, accompanied by a down-turn in consumer spending, turn many retail parks into the new commercial waste lands of the 1990s? Someone must be taking a sensible overview and trying to find a reasonable match between the use of assets like land and buildings and local needs. Some overprovision, of course must be built in to encourage competition and safeguard consumers. That is really what planning is about.

But a nonsense situation has developed in Nottingham in relation to possible development sites. The Government appears to have given encouraging signals so far as retail applications on inner city sites and old disused industrial sites are concerned. Nottingham now has numerous sites completely sterilized for development for any purpose other than retailing. Anyone looking for a large well located site for a new industrial or commercial development will invariably find that the best sites are subject to retail planning applications or appeals, or have already obtained a consent for retail development.

Vendors have their expectations of price raised to a level which makes them unable to accept the rate for a commercial or industrial development. A good industrial site of say 15 acres, well located with easy access to the motorway, would fetch perhaps £1.5 – £2m. But the same site, with a consent for a retail park of 250 000 sq.ft, would probably realize over £10m – perhaps substantially over. Is it any surprise that the best sites for non-retail businesses seeking to come into the area, or for the expansion of existing businesses, are being withheld from them by reason of the new retail hope value which has been generated in the minds of the owners of these sites? Priority should be given to the land requirement of new and expanding industrial and commercial enterprises.

So the Government's desire to see redevelopment of these sites is actually getting in the way of what is supposed to be the main thrust of its economic strategy – to stimulate the growth of new and existing industrial and commercial enterprise.

## EVALUATING POTENTIAL SITES

The first question posed at the start of the chapter is: 'How do developers evaluate the potential of a site?' Site evaluation is not of course an exact science, although most developers employ similar techniques.

It would be easy to suggest that new development sites are chosen because they are in an area where they would fulfil an obvious need. Today this is rarely the case. There are of course areas of need, but the very fact that the need still remained in 1987 suggests that there are very good reasons why it has not been satisfied. It is probably a need which is uneconomic to satisfy; for example no-one wishes to build a superstore in a rural village. A developer will evaluate a site on its ability to generate a return on capital which will provide him with an acceptable level of profitability. This depends among other things on location, size and type of unit or units, and on the strength of other competitors already established within the catchment projected for the new development.

With the high and growing level of car ownership, more and more people are looking for ease of parking. Of course the same growth in car ownership has resulted in city centres and city centre car parks being more and more difficult for the car-borne shopper to negotiate. So the provision of edge-of-town, or out-of-town facilities, with ample free parking, is a big inducement to car-borne shoppers. The bulk of food shopping is now conducted in this way; so also is DIY.

Comparison shopping is still done predominantly in established shopping centres, although the growth in out-of-town superstore shopping for furniture, carpets and electrical merchandise is much in evidence. If an out-of-town or edge-of-town shopping development can be large enough to offer a reasonable range of shops and products, then with car parking and convenience added, it may constitute a strong centre in its own right which will be able to challenge the established centre and divert a substantial part of its trade.

Site evaluation is generally about estimating how hard a new outlet can impact on existing centres or business to divert enough trade to make the new development worthwhile. The stronger the new development relative to the established centre, the more successful it will be.

That is why claims of producing 400 new jobs, for example, are a bit of a nonsense. Diverting 400 perhaps or re-employing 400 of those made redundant elsewhere is nearer the truth. Developers do their credibility no good when they say, 'We will build these new highly efficient retail units and operate them in a very cost-effective way and that will result in 400 more people being employed.'

## FINANCING RETAIL DEVELOPMENTS

Finally then, how is a proposed new development to be financed? If the development makes sense after a proper site evaluation and costing exercise has been carried out, the site will probably be secured subject to planning. Having obtained planning consent the provision of finance should be the easy part.

A developer who is not also going to be the main user will be endeavouring to pre-let his proposed development. Between outline and detailed planning consent he will hope to achieve this, and indeed the final detail will be substantially influenced by the eventual users.

He may then obtain finance to complete the development by finally selling on to an institution. Or he may of course wish to retain all or part of the development as an investment. Or he may sell the site on with planning consent to someone else who will undertake the development. This may be another development company, or a retailer.

There are so many permutations and so many people and corporate bodies wanting to provide funding, that no worthwhile development should ever fail to attract finance. It is simply a case of trying to select the method which is most cost-effective and best suits the company's business strategy.

The Greater Nottingham Co-operative Society adopts a very simple approach. It wants to retain the freeholds or ground leases, for example, so it does not sell and lease back any new developments. It still owns all the retail developments which it carried out. The most difficult one to fund was the first, because 10 years ago it had very few free assets to offer as security. However eventually a suitable secured loan was raised to fund the first superstore. That superstore when completed was used as security to raise the funds for the second and so on, leapfrogging like that for a few years until, with rising profits, and a growing asset base, new units were actually being built without having to charge more assets. This happened around number five or number six.

It seems that funding can be simple or complicated depending on preferences. Some of the more elaborate schemes are of course geared more to allowing what is euphemistically referred to as 'flexibility' in the preparation of the company's final accounts. This is more about fudging than funding.

With a cooperative society there is no share quotation to worry about, so they do not capitalize any interest or pre-opening costs. They are all charged against profits as and when incurred. This is obviously a very conservative method, which tends to understate profitability.

On the other hand finance has been offered which can go to the other extreme. For example a new unit is built at a total cost of, say for simplicity, £10m. (The bank or funding institution pays the costs as incurred − £10m.) The unit at this stage belongs to the bank and it is not on the retailer's balance sheet at all. Neither are any borrowings. It is, as they say, 'off balance sheet', so it does not affect the gearing ratio. The retailer trades in the unit for two years and he pays no interest on the loan, or rental for the premises during that two-year period. So his profit and loss account is not adversely affected in the early years of the development. In year three he buys the unit from the bank at cost, the cost of course including accrued interest for the two years that none was paid. He funds this purchase from the bank by means of a loan from the bank, repayable over an agreed number of years, or at the end of an agreed number of years.

It can readily be appreciated how open to abuse some such systems can be. Indeed how far some funding arrangements, as applied, measure up to the concept of 'a true and fair view' in the company's accounts must be open to question.

There are of course many other ways of financing developments. The methods discussed here are simply a few of those which are currently adopted.

# 19
# New roles for building societies

*Douglas Wright*

This chapter looks at the way in which building societies are becoming actively involved in property development and examines the distinctive contribution they can make. It concentrates particularly on the work of the Nationwide Housing Trust set up by the Nationwide Anglia Building Society.

## THE NATIONWIDE HOUSING TRUST

The Nationwide Housing Trust was formed in 1982. The company was set up with a small amount of capital and was hampered in the earlier years in not being properly capitalized. Clearly the lack of working capital did not help in trying to get many schemes off the ground. Within the Nationwide Anglia Building Society group the Housing Trust is looked at as a free-standing property developer. It is not subsidized at all; overheads must be covered and Nationwide expects the Trust to make a return on capital of around the mortgage rate. That is obviously less than a traditional private building firm would expect to earn.

The Trust is not out to compete with traditional developers. There is no question of trying to implement schemes like those of David Wilson, or to operate on the same scale as Barratts or Tarmac. It looks for certain niches in the market, where something distinctive can be offered: perhaps a site that may not be profitable to develop otherwise or one where a local authority wants a type of housing development which would not be built if the scheme went out to general tender.

## HIGHER STANDARDS AND NEW PARTNERSHIPS

The Trust has four basic aims. One is to promote higher standards of design, architecture and layout. Nationwide is not really into the numbers game. It is not interested, for example, in buying 50 units of a block of a scheme from a developer who wants to sell them towards the end of his financial year to increase his turnover. Nationwide are interested in trying to promote higher standards of quality layout at the bottom end of the market − higher standards for the quality of the unit, and higher standards of design for the layout and general architecture of the houses. These standards are not yet always visibly achieved in all cases, but this is a clear long-term objective.

The second aim of the Trust is to act as a catalyst. What Nationwide Anglia is trying to do is to use financial strength to enlarge the total number of finished schemes in the housing market. It is prepared to accept a low return on capital so that schemes will be developed that might not happen otherwise. It is trying to bring together the bodies involved in housing − the local authorities who might have the land, and the contractors who actually build the houses themselves and who have the finance.

The third aim is to provide homes for a particular sector of the market, like first-time buyers, the elderly, or mixed family housing schemes including the provision of more and better housing in the inner cities using the urban development grant and derelict land grant.

By 1989 Nationwide had built approximately 1500 houses over the whole country. There are approximately 1500 under construction at present and it is hoped to get up to 2000 houses being turned over a year by the early 1990s.

The fourth aim is to do all this work through partnerships. Nationwide do not want to be on their own in the housing field but to act in partnership especially with local authorities who provide 90 per cent of the sites. Partnerships are being sought in all parts of the country which would produce developments that meet their assessed housing need.

Another kind of fruitful partnership is with contractors. Nationwide cannot build houses itself so it works in partnership with contractors. The Trust looks for a full joint venture with full profit and risk sharing with the contractors. Many of the schemes are unlikely to yield both a construction profit and a development profit, so the contractor foregoes his contracting profit. He builds the scheme at net cost plus overheads which are charged to the joint venture. This means that there is one profit for the scheme — if there is a loss both parties share it and if there is a profit that is also equally shared.

The reason for preferring partnerships is that they are more likely to produce the type of development that the local authority is looking for and therefore to satisfy the housing need for the area. Working with the contractors avoids the normal conflict between contractor and employer. There have not been any of the problems with planners that traditional developers have, mainly because the sites tend to come from local authorities. The Trust can therefore consult the planners very early on and develop the scheme in a close working relationship with them. As a result there is very little real conflict in the planning process.

## EXAMPLES OF DEVELOPMENTS

The kinds of scheme which are being developed are at the bottom end of the market. Even so the aim is for a high quality of layout and design. It is important to avoid having rows of semi-detached houses, all looking the same, standing next to each other without any variety.

One example is a site acquired from Birmingham City Council which would be eminently suitable for four-bedroomed detached housing over the whole site. Birmingham did not want to see it go for detached housing. They approached Nationwide, specifying a land value which had to be achieved, and asking for a mixed development on the site.

The result is 25 three-bedroomed semi-detached houses, 13 small two-bedroomed bungalows aimed towards the elderly and just one up-market cul-de-sac. This is out of a total of 66 units of which a number are going back to the city in exchange for the site. There is internal cross subsidy within the scheme — the little cul-de-sac of 13 detached units pays for the development profit of the whole site. There is no profit at all on the semi-detached houses. If the site went on the open market, that could not happen. The whole site would probably have been developed for three- or four-bedroomed detached houses (see Figures 19.1 and 19.2).

Styles are varied where possible. Even though there were only 25 semi-detached houses on that site, three different versions were built to try to avoid rows of semi-detached houses all looking identical. Roof-lines are broken by having a bungalow semi-detached with a house. Attempts are also made to try to vary the road pattern.

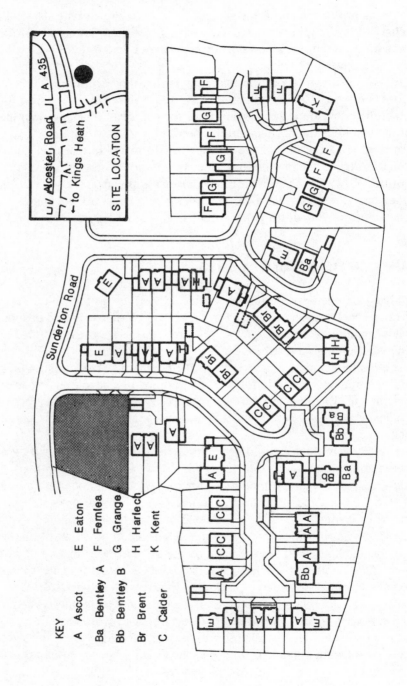

KEY

| | | | |
|---|---|---|---|
| A | Ascot | E | Eaton |
| Ba | Bentley A | F | Femlea |
| Bb | Bentley B | G | Grange |
| Br | Brent | H | Harlech |
| C | Calder | K | Kent |

**Figure 19.1 Layout of a mixed housing development**

THE BENTLEY

Two bedroom bungalow,
designed for easy maintance.

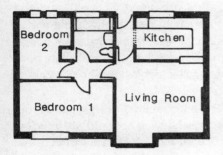

THE EATON

Two bedroom bungalow,
designed for easy maintance.

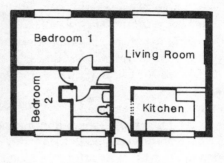

THE ASCOT

3 bedroom house in semi detached
and detached form for a growing
young family.

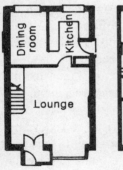
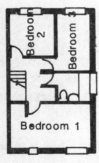

THE HARLECH

3 bedroom house in semi detached
and detached form for a growing
young family.

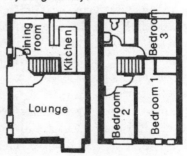

**Figure 19.2   House types for a mixed housing development**

## AN INNER CITY DEVELOPMENT

The second example is a very dense development in a tight inner city site — 25 units on a site of only 1.2 acres. The local authority made the requirement that it must remain a low-cost housing site. Even though this was a high-density site it was still thought important to avoid having a long row of terraced houses all looking the same. Best quality facing brick was used rather than London brick, and there were hardwood front doors, and high performance windows. A high level of specification has been developed for use in partnerships with contractors whenever this can be afforded.

Thus at the bottom end of the market there is good design and layout and a high specification within the houses. Houses are sold at the same price as they would be in the market without these features. Some of the potential profit is therefore foregone in order to improve the design and specification of the unit. There is also a high level of varied landscaping in the paving and in the treatment of the drives. This produces a high quality environment even on a very dense inner city site.

## NURSING HOMES AND FLATS

The Nationwide Housing Trust is currently taking an interest in nursing homes because they are, in general, not being built to a very high standard in the private sector. Standards for nursing homes have been drawn up in conjunction with the medical profession, the nursing profession and other involved bodies, and the first project in that area is just starting. Such schemes are attractive to the Trust but they are only economic in areas where the value of the land is fairly low. However nursing homes could be built on other sites where the local authorities are prepared to put the land in at a subsidized price.

There has also been a very successful scheme in Bristol to redevelop half of the old Bristol Docks. This fairly dense development of flats has turned out to be an imaginative scheme of reasonable quality. Another scheme in Sefton raised the tone of a problem area by taking off the top two storeys of four-storey maisonettes and converting them to reasonable looking houses of some quality. There is also a mixture of flats and bungalows for the elderly in Worcester for which the Trust provided all the finance, and in Swindon a joint venture to build the first development of flats within the area, aimed at the bottom end of the market.

## FINANCE

Nationwide Housing Trust gets all its finance from the Nationwide Anglia Building Society. It is necessary to purchase the land outright and development finance for the scheme comes from Nationwide Anglia Building Society. There is no favourable treatment in terms of the interest rate, but there is preferential treatment in the provision of mortage funds equal to 100 per cent of the cost. The Housing Trust is not a profit-maximizing organization; it works on a range of profits. The overall rate of return is set by Nationwide Anglia, but individual housing department managers in the regions can vary the average. For example in a year when the average required is a 5 per cent return on sales, individual schemes can yield as little as 2 or 3 per cent, and be balanced by others that might make 7 or 8 per cent.

Once the required return on capital is achieved the Trust will examine ways of putting the additional profit back into housing. This can happen in two ways. In the Birmingham scheme the Trust took an equity stake in the properties. Thus if they could sell say at £25 000, and the local authority would like to see the houses on the market at less than that, the Trust would take an equity stake of say £5000 in the property and put the houses on the market at £20 000. This might enable people to get into the housing market by purchasing cheaply.

The second way is by taking some units in lieu of overall profit. So if the profit was sufficient to purchase four units on a site, they might be bought and then rented on an assured tenancy level.

The profits are normally shared with the contractor but there are also sole developments where both the Trust and the contractor would take their full profit. There are a couple of small schemes where it has been agreed that any profits over a certain level will be shared on an equal basis. The Trust would be happy to share the profits with the local authorities on a full risks basis but local authorities are not keen on the risk element.

## EVALUATING SCHEMES

Schemes usually originate from the local authority who specify the sort of mix they want for a site. The Trust must first ensure that there is a demand for that type of housing mix on that site in that locality. There is therefore a very detailed appraisal, including much market research. There is consultation with the Nationwide Anglia Building Society surveyors who have local detailed knowledge, with the local branch, with the local estate agents and a look at the general state of competition in the market. Then there is an initial feasibility study followed by a scheme layout.

This is discussed with the planners and the local authority, and then priced in detail by the contractor. This may need to be done a number of times because there are often many revisions before there is a scheme that everyone — local authority, planners, and the Trust — is happy with, and a scheme that can be built for a price that will make it work.

## RETURN ON DEVELOPMENT

What sort of returns are considered adequate? Two examples from recent schemes with local authorities will give an idea of the return expected. The first example is of some old council offices, Grade 2 listed buildings that the local authority put on the market but could not find a a purchaser for. It was decided to develop a small area of the site to get this listed building back into use. Nine bungalows were built in the grounds of the building and five flats in the conversion of the house itself. This brings a total income of £570 000. The cost of refurbishing the house was such that it would not have been economic on its own but now the profits from the nine bungalows are being used to subsidize the conversion of the house.

The local authority wanted to be paid for the house in two ways; first a fairly nominal cash sum of £28 000 for the value of the land, and second, the balance of the purchase price from the rebuilding of an elderly persons' club which is on part of the site. This is being replaced with a brand new building.

The total costs were £552 000 after adding the scheme cost which leaves a balance of profit, should everything go according to plan, of £17 942. There is a fixed price for the land, a fixed price building contract, and marketing is costed as far as possible by accurate estimates; the fees and the costs are also fixed, so that the only real variable is interest which depends on how quickly the units can be sold. If the units take longer to sell the profit will be reduced, but if they sell quickly it will go up. That profit of £17 000 is obviously a very small return — only 3 per cent of sales. In this particular case if profits were more than 4 per cent it was agreed that they would be shared with the local authority.

The other example can be taken from the dense inner city development discussed earlier. The scheme was developed for 33 units and was reduced to 25 units after discussion with planners. Income would have been £929 000 and expenditure £889 000, leaving a profit of £40 000 which represented a return of just under 5 per cent of sales. This again was a fairly low return on sales and on capital. The Trust is there because it is doubtful whether the developers would undertake a scheme with such a low return. This is a fairly high risk area and sales would possibly be fairly slow.

To try to balance out these low return schemes, it is important to have the odd scheme that is reasonably profitable such as the first one described from Birmingham. The income from that is £2 200 000 and the total costs £2 040 000, so it leaves a profit of £160 000. That represents 7½ per cent of sales which would be considered a fairly healthy return by a building society but not by most developers.

## SOME PRACTICAL PROBLEMS

One of the frustrations with the present system is that building societies are asked to look at many pieces of land, and prepare submissions which involve time-consuming work, only to find that the local authority, nine or twelve months later, has changed its mind and decided not to release the land.

There are also occasions when fully workable schemes have been agreed with the planners, and the contractors are ready to start when at the last minute the local authority decides to put out to tender a scheme based on the one that the building society has developed and the benefit of 12 or 18 months' work goes to someone else.

It would be better if, before local authorities came to building societies to ask them to undertake development, they were to make sure that they really do want the development of a particular type on a particular piece of land. Moreover if there were an officer within the local authority who could coordinate all the various departments involved, it would avoid the societies going through many different committees and authorities before getting final approval. It is possible to get through nine-tenths of such a journey and then find that, say, the Education Department, which is also involved in the scheme, has decided against it and so the whole thing is called off. If they had been consulted early on much work could have been saved.

# Index